Abraham Lincoln

and

Liberal Democracy

American Political Thought
Wilson Carey McWilliams and Lance Banning
Founding Editors

Abraham Lincoln and Liberal Democracy

Edited by Nicholas Buccola

University Press of Kansas

© 2016 by the University Press of Kansas
All rights reserved

Published by the University Press of Kansas (Lawrence, Kansas 66045), which was organized by the Kansas Board of Regents and is operated and funded by Emporia State University, Fort Hays State University, Kansas State University, Pittsburg State University, the University of Kansas, and Wichita State University

Library of Congress Cataloging-in-Publication Data

Names: Buccola, Nicholas, editor.
Title: Abraham Lincoln and liberal democracy / edited by Nicholas Buccola.
Description: Lawrence : University Press of Kansas, 2016.
Series: American political thought | Includes index.
Identifiers: LCCN 2015040954
ISBN 9780700622160 (cloth : alk. paper)
ISBN 9780700622177 (pbk. : alk. paper)
ISBN 9780700622184 (ebook)
Subjects: LCSH: Lincoln, Abraham, 1809–1865—Political and social views. | Lincoln, Abraham, 1809–1865—Philosophy. | United States—Politics and government—1861–1865. | Democracy—Philosophy.
Classification: LCC E457.2 .A143 2016 | DDC 973.7092—dc23
LC record available at http://lccn.loc.gov/2015040954.

British Library Cataloguing-in-Publication Data is available.

Printed in the United States of America

10 9 8 7 6 5 4 3 2 1

The paper used in this publication is recycled and contains 30 percent postconsumer waste. It is acid free and meets the minimum requirements of the American National Standard for Permanence of Paper for Printed Library Materials Z39.48-1992.

Contents

Acknowledgments   vii

Introduction   1
    —Nicholas Buccola

PART ONE. LINCOLN AND DEMOCRACY
1. Prosperity and Tyranny in Lincoln's Lyceum Address   13
    —John Burt
2. Providentialism and Politics: Lincoln's Second Inaugural Address and the Problem of Democracy   44
    —Michael Zuckert

PART TWO. LINCOLN AND LIBERTY
3. Lincoln and the Ethics of Emancipation: Universalism, Nationalism, Exceptionalism   73
    —Dorothy Ross
4. What If Honest Abe Was Telling the Truth? Natural Rights, Race, and Legalism in the Political Thought of Lincoln   110
    —Nicholas Buccola

PART THREE. LINCOLN AND EQUALITY
5. "The Vital Element of the Republican Party": Antislavery, Nativism, and Lincoln   139
    —Bruce Levine
6. Lincoln's Competing Political Loyalties: Antislavery, Union, and the Constitution   164
    —Manisha Sinha

PART FOUR. LINCOLN AS A LIBERAL DEMOCRATIC STATESMAN
7. Four Roads to Emancipation: Lincoln, the Law, and the Proclamation   195
   —Allen Guelzo
8. Abraham Lincoln's Kantian Republic   216
   —Steven B. Smith

Contributors   239

Index   241

Acknowledgments

Most of the essays collected here were presented at a conference I hosted titled "The Political Thought of Abraham Lincoln" at Linfield College in McMinnville, Oregon. The chief sponsor of the conference was the Frederick Douglass Forum on Law, Rights, and Justice, a program I direct at Linfield. The forum's activities are made possible by the generosity of many foundations, including the Apgar Foundation, the Open Society Foundation, and the Jack Miller Center, and private donors, including Sheila Auster and Thomas Klingenstein. Without the support of these foundations and individuals, we would not have had the opportunity to gather and discuss Lincoln, and this volume would not exist. For this reason and many others, I am grateful to all those who make the work of the Douglass Forum possible. In addition, I would like to thank Susan Barnes Whyte, director of the Nicholson Library at Linfield; the amazing staff at the Nicholson Library; and the undergraduate Douglass Fellows for making the conference such a success.

In the process of transforming a series of conference papers into this volume, I incurred many debts. Maggie Hawkins, Ellie Forness, and Hannah Roberts provided vital editorial assistance. Richard Ellis, David Gutterman, Bill Curtis, Andrew Valls, Margot Minardi, members of the Portland Political Theory group, and anonymous reviewers for the University Press of Kansas provided valuable feedback on drafts of the essays included here. I am grateful to Fred Woodward at the University Press of Kansas for his patience and wisdom. Last but not least, my wife, Emily, displayed her usual grace and resilience as I worked on this project while we adjusted to the wonders and challenges of welcoming our first child, Luna, into the world.

Nicholas Buccola

INTRODUCTION

Nicholas Buccola

Abraham Lincoln was not a systematic political philosopher, but he did—through word and deed—grapple with several ultimate questions in politics. What is the moral basis of popular sovereignty? What are the proper limits on the will of the majority? When and why should we revere the law? How does our conception of God shape our political views? How is our devotion to a *particular* nation related to our commitment to *universal* ideals? What are we to do when the letter of the law is at odds with what we believe justice requires? What are the political consequences of the idea of natural equality? What do we do when our political loyalties are in conflict? What is the best way to protect the right to liberty for all people? The contributors to this volume have examined Lincoln's responses to these and other ultimate questions in politics. What results is a fascinating portrait of not only Abraham Lincoln but also the promises and paradoxes of liberal democracy.

The basic liberal democratic idea is that individual liberty is best secured by a democratic political order that treats all citizens as equals before the law and is governed by the rule of law, which places limits on how citizens may treat one another and on how the state may treat its citizens. These ideas exhibit a wonderful coherence in theory, but the real world of politics never quite follows the best-laid plans of theoreticians. Lincoln was, in many ways, the embodiment of both the promises and the paradoxes at the heart of liberal democracy. He was "naturally antislavery" but unflinchingly committed to defending proslavery laws and clauses of the Constitution; he was a defender of the common man, yet he worried about the excesses of democracy; he was committed to the idea of equal natural rights yet could not imagine a harmonious, interracial democracy in which all citizens had equal political rights. The fact that Lincoln embodies so many of these paradoxes makes it all the more edifying to take him seriously. He was, after all, attempting to work out the meaning and coherence of the liberal democratic project in practice. Lincoln cared deeply about "government of, by, and for the people," the promise of individual liberty for all, and our "ancient faith" in human equality. And, of course, he revered the law. Over the course of his political career, though, he came to see the myriad ways in which the neatly interlocking facets of liberal democratic theory often fall apart in practice. What is a principled statesman to do when the letter of the law is at odds with the liberal promise of liberty for all? How should a liberal democratic statesman respond when a faction in his party insists on excluding members of new immigrant groups from equal citizenship? How can a principled leader use rhetoric to curb the excesses of democracy? The contributors to this volume show that Lincoln confronted these and many other big questions during his political career, and the aim of this book is to take his answers seriously.

The essays collected here are surely not the first attempts to come to grips with Lincoln's status as a political thinker. Many of Lincoln's biographers have appreciated the philosophical dimension of his statesmanship, and the nature of his political thought has been the subject of robust debate in the fields of political theory and intellectual history. In *Crisis of the House Divided* and *New Birth of Freedom*, for example, Harry Jaffa presents us with a portrait of Lincoln as a thinker who brilliantly combined classical natural law and modern natural rights doctrines. Intellectual historian John Patrick Diggins's *The Lost Soul of American Politics* celebrates Lincoln's infusion of liberalism with the conscience of Calvinism. According to political scientist J. David Greenstone, the "Lincoln persuasion" combines Kantian ethics, Protestant theology, and liberal politics. In *Lincoln's Tragic Pragmatism*, John Burt argues that Lincoln's reaction to moral conflict anticipates developments in contemporary liberal theory. And then, of course, there are interpreters on the Far Right and Far Left who have read Lincoln as the quintessential teacher and practitioner of political evil.[1]

In the face of these many interpretations of Lincoln, how can we make sense of such a compelling and elusive figure in American political thought? It seems to me that if we want to catch a glimpse of the truth about Lincoln's political thought, we must view it from a variety of perspectives and through multiple lenses. We need philosophical lenses to determine the coherence and normative appeal of Lincoln's ideas, and lest we get seduced by the brilliance of his words, we need historical lenses to pull us back to the ground so we can appreciate the intellectual and political contexts in which he wrote and spoke.

These multiple lenses are essential to understanding American political thought in general and Lincoln in particular. In the study of American political thought, we are confronted—more often than not—with subjects who conceived of themselves as political actors, not as expositors of philosophical systems. Lincoln exemplifies what might be called the problem of American political thought: in a political culture where "doers" have been far more prevalent than "thinkers," where and how are we supposed to find political *thought* that is worthy of our attention?

The question of where to look is definitely easier to answer. Throughout the history of American political thought, we find reformers and statesmen who utilized their pens and their voices to justify their political "doings." These justifications are, in their own way, responses to the ultimate questions presented at the beginning of this introduction. They are, in other words, responses to the sorts of questions that interest political theorists—questions about rights, the role of government, legitimacy, equality, and so forth. Although every era in American political history has produced many voices worthy of our attention, our search for these voices often pulls us to moments of great conflict and social change, such as the founding, the antebellum and Civil War era, the Progressive Era through the New Deal, and, more recently, the revolutions of the 1960s and the conservative backlash against those revolutions. Our tendency to be drawn to such eras is not surprising because, in the words of political theorist Sheldon Wolin, during periods of political turmoil, "the range of possibilities appears infinite," and we are confronted with the opportunity to "reconstruct a shattered world of meanings and their accompanying institutional expressions" and "fashion a political cosmos out of political chaos." In this passage, Wolin's focus is on why great "political philosophers" tend to emerge when they do, but the idea applies just as well to the study of American political thought. In moments of political turmoil, we find reformers and statesmen grappling with big questions and offering answers rooted in both principle and the demands of pragmatic politics.[2]

The more difficult question presented by the problem of American political thought is *how* we should attempt to make sense of the political ideas of the reformers and statesmen we study. Here is where the approach to Lincoln taken in this volume can be helpful. Although there is much disagreement about Lincoln in this book, it is fair to say that all the contributors believe that Lincoln has something significant to say in response to ultimate political questions. Lincoln was, first and foremost, a politician who was attempting to achieve particular aims. To understand precisely what those aims were, why he chose certain objectives and means, and the context in which he employed those means in pursuit of those objectives, the lens of the historian is essential. Whereas theorists are (hopefully) not insensitive to the concrete, historical context of Lincoln's life in politics, they attempt to make sense of him in a fundamentally different way. For the theorist, the task of coming to grips with a figure like Lincoln is both interpretive and normative. As an interpretive matter, the theorist (along with the intellectual historian) adds to our understanding by attempting to make sense of where someone like Lincoln fits within the many traditions of political thought. Contributors to this volume, for example, ask the following questions: How did Lincoln (knowingly and unknowingly) advance or challenge the various ways of thinking that preceded him and that dominated his own milieu? Does it make sense to see Lincoln as an important figure in the American Enlightenment? Was Lincoln a purveyor of the doctrine of American exceptionalism? Did Lincoln accept the exclusionary ideologies of nativism and racism, which constituted such powerful strands in the tapestry of American political thought? Where do Lincoln's actions and reflections on self-government fit within the tradition of democratic theory? These are just a few of the interpretive questions the theorist might ask about Lincoln. When these questions are paired with the attention to detail and analysis of causality provided by the historian, we can attain a much deeper understanding of why Lincoln said and did particular things and where those words and deeds fit within the complex traditions of thinking about morality and politics.

The second major branch of the theorist's enterprise is to consider the normative questions raised by the words and deeds of a figure like Lincoln. Was Lincoln's legalist "political religion" morally defensible? Did Lincoln's antebellum views of the slavery question respect the dignity of African Americans? Should statesmen use religion to curb the excesses of political zeal? How should political actors balance *universal* moral demands with the *particular* moral demands of history, culture, and community? These are contentious moral questions, and as we reflect on how to come to grips with Lincoln's responses, a brief word must be said about the ideological commitments we bring to the study of American political thought. One of the most striking things about the existing literature on Lincoln's political thought is its heavily rightward tilt.[3] While conservative and libertarian scholars have contributed much to our understanding of Lincoln, there is a lot to be gained from normative judgments about his thought from other ideological perspectives. However much we strive to achieve "objectivity" in our study of American political thought, we are inevitably influenced by our ideological commitments. Conscientious scholars are obligated, of course, to offer fair and honest interpretations of the reformers and the statesmen they study. But the questions they ask about these individuals will be shaped, at least in part, by their own normative commitments. The normative evaluations of the political thought they interpret will also be rooted in these normative commitments. A conservative scholar who holds up the rule of law as an essential safeguard of the social order, for example, will have an easier time accepting Lincoln's legalism. A libertarian scholar who laments the growth of the federal government throughout American history is likely to approach Lincoln's statesmanship with a great deal of skepticism. A liberal or radical scholar is less likely to find Lincoln's antiabolitionism morally acceptable. And so on.

In sum, we are most likely to understand Lincoln's significance in American political thought if we interpret him through multiple methodological lenses and if we judge him from a variety of normative perspectives. To my knowledge, this volume represents the first gathering of an ideologically and methodologically diverse group of scholars to assess the nature and value of his political thought.[4] We hope it inspires additional collections on Lincoln and many of the other great voices of American political thought.[5]

The essays in this volume coalesce around a central question: what does Lincoln teach us about the theory and practice of liberal democracy? They could have been assembled in a variety of ways, since each essay addresses multiple aspects of Lincoln's thought and the liberal democratic project. I have chosen to divide the essays under four broad headings: Lincoln and Democracy, Lincoln and Liberty, Lincoln and Equality, and Lincoln as a Liberal Democratic Statesman. The essays in part I reveal that Lincoln had a complicated relationship with democracy. On the one hand, he was one of the great defenders of equality, which is undoubtedly the moral core of the democratic idea. On the other hand, Lincoln's attitude toward popular sovereignty, which is the political core of the democratic idea, was deeply ambivalent. The essays in part I examine Lincoln's complex relationship to democracy through close, contextually sensitive readings of two speeches that are virtual bookends in his remarkable oratorical career: "The Perpetuation of Our Political Institutions," an address delivered at the Young Men's Lyceum in 1838, and his Second Inaugural address, delivered in 1865. In "Prosperity and Tyranny in Lincoln's Lyceum Address," John Burt examines the "cultural preconditions of democratic rule" by taking seriously Lincoln's call to "revere the law." By deepening our understanding of what it is "one has reverence for when one has reverence for the law," we are able to discover, Burt shows, "the charisma of democracy," which can serve not only as a check against tyranny but also as the basis for a reconception of democratic lawmaking as an invigorating and liberating task.

In "Providentialism and Politics: Lincoln's Second Inaugural Address and the Problem of Democracy," Michael Zuckert presents this famous speech as a "political act" intended to achieve two goals: the immediate goal of bringing the Civil War to an end and "bind[ing] up the nation's wounds," and the more abstract—but no less important—goal of convincing his audience to rethink the nature of sovereignty. In place of the radically democratic idea that "God's will makes itself known through the voice of the people," Zuckert contends that Lincoln developed his complex conception of a "providential" God. In the face of democratic excess, whether in the form of mob violence or in Stephen A. Douglas's doctrine of popular sovereignty, Lincoln defended "providentialism" as an ultimate check on the sovereignty of human will.

In part II we turn our attention to Lincoln's reflections on the idea at the heart of liberalism: individual liberty. In "Lincoln and the Ethics of Emancipation," intellectual historian Dorothy Ross examines the interplay of liberty, nation, and exceptionalism in Lincoln's thought. What interests Ross is how Lincoln reconciled his particularist and often exceptionalist commitment to nation with the universalist idea of a natural right to liberty. Ross's analysis reveals that nationalism both enhanced and undermined Lincoln's commitment to universal emancipation. En route to this conclusion, Ross presents us with a systematic reconstruction of Lincoln's understanding of liberty and provides a powerful explanation of how his commitment to this idea fit with other values.

In "What If Honest Abe Was Telling the Truth?" I explore the possibility that Lincoln genuinely believed in universal natural rights yet rejected an obligation to abolish slavery, and I provide an explanation of how he reconciled these seemingly irreconcilable views. I argue that the key can be found in his legalism, which allowed him to reconceive the moral requirements of natural rights–based political morality and keep the "public mind" at rest in the hope that slavery was on the road to "ultimate extinction."

In part III we place Lincoln's views side by side with two of the most important political movements of his time—nativism and abolitionism—to reveal his understanding of another central idea of liberal democracy: equality. In "The Vital Element of the Republican Party," Bruce Levine shows that (contrary to some scholars who suggest otherwise) Lincoln thoroughly repudiated the nativist movement. To counter those who have argued that Lincoln was less than emphatic in his denunciation of the nativists, Levine points out that he "identified antiforeign and anti-Catholic measures as fundamentally alien and opposed to his deepening commitment to the democratic tenets represented by the Declaration of Independence." In both public and private statements, Lincoln rejected the nativist movement because it represented a betrayal of the idea of human equality at the heart of liberal democratic politics. The vital element of the Republican Party, Levine reminds us, was "anti-slavery sentiment," not nativism.

But how far was Lincoln willing to take his commitment to equality? While he hated slavery and believed that the natural rights described in the Declaration of Independence applied to all men, he was no abolitionist. Why not? This is the animating question of Manisha Sinha's contribution to this volume, "Lincoln's Competing Political Loyalties." Whereas some explain Lincoln's reluctance to embrace abolitionism by downplaying his egalitarianism and antislavery credentials, Sinha shows that he tried to reconcile his "conflicting political loyalties" to antislavery, the Union, and the Constitution. Lincoln's egalitarianism led him to a firm antislavery position prior to the Civil War, Sinha argues, but his commitment to the Union and the Constitution prevented him from taking the next step into the abolitionist camp. To illustrate the nature of the competition between Lincoln's political loyalties, Sinha places his ideas side by side with those of several leading abolitionist constitutional theorists such as Gerrit Smith, Lysander Spooner, and Frederick Douglass. In the end, the war allowed Lincoln to resolve his conflicting loyalties by "decoupling slavery from the Union and the Constitution." This decoupling allowed Lincoln and other moderate Republicans, Sinha concludes, to "become emancipationists, if not abolitionists."

Lincoln's role as a liberal democratic statesman is the focus of the two essays in part IV. Allen Guelzo's "Four Roads to Emancipation" provides a careful explanation of the *how* of emancipation. Lest we think this is irrelevant to a book on Lincoln's thought, Guelzo reminds us that Lincoln's choice of which road to take reveals much about him as a man of ideas. Lincoln's road to emancipation was marked by prudence and a continuing commitment to the rule of law, and it was, Guelzo argues, the road best suited to the achievement of lasting freedom. The principled and forward-looking nature of Lincoln's emancipation policy leads Guelzo to conclude that it is a "hallmark" of liberal democratic statesmanship.

In contrast to Guelzo's emphasis on Lincoln's prudence, Steven Smith emphasizes the "egalitarian, universalist, and progressive character to his statecraft" in "Lincoln's Kantian Republic." Smith offers this interpretation as an explicit challenge to Guelzo and other scholars who focus on the centrality of prudence in Lincoln's thought. While Guelzo provides us with a useful explanation of Lincoln's statesmanship from the "ground up" as he navigates his way to the Emancipation Proclamation, Smith reflects on Lincoln's statesmanship from the bird's-eye view of the political theorist as he helps us think through the theoretical framework that animated Lincoln both explicitly and implicitly.

In the world around us, citizens and statesmen continue to grapple with questions about liberal democracy that echo those asked in the age of Lincoln. What is the proper balance between the will of the majority and the rights of the individual? When does the law deserve our reverence, and when does it deserve our resistance? How does our understanding of God shape our politics? How does patriotism promote, and how does it undermine, universal freedom? How does our commitment to the rule of law enhance and at the same time inhibit our own emancipatory projects? How should new immigrants and religious minorities be treated? How can one balance competing political loyalties? What are the hallmarks of liberal democratic statesmanship? As we continue to confront these questions, we would do well to remember Lincoln, who provides us with many profound answers while at the same time reminding us why these questions are perennial.

NOTES

1. Harry Jaffa, *Crisis of the House Divided* (Chicago: University of Chicago Press, 1999); Harry Jaffa, *New Birth of Freedom* (Lanham, MD: Rowman & Littlefield, 2004); John Patrick Diggins, *The Lost Soul of American Politics* (Chicago: University of Chicago Press, 1984); J. David Greenstone, *The Lincoln Persuasion* (Princeton, NJ: Princeton University Press, 1993); John Burt, *Lincoln's Tragic Pragmatism* (Cambridge, MA: Belknap Press, 2012); Thomas DiLorenzo, *The Real Lincoln* (New York: Three Rivers Press, 2002); Lerone Bennett, *Forced into Glory: Abraham Lincoln's White Dream* (Chicago: Johnson Publishing, 1999).

2. Sheldon Wolin, *Politics and Vision* (New York: Little, Brown, 1960), 8.

3. See Joseph Fornieri and Kenneth Deutsch, *Lincoln's American Dream* (Dulles, VA: Potomac Books, 2005).

4. The only major collection of essays focused on Lincoln's political thought is Fornieri and Deutsch's *Lincoln's American Dream*. Although it is a valuable volume, it suffers from two major shortcomings. First, it is largely a compendium of essays published previously. Second, the volume consists almost entirely of essays from one side of the political spectrum. The volume contains opposing views of Lincoln, but it is focused almost exclusively on disagreements between Straussian conservatives and paleoconservatives. Two other volumes worth mentioning are *The Cambridge*

Companion to Abraham Lincoln (Cambridge: Cambridge University Press, 2012) and *Our Lincoln* (New York: W. W. Norton, 2008). A small fraction of the essays included therein addresses Lincoln's political thought, but that is not the overall focus of either volume. The most recent contribution to the Lincoln literature is Lucas Morel, ed., *Lincoln and Liberty: Wisdom for the Ages* (Lexington: University Press of Kentucky, 2014). Morel's collection falls somewhere between *Lincoln's American Dream* and the *Cambridge Companion*. It focuses largely, though not exclusively, on Lincoln's thought, and it is largely, though not exclusively, a collection of essays by conservative scholars.

5. The essays collected here are by no means a comprehensive examination of Lincoln's political thought. There are many areas—such as his views on economic development, technology, and civil liberties in wartime—that we did not include due to space limitations. My hope is that the approach taken here—viewing Lincoln through multiple disciplinary lenses and from a variety of theoretical perspectives—will serve as a model for future studies.

PART ONE

Lincoln and Democracy

CHAPTER ONE

Prosperity and Tyranny in Lincoln's Lyceum Address

John Burt

Lincoln's 1838 address to the Young Men's Lyceum of Springfield, Illinois, "The Perpetuation of Our Political Institutions," was not his first political speech, but it was the first articulation of many themes that would become prominent in his more mature oratory. Among these was the claim that stable political institutions require the cultivation of habits of thought and behavior that fit people for democratic living. Further, these habits, though arising from the demands of reason, must ingrain themselves beneath reason into the structure of popular feeling so as to become an intuitive, and never fully reflected on, ground of habit—something Lincoln refers to as "political religion" in the Lyceum speech and as "the public mind" in his 1858 debates with Stephen Douglas. These structures of feeling are hard to establish and fragile, and the natural course of political life inevitably subjects them to strains they may not be able to withstand. That is, the normal pulling and hauling of politics, not merely the emergence of charismatic and tyrannical personalities, expose the fissures in the democratic order and weaken the people's attachment to that order, unless special care is taken to preserve the cultural preconditions of democratic rule. As he would do twenty years later in the "House Divided" speech, Lincoln lists in the Lyceum speech a series of recent events that provide early warnings of

---

An earlier, less developed version of this essay appeared as "Lincoln's Address to the Young Men's Lyceum: A Speculative Essay," *Western Humanities Review* 51, 3 (1997): 304–320.

the threat to the culture of democracy and proposes measures, as much cultural as political, to answer that threat.

According to John Channing Briggs, the idea that democracy was in danger of eroding from within was a commonplace of late 1830s oratory. Many of the incidents to which Lincoln alludes—the 1835 lynching of professional gamblers in Vicksburg, the 1836 burning of Francis McIntosh in St. Louis, and the November 1837 assassination of abolitionist editor Elijah Lovejoy in Alton, Illinois—were, along with the 1834 burning of the Ursuline convent in Charlestown, Massachusetts, commonly cited by those who feared a breakdown of the culture of law. Lovejoy himself alluded to all these events (except, of course, his own murder, which he did, however, predict) in an article in his *St. Louis Observer*, and he was driven out of St. Louis to Alton for his pains.[1]

It is easy to underestimate the Lyceum address. Relative to the speeches of Lincoln's maturity, its rhetoric seems florid and inauthentic. Relative to the diamond precision of the tricolon within a tricolon with which he ends the Gettysburg Address, the elaborately structured periodic sentence in which Lincoln imagines Washington arising at the sound of the last trumpet to inquire what became of the nation sounds like a rhetorical paste gem, something one can imagine the young Lincoln practicing before a mirror. Even the main answer the speech proposes to the threat that a charismatic tyrant may seek to overthrow democratic rule, the inculcation of a spirit of submission to the law, seems thin and unsatisfactory.

Because of these weaknesses, a traditional reading of the speech sees it, for the most part, as a paint-by-numbers Whig attack on Jackson and his followers, who were indeed considered threats to stable republican rule on account of their willingness to whip up popular feeling or to follow popular will wherever it led, however ugly that place might be.[2] More recently, Michael Burlingame has advanced the idea that the speech was an oblique move in the 1838 congressional campaign, with Stephen Douglas himself in the role of the "towering genius" the speech critiques. Lincoln had in fact mocked the very short-statured Douglas as a "towering genius," like the similarly short Napoleon Bonaparte, in a piece he published the same day the Lyceum speech was delivered. In addition, the speech's critique of mobocracy in many ways resembles other critiques emanating from Whiggish circles in Illinois the same year, including earlier speeches at the Young Men's Lyceum.[3]

It is only on third or fourth thought that one sees anything in the Lyceum address beyond stale filial piety and rote partisanship. To do that requires recognizing, as Harry Jaffa did long ago in *Crisis of the House Divided*

(1959), that Lincoln not only warns against charismatic tyranny but also diagnoses its fatal weakness—that the quest for power is always futile, that the dreams of Callicles and Thrasymachus are not visions of greatness but grandiose fantasies whose ultimate consequence is empty self-abasement. The charismatic tyrant is a product of the wear and tear of democratic politics, which seems to provide no meaningful task for masterful personalities to do; yet, when closely examined, tyrannical rule does not turn out to be a meaningful task worthy of a masterful personality either. Finding that meaningful task, the task that saves the republic from the charismatic tyrant and is worthy of the masterful personality's greatness, requires seeing democracy as having its own charisma, so that the would-be tyrant better serves his charisma by protecting democracy rather than threatening it. Discovering the charisma of democracy, in turn, requires one to ask what it is, when all is said and done, that one has reverence for when one has reverence for law.

Ultimately, what one has reverence for is the positive moral content of a democratic ethos, its prophetic call to the moral equality of all people. But not every conception of the democratic ethos embodies that call. To see a democratic society, for instance, as merely a fair-minded arbiter of conflicts among parties with different interests, to see it as an instance of what J. David Greenstone, in his important book *The Lincoln Persuasion* (1993), calls "humanist liberalism," is to see it as merely an agreement among ingroups about how to divide the spoils of social life among themselves. Such a society inevitably calls forth the challenge of charismatic tyranny (since the tyrant feels in his own person, and provides for the republic, that sense of calling that a humanist liberal society, by definition, lacks). Years later, in the Peoria speech of 1854, Lincoln would develop a fuller critique of the idea that the democratic ethos is essentially one of neutral deal making among parties with different desires. There, he would object to the idea, which he believed Stephen Douglas's Kansas-Nebraska Act embodied, "that there is no right principle but interest." This view, Lincoln argued, subverted the promises of the opening sentences of the Declaration of Independence and reduced the meaning of freedom to the idea that if one man chooses freely to make a slave of another, no third man can be allowed to object.

The Lyceum speech argues that only what Greenstone calls "reform liberalism" is capable of maintaining a stable democratic order, since it has a positive vocation, rooted in "a broadly Kantian ethic that is rooted in the New England Puritan tradition," to provide individuals with the means of fulfilling their obligations; "to cultivate and develop their physical, intellectual, aesthetic, and moral faculties"; and to help others do the same.[4] The positive, liberating moral vocation of reform liberalism provides the practical means by which political agents recognize and acknowledge their moral equality with one another, earning the possibility of moral agency by recognizing and fostering moral agency in others. It is in this vocation that we seek the meaning of what Hannah Arendt, in *The Human Condition* (1958), calls *action*.[5]

CHARISMATIC TYRANNY

What stands out for most readers of Lincoln's 1838 Lyceum address is his startlingly Miltonic description of the character of the tyrant.[6] Aware that "men of ambition and talents" will continue to arise in America, Lincoln asks how such people, now that the Revolution is over, can put those ambitions and talents to use. In the revolutionary era, the greatness of heroic personalities, as well as their will to power, was fully realized in, and to an extent neutralized by, the grandeur and difficulty of the revolutionary task. But since that time, the only task equal to the grandeur of genius has been tyranny:

> The question then, is, can that gratification be found in supporting and maintaining an edifice that has been erected by others? Most certainly it cannot. Many great and good men sufficiently qualified for any task they should undertake, may ever be found, whose ambition would aspire to nothing beyond a seat in Congress, a gubernatorial or a presidential chair; *but such belong not to the family of the lion, or the tribe of the eagle*. What! think you these places would satisfy an Alexander, a Caesar, or a Napoleon? Never! Towering genius disdains a beaten path. It seeks regions hitherto unexplored. It sees *no distinction* in adding story to story, upon the monuments of fame, created to the memory of others. It *denies* that it is glory enough to serve under any chief. It *scorns* to tread in the footsteps of *any* predecessor, however illustrious. It thirsts and burns for distinction; and, if possible, it will have it, whether at the expense of emancipating slaves, or enslaving freemen.[7]

It is the last sentence, of course, that has attracted the most notice, leading Edmund Wilson (1962) to argue that Lincoln is warning the country against himself (as both the emancipator of slaves, through the Thirteenth Amendment, and the enslaver of freemen, through the suppression of habeas corpus).[8] The same passage led psychohistorians such as Dwight G.

Anderson to posit an Oedipal relationship between Lincoln and the founding fathers.[9] While it is a mistake to see this passage as either a prophecy of Lincoln's policies a quarter century later or an explanation of the neurotic basis of those policies, certainly Lincoln (like Milton) felt the magnetism of the role he describes and critiques. And just as certainly, what Lincoln describes here is not just the familiar tyrant from the civic republican literature of the previous century or even the Machiavellian man of virtu, but the demonic hero familiar to us from the Romantic reading of Milton articulated by Blake, Shelley, Byron, and Melville.[10]

What is especially Miltonic about Lincoln's tyrant is not only his unwillingness to play a small part in a great drama that centers on some other person's greatness but also his resentment of a world that does not owe its creation to him and that, by offering him security and prosperity while asking in return only the comparatively small price of grateful acceptance of its bounty, shows him all too painfully that it has no essential need of him. It is in possessing a real but inconvenient grandeur that Lincoln's tyrant is most like Milton's Satan—and unlike the lesser tyrants that haunt the civic republican imagination. Lincoln feels the force of the tyrant's charisma just as Milton felt the charisma of his own Satan; he understands the logic of his personality and the dramatic attractiveness of his ambitions. Like Milton, Lincoln registers the force of his character's charisma but holds it at arm's length; like Milton, he ultimately breaks the power of that charisma and sees it as self-emptying and futile. And like Milton in *Paradise Regained*, he finally replaces a discredited ideal of charismatic power with a more genuine but less dramatic ideal of restraint and submission to law, aware of both the price and the promise of this replacement, so that the "figure of towering genius" is to George Washington what Milton's Satan finally is to Milton's Jesus.[11]

The tyrant Lincoln imagines, then, is not a creature of mere vice. More surprising still, the tyrant Lincoln imagines is not, like Robespierre or Lenin, enraged into destroying the political world by a maddening vision of the misery to which he sees himself responding. He is rather, again like Milton's Satan, a creature of the success of the order he seeks to overthrow.

THREATS TO DEMOCRACY

Lincoln was not alone in locating a major threat to American democracy in its material and political success. What the tyrant rejects is, after all, not very different from what Thoreau would call a life of quiet desperation eight years later. Nor is it very different from the purely instrumental life devoted to getting and spending that Emerson criticized in "The American Scholar" in 1837. Indeed, the life of the private citizen, devoted to patient and modest accumulation and with little invested in the public world—the life that Lincoln himself would praise in his speeches at the Wisconsin State Agricultural Society in 1859 and in New Haven the next year, his classic statements of what Eric Foner calls the "free labor ideology"—seems in this speech to be a life of dreary conformist emptiness.[12] When Lincoln describes the task of his generation, is it only to my ear that he seems somewhat grudging about it, as if he had been given a beautiful suit of clothes but nothing to do with it except keep it from getting dirty?

> We, when mounting the stage of existence, found ourselves the legal inheritors of these fundamental blessings. We toiled not in the acquirement or establishment of them—they are a legacy bequeathed us, by a *once* hardy, brave and patriotic, but *now* lamented and departed race of ancestors. Their's [*sic*] was the task (and nobly they performed it) to possess themselves, and through themselves, us, of this goodly land; and to uprear upon its hills and its valleys, a political edifice of liberty and equal rights; 'tis ours only, to transmit these, the former, unprofaned by the foot of an invader; the latter, undecayed by the lapse of time, and untorn by usurpation—to the latest generation that fate shall permit the world to know. This task of gratitude to our fathers, justice to ourselves, duty to posterity, and love for our species in general, all imperatively require us faithfully to perform.[13]

Even when Lincoln rules out invasion by a foreign power as a source of danger and argues that whatever danger the republic faces must come from within, does not danger seem at least bracing? And does not the thought of an immortality without danger seem as burdensome to Lincoln as it was to Tithonus? "At what point then is the approach of danger to be expected? I answer, if it ever reach us, it must spring up amongst us. It cannot come from abroad. If destruction be our lot, we must ourselves be its author and finisher. As a nation of freemen, we must live through all time, or die by suicide."[14] Note that this passage looks like an argument by elimination (we do not expect danger from X, so we can only be threatened by Y), but in fact it is a causal argument: *because* the United States does not face danger from abroad, *therefore* it faces danger from itself. For one thing, given the success of the Revolution, those ugly feelings that may be a larger part of great natures than of small ones have been left with no safe mode of expression. Lincoln is very frank about the role dark feelings played in the Revolution—perhaps he has in mind something like the old inner identity Machiavelli described between the outlaw and the founder of cities—and he is also frank in admitting that ugly passions do not vanish when the occasions for those passions do. Speaking of the mobilization of passions by the Revolution, Lincoln argues:

> By this influence, the jealousy, envy, and avarice, incident to our nature, and so common to a state of peace, prosperity, and conscious strength, were, for the time, in a great measure smothered and rendered inactive; while the deep rooted principles of *hate*, and the powerful motive of *revenge*, instead of being turned against each other, were directed exclusively against the British nation. And thus, from the force of circumstances, the basest principles of our nature, were either made to lie dormant, or to become the active agents in the advancement of the noblest of cause—that of establishing and maintaining civil and religious liberty.[15]

Over these same years—the heyday of American braggadocio—the idea that stability and prosperity would breed a debased culture was very much in the air. What Lincoln, Emerson, Thoreau, and Tocqueville feared was not the modern nightmare about early market economies—that they descend into societies of rapacious exploiters who serve accumulation with ruthless dedication and are interested in public culture only to the extent it provides security for their possessions and the opportunity to seize more of them. What they feared in different ways was that even a more modest political culture, one interested in securing a steady if undramatic advancement of its material conditions (the culture of fair-minded, worldly, and enlightened traders and negotiators described by Martin Diamond), would somehow result in a habit of life that was less than fully human.[16]

Emerson's critique of this habit of life is well known. Tocqueville's is less so but more telling, since what he describes as a nightmare—a tyranny that degrades rather than torments its victims because it unfailingly supplies them with what they think they want and subjects them to the irresistible power of their own desires—is not terribly different from what both political parties then and now have always described as a dream. Accustomed to confining his attention to private concerns, the American, Tocqueville predicts, will also accustom himself to thinking of larger concerns as cloudy and unreal; he will "confine the activity of private judgment within limits too narrow for the dignity and happiness of mankind," until he is finally induced to give up thinking at all.[17] The result is a kind of despair in which only concerns related to money or pleasure or comfort have any essential reality, and ultimate realities are, if not actually dismissed as illusions (or as disguised versions of seeking money, pleasure, or comfort), mystified as value judgments and leaps of faith that, because they are never quite rational, are honored with a slight edge of contempt, since what one cannot reflect on in a critical way cannot matter much either.

What is to be feared about this state of despair is not that the vision of life it embodies is not a human one or that lives lived in such a state will be empty, although both these things are true. Rather, the fear is that despair causes one to do desperate things. As Tocqueville darkly argues:

> Each man gets into the way of having nothing but confused and changing notions about the matters of greatest importance to himself and his fellows. Opinions are ill-defined or abandoned, and in despair of solving unaided the greatest problems of human destiny, men ignobly give up thinking about them.
>
> Such a state inevitably enervates the soul, and relaxing the springs of the will, prepares a people for bondage.
>
> Then not only will they let their freedom be taken from them, but often they actually hand it over themselves.
>
> When there is no authority in religion or in politics, men are soon frightened by the limitless independence with which they are faced. They are worried and worn out by the constant restlessness of everything. With everything on the move in the realm of the mind, they want the material order at least to be firm and stable, and as they cannot accept their ancient beliefs again, they hand themselves over to a master.[18]

The failure to find a good use for freedom, whether by the people or by the would-be tyrant, Tocqueville argues, invites both of them to invent a dramatically bad use for it. People turn themselves over to a master because materialism, "coming between themselves and God," afflicts them with "a strange melancholy" in which they are no longer capable of "thinking," except in impulsive, dogmatic, or uncritical ways, about the "cares of living."[19] By "cares of living," Tocqueville means not plans about material prosperity but concern about the problems of human life, of being born and having to die—problems we cannot expect to solve, but we cannot be human unless we try to. What Tocqueville calls "a strange melancholy" is what Thoreau later calls "a stereotyped but unconscious despair,"[20] a despair so deep that it even loses consciousness of itself as despair.

The reader will recognize in Tocqueville's description of the despairing materialist society a collective version of the crisis of vocation that Lincoln attributes to the tyrant: the demonic hero and the despairing society are each other's creatures. Both are fanatics, not out of a violent devotion to a violence-justifying idea, and not out of pure will to power either, but out of a panicked sense that only by fanaticism can they face down the inner deadness of a life of materialist accumulation and consumption. The tyrant seeks power as a way of shouting down his sense that life—not just *his* life, but life itself—is empty. And followers of that tyrant follow him in an attempt to persuade themselves that something still matters to them.

MOB RULE

When Lincoln surveys his society, he finds several examples of mob rule capable of shaking the populace's faith in the democratic order and preparing them to hand their liberties over to a tyrant who might at least provide order and security. But these acts of violence seem to arise not from the alienation I just described but from fanaticism. Indeed, it would be fairer to call the murders of Lovejoy and McIntosh and the lynching of the gamblers at Vicksburg examples of unhinged racism than of alienation or anomie. On their face, these incidents do not really prove that the slackening of the fervor of the revolutionary age has put the republic at risk; they prove that the republic is at risk because of its deadly differences of opinion about slavery and race. One could imagine that the evidence Lincoln cites in the Lyceum speech would better support the case he makes later in the "House Divided" speech—that the machinations of the slave power are corrupting the springs of democratic thought—than the case he makes here.

Lincoln's portrayal of racist mobbing in the Lyceum speech is strikingly different from his portrayal of the conflict with the slave power in the "House Divided" speech. For one thing, in the Lyceum speech Lincoln discerns beneath the savagery of mob violence not a sinister conspiracy to nationalize the peculiar institution but an angry and misguided but nevertheless earnest demand for what the mob sees as immediate justice.

Why on earth would Lincoln grant the lynchers of McIntosh and the assassins of Lovejoy such a concession? Surely he had no intention of defending either. Partly, Lincoln may have been motivated by prudence or perhaps even fear, considering the virulence of the against abolition he himself had witnessed in response to a resolution in the Illinois legislature the previous year. But there is more to it than this. The lyncher, as Lincoln portrays him, is usually someone in the grip of an urgent and violent passion, a passion to see justice done, a passion so strong that it justifies ignoring every procedural nicety and treating those procedural niceties as hindrances to justice and, what is more, as a kind of complicity in injustice. One might think that the connection between the lyncher and the tyrant is that the latter poses as someone who can satisfy the former's rage for justice by brushing aside the institutions of legitimacy that stand in the way of that justice. Indeed, the tyrant's ability to do just that is his usual defense of himself: he is someone who seeks power and gets it by persuading people to see him as the harsh servant of enraged justice. But when one examines the specifics of the lynching incidents Lincoln describes, one finds at the heart of the lyncher's enraged lust for justice an emptiness and futility not much different from the emptiness and futility at the heart of the tyrant's enraged lust for power.

The most famous lynching Lincoln discusses, of course, is his oblique yet unmistakably pointed treatment of the November 7, 1837, murder of abolitionist editor Elijah Lovejoy by a mob in Alton, Illinois. The event was recent enough at the time of the speech that even Lincoln's delicate and indirect allusion could not help but bring it fully to mind among his contemporary audience. Lincoln's treatment of the Lovejoy case is peculiar, especially in light of his later political friendship with Elijah's brother Owen Lovejoy. He treats the mob not as a crowd brought to violence by a positive interest in slavery or simply by its own native wickedness but as a group of people who may have a genuine grievance but are impatient of the law's ability to respond to that grievance. After an offhand reference to crowds who "throw printing presses into rivers" and "shoot editors," Lincoln launches into a rather abstract (and to my mind, rather thin) argument about why people with grievances should not resort to mob action:

> There is no grievance that is a fit object of redress by mob law. In any case that arises, as for instance, the promulgation of abolitionism, one of two positions is necessarily true; that is, the thing is right within itself, and therefore deserves the protection of all law and all good citizens; or it is wrong, and therefore proper to be prohibited by legal enactments; and in neither case, is the interposition of mob law, either necessary, justifiable, or excusable.[21]

That the "promulgation of abolitionism" might be grounds for grievances deserving of the slightest respect might strike us as odd. But certainly, Lincoln is only making a strategic concession here, arguing that even if abolitionism *were* grounds for grievance, mob action would still not be justified. Even so, seeing Lincoln's concession this way does not quite wipe away the oddness of his assumption that he is addressing an audience of people more like the lynchers than their victim. In the paragraph just cited, Lincoln is aware that abolition is a risky conviction, and his strategic concession is charged with a nervous pretense that he has at least some sympathetic insight into the volatile feelings of his audience, whom he addresses in the soothing language one might use when faced with a strange dog.

Lincoln's argument turns on a false dichotomy: in every case, something is either right, and should therefore be left alone, or wrong, and should therefore be the business of the law, not mobs of private citizens. The difficulty with Lincoln's position is that it applies not only to mob law but also to any manifestation of excited public feeling. If you are enraged by some manifest injustice, you are separated by the thinnest of lines from the lyncher, perhaps only by the fact that you have not yet acted on your rage. Lincoln all but argues that the only legitimate place for moral excitement about political topics is a legislature and that moral excitement outside of a legislature is a form of mob rule. Given an unjust law, for instance, Lincoln permits the citizen no recourse other than to obey it, and the government has no recourse but to rigorously enforce it until it is changed. This is especially odd, since the moral transformations of our society usually come to a boil elsewhere before they engender formal legal or policy deliberations. Lincoln's sanction is as likely to hobble agitation in a good cause as it is in a bad one. Lincoln's argument seems too sweeping, for it rules out not just lynching but also the idea that popular feeling plays any role at all in politics, and he describes all pressure put on politics by popular feeling as if it were the moral equivalent of lynching.

For Lincoln, a deliberative lawmaking body and an aroused populace entertain convictions in very different ways. For one thing, governments, unlike "the people," can make specific promises to which they can be held. For another thing, whereas the people's convictions exist mostly in the comparatively blunt form of pressure in favor of the cause they are aroused about, governments are capable of entertaining many convictions at many levels of intensity and over many time scales and can therefore make considered trade-offs and prudent bargains. (One of the reasons it is so difficult to negotiate with representatives of popular movements is that someone else can always claim to represent the popular movement more authentically, rendering negotiation empty: one can make and keep promises with a government, but not with a popular movement. Nobody really speaks for a popular movement, and popular movements are, by definition, incapable of exercising responsibility or being held to it.)

What is ultimately at stake in this peculiar passage about mob law is the difference between government as the expression of deliberation and principle ("reform liberalism") and government as the expression of will ("humanist liberalism"). That is why an argument that should be a passionate denunciation of bloody misrule by lynchers turns into a rather pallid admonition that people should continue to obey bad laws until they are changed:

> When I so pressingly urge a strict observance of all the laws, let me not be understood as saying there are no bad laws, nor that grievances may not arise, for the redress of which, no legal provisions have been made. I mean to say no such thing. But I do mean to say, that, although bad laws, if they exist, should be repealed as soon as possible, still while they continue in force, for the sake of the example, they should be religiously observed.[22]

Lincoln here, as in his 1858 debates with Stephen Douglas, is skeptical about the role of popular will in legitimate government. He sees popular will not as the lifeblood of a democracy but as a kind of intoxicating stimulant that corrupts a republic's judgment. Douglas, unlike Lincoln, argues that, for the most part, citizens hold their convictions in a stable way, and the work of government is to weigh all those convictions against one another and work out the sum. If the people of the Kansas Territory want to have slavery, for example, that would be up to them to decide (through their legislature). The only question would be whether their legislature really reflects the wishes of the people of the territory. Whatever the law is, for Douglas, it expresses imperatives that arise from a stratum beneath the positive law—the stratum of popular feeling. Lincoln, by contrast, describes "squatter sovereignty" as an exercise in mob rule that is not much different from lynching (which is why he echoes his 1838 language in his debates with Douglas): under "squatter sovereignty," the mob of people that first seizes control of the territorial machinery gets to write the laws for everybody else.[23]

Law for Lincoln is not the expression of popular will but the upshot of long deliberation about principle, and what underlies law is not popular feeling but the more or less durable set of common assumptions and habits that make for a common public life, what Lincoln refers to in 1858 as the "public mind." The Kansas Territory cannot decide to make slaves of people because no legislature gets to decide who is a human being and who is not, and whatever freedom is, it is not the freedom to rule other people without their consent. The distinction between founding the legitimacy of law in its accurate reflection of public will, or its ability to trade off conflicting wills in a fair-minded way, and founding the legitimacy of law in reflected-upon insights into common and deeply held but always imperfectly understood principles is parallel to the distinction Greenstone develops between humanist liberalism and reform liberalism.

What is at issue in Lincoln's treatment of the Lovejoy case is not only that mob violence encourages people with passionate grievances to ignore the law and encourages those who seek security and order from the state to despair of the state's ability to provide it. What is also at issue, as Jaffa notes, is the necessity of restraining the people's exercise of sovereignty lest they become so intoxicated by sovereignty that they undo freedom. Freedom is not the ability to do as one pleases or even the ability to do as one pleases so long as nobody else gets hurt by it; freedom is the exercise of moral autonomy, and it is distinguished from enslavement to one's own whims and desires by the seriousness with which it holds itself, through circumspect deliberation, to moral absolutes that have not been designed to serve its own convenience.[24]

The distinction between what a crowd wants and what has been formally enacted by a deliberative body does not exhaust Lincoln's argument, since legislators, intoxicated by the people's sovereignty, are just as capable as mobs of betraying the circumspection and reflection necessary for legitimate government. The authority of law does not arise merely from the fact that it has been enacted by a legislature but also because, as Lincoln says, it is "right within itself and therefore deserves the protection of all law and all good citizens." In other words, for Lincoln, law is founded on a layer of collective moral reflection that is embodied in the established sense of a culture's felt values and in the critical examination of both particular courses of action and traditional cultural values.

Even describing the tension between law as the expression of popular will and law as the expression of principle and tradition, however, misses a central fact about the tension between consent and principle that underlies the legitimacy of law: that is, when pressed hard, each term seems to dissolve into the other. When, for instance, we ask what a particular act of the will entails, we are asking what is included in its intention. Every act has a chain of consequences, not all of them anticipated, and every act must be seen against an unfolding set of circumstances; therefore, the question of what an act really means is always a live one, subject not only to readjustment but also to wholesale rethinking. One can make sense of popular will only by seeing it as Ronald Dworkin does in *Law's Empire* (1986), as a kind of groping about for a difficult-to-articulate principle that is never fully represented—and always partly betrayed—by its enactments. When I view law as "whatever it is I happen to want," I raise the question of "what is it that I want, really?" This raises the further question of "what would be most expressive of what I most deeply am, what would be worthy of me to want?" And I cannot answer this question unless—as Socrates demanded of Callicles—I discover that something like principle stands in a critical relation to what I think my will is.[25]

It is only by seeing that will stands in some engaged relationship to principle that we can work through the otherwise paralyzing ambiguities in the act of willing itself, whether we are speaking of the will of individuals or will in some public form. When we look hard at will, it seems to vanish into a thicket of heterogeneous intentions. We sometimes naïvely suppose that authentic acts of will spring out of a lucid and intense present in which I *am* as I *am*, and what I am is known to me in a wholly satisfying although perhaps wholly implicit way. But the first fact I learn about my own will is its ambivalence. What finally issues from me as an act is only what survives from a tangle of contradictory impulses, hesitations, and desires, some of which I recognize as transitory and "not really what I am about," and others that strike me as deep but also obscure, as things I do not fully understand but wish to follow out. (This is why Emerson's demand in "Self Reliance"—that we do the work that is authentically ours to do—looks so easy to satisfy from the outside: because outsiders have little in the way of testing whether that demand has been satisfied. Yet, from the inside, it is almost impossible to fulfill: "If any one imagines that this law is lax, let him keep its commandment one day.")

The person who is free only because he is not subject to constraints is not free. The person who does whatever it occurs to him to do is not free; he is enslaved by his impulses, a person who cannot help himself. The only free person is someone whose acts are the outcome of reflection, and reflection inevitably raises the question of principle.[26]

Principle, likewise, is opaque to Whiggish minds like Lincoln's without a live engagement with will. If one sacrifices will to principle, crying out "Let God's will be done though the earth perish!" it turns out that one is not serving principle after all. Principle can be served only through judgment and reflection; it is served not through calculation but through playing the principle on the pulse. A live principle has a vitality so formidable and so rebuking to self-love that I can never claim to have it under my thumb, and I cannot be certain that my political opponents will never be in a position to instruct me about it. If I do not see my values in this way—as something I know the way I know a person (which is to say, as something I know by unknowing)—then I am serving not my values but merely a louder-voiced variety of will. If I deduce a principle that some other person does not deduce, and if I trample that person in the name of that principle (arguing, perhaps, that I need not seek that person's consent because my principle is so compelling), that person would be justified in claiming that deduction-plus-force is not much different (from my point of view as well as from his) from the most naked will to power.

A principle is not so much a proposition as a poetic insight into a fully human habit of moral life, and as such, it has ties to both feeling and thought. Certainly, if we have any rational engagement with our values at all—if we are neither ethical machines nor makers of "value judgments"—we must be capable of enough circumspection about our values, even as we commit to them, to at least weigh different developments of them as time and thought turn them around and around before us.

"Reason also is choice," Milton's God crabbily remarks, meaning roughly the same thing I do: that only a principle entertained in a live if provisional way, in reflective equilibrium, can ground truly autonomous action. Principle and will are often seen as opposites, and political conflict is often seen as a contest between parties of principle and parties of will. But principle and will are deeply engaged with each other in all forms of political legitimacy, since only principle allows will to clarify itself out of the chaos of willing, and only a live reckoning with the wills of others enables one to see principle as anything other than a louder-voiced variety of will.

ENRAGED JUSTICE

The tension between consent and principle is not precisely parallel to that between interest politics and ethical politics. However, those who embrace ethical politics see consent as the resort of the unprincipled, and those who embrace interest politics see principle only as a rationalization of one interest group's urge to trample the interests of others. The most potent kinds of intoxicating popular sovereignty are, after all, not those that arise out of desire and interest but those that arise out of an angry love of justice. When confronted with this kind of popular movement, the attempt to bring principle and consent into harmony is of almost no use, for under these circumstances, the people, in their rage, believe they are in the grip not of an urgent desire but of a principle. People who believe they are acting on principle are responsible to something that is worth everything to them, and for that reason, they are capable of anything.

Lincoln introduces two additional discussions of mob violence to make this point. Like the Lovejoy case, both these cases turn on issues of slavery and race. One of the things that caused Lovejoy to be attacked was his defense of the victim of mob violence (or, more precisely, his denunciation of the victim's attackers) in his newspaper. Lovejoy's treatment of these cases in the *St. Louis Observer* is, in fact, so close to Lincoln's that it persuades Briggs to see Lincoln as obliquely following Lovejoy's lead:

> We have drawn the above gloomy and hideous picture, not for the purpose of holding it up as a fair representation of the moral condition of St. Louis—for we loudly protest against any such conclusion, and we call upon our fellow citizens to join us in such a protest—but that the immediate actors in the horrid tragedy may see the work of their hands, and shrink in horror from a repetition of it, and in humble patience seek forgiveness of that community whose laws they have so outraged, and of that GOD whose image they have, without his permission, wickedly defaced; and that they may all see, (and be warned in time) the legitimate results of the spirit of mobism, and whither, unless arrested in its first out-breakings, it is sure to carry us. In Charlestown it burns a Convent over the heads of defenceless women; in Baltimore it desecrates the Sabbath, and works all that day in demolishing a private citizen's house; in Vicksburg it hangs up gamblers, three or four in a row; and in St. Louis it forces a man—a hardened wretch certainly, and one that deserved to die, but not *thus* to die—it forces him from beneath the aegis of our Constitution and laws, hurries him to the stake and burns him alive.[27]

Lincoln's own description of the St. Louis burning case is stark:

> Turn, then, to that horror-striking scene at St. Louis. A single victim was only sacrificed there. His story is very short; and is, perhaps, the most highly tragic, of any thing of its length, that has ever been witnessed in real life. A mulatto man, by the name of M'Intosh, was seized in the street, dragged to the suburbs of the city, chained to a tree, and actually burned to death; and all within a single hour from the time he had been a freeman, attending to his own business, and at peace with the world.[28]

The last few sentences give the impression that the victim had been seized at random by an enraged mob, like the African American victims murdered during the New York City draft riots of 1863. Indeed, the depictions of him as "a freeman" and "at peace with the world" imply that Lincoln intends to tell a story of pure victimization. The case was a well-known one, alluded to by Horace Bushnell of Hartford in a letter to Henry Clay as an example of the increasing threat to society posed by mob rule. But Lincoln goes on to elaborate the case in such a way as to make it clear that its horror is a function not of the innocence of the victim but of the extralegality of the murder.

McIntosh, a steward on the steamboat *Flora*, had killed a sheriff and wounded a constable after they arrested him for interfering with their attempts to arrest two other sailors. He certainly feared that they intended to imprison him for a long term, and he may have feared that they intended to convey him into slavery.[29] "He had forfeited his life, by the perpetration of an outrageous murder, upon one of the most worthy and respectable citizens of the city; and had he not died as he did, he must have died by the sentence of the law, in a very short time afterwards. As to him alone, is was as well the way it was."[30] What offends Lincoln is that the right person was lynched only by accident, for enraged mobs (who are likely to subject Clara Petacci to the same punishment they visit on Benito Mussolini) cannot be expected to render fine distinctions of guilt:

> When men take it in their heads to day, to hang gamblers, or burn murderers, they should recollect, that, in the confusion usually attending such transactions, they will be as likely to hang or burn some one, who is neither a gambler nor a murderer, as one who is; and that, acting upon the example they set, the mob of to-morrow, may, and probably will, hang or burn some of them by the same mistake.[31]

Contempt for the forms of justice is contempt for moral autonomy, because only the deliberative machinery of justice enables one to distinguish between actual justice and a rage for justice that is all too often driven by some other urgency. Without deliberation, the rage for justice is indistinguishable from any other impulse and is no more deserving of respect than any other impulse. Those who become intoxicated with freedom and become lynchers and those who, seeing what lynchers do, become disgusted with freedom and embrace tyranny entertain only slightly different versions of the same thought: both rage against the political community because they feel that it is incapable of dispensing justice. The disgruntled good citizen is only one step behind a lyncher in his political development:

> Good men, men who love tranquillity, who desire to abide by the law, and enjoy their benefits, who would gladly spill their blood in the defence of their country; seeing their property destroyed; their families

insulted, and their lives endangered; their persons injured; and seeing nothing in prospect that forebodes a change for the better; become tired of, and disgusted with, a Government that offers them no protection; and are not much averse to a change in which they imagine they have nothing to lose.[32]

Still more startling is Lincoln's treatment of the Vicksburg lynching case:

In the Mississippi case, they first commenced by hanging the regular gamblers: a set of men, certainly not following for a livelihood, a very useful, or very honest occupation; but one which, so far from being forbidden by the laws, was actually licensed by an act of the Legislature, passed but a single year before. Next, negroes, suspected of conspiring to raise an insurrection, were caught up and hanged in all parts of the State: then, white men, supposed to be leagued with the negroes; and finally, strangers, from neighboring States, going thither on business, were, in many instances, subjected to the same fate. Thus went on this process of hanging, from gamblers to negroes, from negroes to white citizens, and from these to strangers; till, dead men were seen literally dangling from the boughs of the trees upon every road side; and in numbers almost sufficient, to rival the native Spanish moss of the country, as a drapery of the forest.[33]

Lincoln is referring here to the famous Madison County slave insurrection hysteria of July 1835. The case was widely reported in the newspapers, and the citizens of Livingston, Mississippi, the county seat, were so angry about the bad press that they published a pamphlet exculpating themselves, adopting what became the common southern strategy of blaming the whole thing on northern agitators. Lincoln got some of the details mixed up. According to that bumptious madman Senator Henry Foote, who was there, the lynching of the gamblers was one of the later consequences of the hysteria, not one of the first.[34]

It is a grim, weird story that even Faulkner could not do justice to but that William Freehling and David Grimsted have recently retold. Briefly, the facts are these.[35] In late June 1835 rumors of an impending slave insurrection, set for July 4, began to surface among the slaves of one Mrs. Latham of Beatie's Bluff. Assiduous beating induced Mrs. Latham's slaves to implicate Peter, a slave owned by Ruel Blake of Livingston. Blake's lack of enthusiasm for whipping Peter focused the vigilance committee's suspicion on himself, and other slaves claimed that Blake's misgivings about slavery had induced him to organize the conspiracy in the first place (and to promise the favors of white women to any male slaves who joined him). They also implicated two itinerant quacks ("Thompsonian doctors"), Dr. Joshua Cotton and Dr. William Saunders, who turned on each other (and Blake) in the (vain) hope of saving their own necks. Their testimony was important, because Blake could not be hung merely on the testimony of slaves. On the scaffold, Blake freed his slaves (which gave color to the mob's suspicions about him). Six more slaves were hung, but not before they were tortured, providing exactly the lurid testimony the mob sought. Dr. Cotton, bargaining for time, claimed the slave insurrection had actually been organized by the famous Natchez Trace bandit John Murrell. Murrell was in jail at the time, but one of his jailers, named Stewart, had published a book claiming that Murrell had planned to lead a slave insurrection on Christmas Day 1835. According to Foote, Stewart's book started the whole thing, and he was the defense attorney for Murrell's alleged coconspirator, the bandit Alonzo Phelps. (Readers of Eudora Welty's stories may recognize some of these names.) By this time, suspicion focused on white men who lived with black women (especially those who were not their own slaves) and on masters with reputations for leniency.

All told, ten whites and thirty or so blacks were killed in Madison County, although there were other incidents all over the state, and many other persons were "whipped from the locality."[36] It all ended when the Madison County militia, enraged that a Hinds County planter named Patrick Sharkey had released two young men named Rawson from the militia's tender care, mounted an attack across the county line to seize Sharkey. This was enough for Hinds County, whose militia fought a pitched battle with its Madison County opposites, and for the state (Sharkey's brother was a supreme court judge), which finally put a stop to the whole thing.

What struck Lincoln about the Madison County hysteria was the rapidity with which it changed its objective. The best modern students of the event, David Grimsted, Laurence Shore, and Christopher Morris, attempt to explain why certain parties came under suspicion at certain times. But it is the nature of historical accounts like theirs to be retrospective and to treat plausible explanations as if they had the force of necessity. It is hard, however, to see how anyone in the thick of the event could have seen anything inevitable about the way it unfolded. Indeed, what was frightening about this hysteria was the rapidity with which it overran even the most powerful ideological agenda that might have operated on it.[37]

That popular passions can turn in unexpected directions is one of the first lessons to be learned about them. Think, for instance, how often class antagonisms erupt and are transformed into racial antagonisms—as occurred in New York in 1863. Enraged people, ignited by a passion for justice, do not merely desire unjust things or avail themselves of unjust means. They lose the ability to control or even to choose what they want—they become possessed by an endlessly changing and endlessly self-overthrowing élan. This is one reason why popular movements are so notoriously difficult to negotiate with: the movement does not want to attain its ostensible objectives so much as it wants to run its course to exhaustion.

Lincoln's consciousness of revolutionary *amor fati* separates his account of mob violence and tyranny from other nineteenth-century accounts. Whereas the traditional account sees the tyrant as an interested man who stirs up popular rage for some end and sees the mob as if it entertains some concrete aim, Lincoln's tyrant, like the modern totalitarian and unlike the classical Caesar, has no interests apart from passion itself: passion is the end, not the means. What else could Lincoln mean when he says that the tyrant will seek distinction, whether at the price of emancipating slaves (like an idealist tyrant, a Lenin) or enslaving freemen (like a cynical tyrant, a Louis Napoleon)? Lincoln's tyrant is not a republican Caesar who uses the people's feelings to destroy popular government and secure a position for himself. He is not even particularly interested in power in the ordinary sense of that word, since power is always the power to do something; what he wants is not so much to do something as to always be doing, restlessly following a kind of vital energy through its endless self-overthrowings. Even racism, in Lincoln's account of the Madison County killings, seems more the occasion than the theme, the means rather than the end.

The reason popular passions turn in unexpected directions is clear when one reflects on the anomie that underlies them, for the aim of the passion is less important than its intensity. If I must be intoxicated with passion to feel alive, I will find a new hatred when an old one is worn threadbare. The instability of popular passions is shocking to those who seek a political rationale for them, because the instability suggests that the political aims of violence are almost retrospective creations, rationalizations. Henry Adams's famous bon mot that politics is the systematic organization of hatreds attests to the fact that the motivations of the lyncher, like the motivations of the tyrant, are driven by the stereotyped and unconscious despair that comes from a sense of life's emptiness.

The acts of mobs are finally almost gratuitous, as if they had discovered in violent arbitrariness a kind of unmediated freedom. But lynchers are enthralled people, not free people. They feel that if they allow themselves to be caught up by a greater-than-everything force—such as the People or History—then they can be agents of that force rather than victims of it, even if the price of that agency turns out to be their own deaths.

REVERENCE FOR THE LAWS

What Lincoln offers as an antidote to the destructiveness of the desire for heroic action, whether entertained by the tyrant or by the lyncher, seems, at first, to be nothing more than repressive conformism:

> The question then recurs "how shall we fortify against it?" The answer is simple. Let every American, every lover of liberty, every well wisher to his posterity, swear by the blood of the Revolution, never to violate in the least particular, the laws of the country; and never to tolerate their violation by others. As the patriots of seventy-six did to the support of the Declaration of Independence, so to the support of the Constitution and Laws, let every American pledge his life, his property, and his sacred honor;—let every man remember that to violate the law, is to trample on the blood of his father, and to tear the character of his own, and his children's liberty. Let reverence for the laws, be breathed by every American mother, to the lisping babe, that prattles on her lap— let it be taught in schools, in seminaries, and in colleges; let it be written in Primers, spelling books, and in Almanacs;—let it be preached from the pulpit, proclaimed in legislative halls, and enforced in courts of justice. And, in short, let it become the *political religion* of the nation; and let the old and the young, the rich and the poor, the grave and the gay, of all sexes and tongues, and colors and conditions, sacrifice unceasingly upon its altars.[38]

Is the idea here that Americans are to be so indoctrinated with filial piety that they are never tempted by heroic virtues? Is the safety of the republic to be entrusted to the thought-controlling power of the state's cultural apparatus to blunt ambitions, so that no person with enough character to threaten the republic may arise within it?

If the aim of the law was only to keep the tyrant in check, Lincoln would be asking for a world that dulls all the excellences of political life. To dull the passion for greatness, or to divert it toward some harmless and trivial aim, would be to devise a cure worse than the disease or to risk an even worse outbreak of that disease. This does not answer the alienation and despair that give rise to the lyncher and the tyrant; it merely diverts their energies in even more alienating and despairing directions.

The most striking fact about the worship of force is its futility, and no person experiences that futility more pointedly than the tyrant Lincoln describes in the Lyceum speech. When Lincoln proclaims in the 1854 Peoria speech that "as I would not be a slave, so I would not be a master," one of the things he recognizes is the corrosive effect of mastery on the political personality. It is not just that being a master accustoms one to doing things one should not do in free societies (as Jefferson had also argued); it is that the desire for mastership itself causes one to sacrifice the only things worth being master of. The master is, as Orwell recognized, a slave to the adulation of the most insignificant of the people he dominates, and he must work continuously to extort the adulation of those whose praise is worth nothing anyway, since extorted praise is no praise at all, and if it is genuine praise, it is foolishly given and thus worth nothing as praise.[39] The master seeks distinction by putting forth a vision that defines all value as merely force, but in so doing, he destroys the only source of the distinction he craves, because there is no trick to winning honor from people who must give it. The only distinction that matters comes from those who have the power to refuse it.

There is no greatness that does not depend on winning the considered allegiance of others whose agency is as real as one's own. Because law breaks the tyranny of the strong, we think of it as winning freedom for the weak. Indeed, an underinterpreted reading of Nietzsche has taught adolescents of every age that law is essentially only a trick employed by the weak to hamstring the strong. But law wins freedom for the strong as well, for it frees the strong from the futility of their strength, a strength whose nature is to compel what compulsion always destroys.

The only cure for tyranny is to demonstrate that it is self-thwarting, that it is a work unworthy of the charismatic personality who aspires to it. Lincoln does not discover that work in the Lyceum speech, and for that reason, adherence to law sounds like a small thing. Only in 1854, when he discovers in the promises of the Declaration of Independence the "sheet anchor" of his moral identity, does Lincoln articulate the work that is worthy of the greatness the "towering genius" wastes on tyrannical ambition. The focus on the Declaration of Independence enables Lincoln to demonstrate that tyrannical force is not a goal worthy of genius and that the highest public task is not tyranny but a passionate apprehension of an order of communal values—not merely what we happen to honor but what our purpose is in living together—that is, some end that we are incompetent to do justice to alone and that requires us to call out the best aspects of one another's freedom. The greatest public task is liberation, and the work of liberation is the making of law, the securing of all people's rights to life, liberty, and the pursuit of happiness by instituting governments that derive their just powers from the consent of the governed.

CIVIL RELIGION

When Lincoln envisions law as the public expression and elaboration of moral freedom, he speaks not only of the positive law but also of the culture of lawfulness from which the positive law springs. Reverence for the law is to be lisped to the prattling babe not to make the babe a legislator but to introduce that babe to a different kind of identity. This identity is not our biological identity as those who suffer from hunger and need and answer that suffering as cunning members of the animal species *Homo sapiens*, nor is it merely the social identity of social creatures caught up in patterns of collective behavior characteristic of the not-quite-human animal *Homo economicus*. What the political culture of law establishes are two kinds of identity, ethical individuality and political citizenship, which differ from biological and social identity in being forms of freedom rather than reflections of necessity.

Lincoln spends a great deal of time in the Lyceum speech worrying about the effect of violent events on the public mind:

> Thus, then, by the operation of this mobocratic spirit, which all must admit, is now abroad in the land, the strongest bulwark of any government, and particularly of those constituted like ours, may effectually be broken down and destroyed—I mean the *attachment* of the People. Whenever this effect shall be produced among us; whenever the vicious portion of population shall be permitted to gather in bands of hundreds and thousands, and burn churches, ravage and rob provision stores, throw printing presses into rivers, shoot editors, and hang and burn obnoxious persons at pleasure, and with impunity; depend on it, this Government cannot last. By such things, the feelings of the best citizens will become more or less alienated from it; and thus it will be left without friends, or with too few, and those too weak, to make their friendship effectual. At such a time and under such circumstances, men of sufficient talent and ambition will not be wanting to seize the opportunity, strike the blow, and overturn that fair fabric, which for the last half century, has been the fondest hope, of the lovers of freedom, throughout the world.[40]

Lincoln's arguments here about the "attachment of the people" are of a piece with his later speculations in the 1858 debates about the effects of Douglas's positions on "the public mind." Lincoln does not mean only the kind of thing a modern pollster would measure, such as the momentary state of public investment in particular views or personalities or the varying intensities of collective feelings about the political topics of the day. By "the public mind," Lincoln means something like the half-conscious structure of habits and commitments that must underlie a democratic political culture. The idea connects with Lincoln's repeated claims that nations have destinies, test propositions, struggle to fulfill promises, attempt to discover their purpose for being, and have a moral history.

What Lincoln fears from the tyrant and the lyncher are not the specific occasions of their violence. Nor does he fear that the tyrant might get the upper hand in American political institutions and turn them to bad ends. What he fears is corruption of the culture of opinion on which freedom (not just the American government) depends. The idea of freedom itself, the idea that moral agency is possible in public life, depends not only on moral imperatives and political first principles but also on a contingent and highly vulnerable structure of opinions and feelings to which we have only indirect access and with which we might lose touch entirely if we are careless. We can choose to corrupt democracy by neglecting the preconditions in opinion on which it depends. But we cannot just choose to re-create it, because the sphere of opinion is not something immediately accessible to will and choice; rather, it is something prior to it—a half-sensed framework of salutary prejudices arising out of the lifeworld of our culture and expressing itself not in the form of specific rational convictions but in the form of sensibility and in never fully articulated assumptions about the nature and aim of human life. The price of the conviction that force is the ultima ratio of politics is not just that one can use that conviction to justify bad acts. The price is that one loses the capacity for freedom if one truly puts that conviction at the center of one's life. And the price of losing the capacity for freedom is devotion to futility and enslavement in destiny.

The only alternative to the ethos of force that Lincoln can develop in the Lyceum speech is an ethos of restraint, and although there can be heroism in restraint (*Paradise Regained* is about it), it is only the pressure of the transcendentals embodied in the Declaration of Independence, which Lincoln keeps not quite referring to, that differentiates a heroic restraint from a conformist one. Lincoln's final claims are based on the restraining power of reason, but his language about reason seems to treat it as something that curbs heroism rather than something that transforms it and directs it toward a more worthy object. It is hard not to find his depiction drab:

> Passion has helped us; but can do so no more. It will in future be our enemy. Reason, cold, calculating, unimpassioned reason, must furnish all the materials for our future support and defence. Let those materials be moulded in *general intelligence, sound morality* and, in particular, *a reverence for the constitution and laws;* and, that we improved to the last; that we remained free to the last; that we revered his name to the last; that, during his long sleep, we permitted no hostile foot to pass over or desecrate his resting place; shall be that which to learn the last trump shall awaken our WASHINGTON.[41]

Reason is thin, sober, and, above all, safe. Lincoln praises it for the plainness and seriousness of its manner, much in the way we have traditionally praised the rhetoric of Lincoln's later speeches. Lincoln uses the kind of language Freud will use when describing the reality principle. But Lincoln also describes reason as cold and calculating, as a Mr. Blifil among the faculties, and certainly the slightly jarring tone of these words indicates a not fully acknowledged disappointment that this is all political life comes down to.

The end of the passage is stranger still: if we properly revere reason, when George Washington is awakened by the last trumpet and wants to know how we turned out, he will learn good things about us. The invocation of Washington here is more than merely a way of calling down a pious blessing on the end of a patriotic speech. Traditionally, Washington is praised for his refusal of a crown, for his refusal in more general ways to be the Man on Horseback. He is praised here for initiating the tradition of refusing to employ the charisma of military glory to subvert civilian politics, a tradition carried on by a succession of military presidents from Harrison and Taylor to Eisenhower—presidents whose studied drabness has had much to do with Americans' difficulty imagining their country under the spell of a Napoleon. (Lincoln indirectly makes a pointed exception of Jackson. But even though the old hero bent and tarnished American institutions, he was scarcely the kind of dictator Washington could have been, had he chosen to be.)[42]

Washington is praised in the Lyceum speech for his wisdom in resisting the temptation to heroism that Lincoln describes in the figure of the "towering genius." Is that restraint itself a kind of genius? Nothing in Lincoln's explicit language about law as the "political religion" or reason as "cold, calculating, unimpassioned reason" suggests that it is. But why awaken Washington by the last trumpet to learn this unless his restraint is heroic? And why invest in law so passionately if it is not an insight into the purpose of being human, into the kingdom of ends?

"As I would not be a slave, so I would not be a master." In other words, I refuse to be a master not because that is the only safe way to live—since slaves might cut their masters' throats—but because one cannot be a master without trampling the moral autonomy of others, and one cannot claim moral agency for oneself unless one respects the agency of others, since those who prepare a yoke for others must ultimately expect to wear it themselves.

Law matters as an arena of liberating moral agency, but making law by itself does not settle questions of justice. Making law engages questions of justice, but justice is only the upshot of a long process of making law. The lyncher and the tyrant alike seek to replace law with charisma, and in so doing, they short-circuit the long process of approximation by which law serves justice. By invoking Washington, whose charisma is as the refuser of charisma, Lincoln seeks to tame the wild justice of the lyncher into something that ultimately bends toward justice, however long the arc. Washington plays the same role in the Lyceum address that he does in the Temperance address: the angry temperance crusader, drunk on his own self-righteousness, is one version of the lyncher. Washington represents in both speeches the power of actual temperance, which is always a matter of upshots and always a matter of ups and downs, as if the lifelong battle waged by just people for justice were like the alcoholic's lifelong battle with addiction.

Few passages capture this spirit better than one Lincoln wrote to himself in a dark period in 1864. Struggling to do right as he saw it, and puzzled by the repeated failures of his cause, he concluded that whatever the divine purpose is, nobody has the right to claim that he has it in his own pocket. Yet at the same time, nothing matters so much as that purpose, inscrutable as it always is:

> The will of God prevails. In great contests each party claims to act in accordance with the will of God. Both *may* be, and one *must* be wrong. God cannot be *for*, and *against* the same thing at the same time. In the present civil war it is quite possible that God's purpose is something different from the purpose of either party—and yet the human instrumentalities, working just as they do, are of the best adaptation to effect His purpose. I am almost ready to say this is probably true—that God wills this contest, and wills that it shall not end yet. He could have either *saved* or *destroyed* the Union without a human contest. Yet the

contest began. And having begun He could give the final victory to either side any day. Yet the contest proceeds.⁴³

NOTES

1. *St. Louis Observer*, May 5, 1836, cited in John Channing Briggs, *Lincoln's Speeches Reconsidered* (Baltimore: Johns Hopkins University Press, 2005), 45–46. For Lovejoy's expulsion from St. Louis being a consequence of his critique of the authorities in the McIntosh case, see William Lee Miller, *Lincoln's Virtues: An Ethical Biography* (New York: Alfred A. Knopf, 2002), 134. Briggs points out that saving the republic from tyranny and anarchy was not the exclusive concern of Whigs fearful of the hegemony of "King" Andrew; indeed, Jackson himself, in his farewell address, and Martin Van Buren, in his inaugural address, expressed similar fears for the Union. In both cases, they located the threat to democracy in the emergence of the abolition movement, which, in their view, was moved by idealist fanaticism, stirred up trouble over slavery that would not have existed otherwise, and dangerously set Americans against each other. Briggs argues that Lincoln's address is something of a riposte to these two speeches. Whereas Lincoln notes that the threat is "not a creature of climate—neither are they confined to the slaveholding, or the non-slaveholding States," most of his key examples—the McIntosh case, the Vicksburg case, and the murder of Lovejoy—are instances of violence in which the defense of slavery, not abolitionist troublemaking, played a key role.

2. See, for example, Allen C. Guelzo, *Abraham Lincoln, Redeemer President* (Grand Rapids, MI: William B. Eerdmans, 1999).

3. Michael Burlingame, *Abraham Lincoln: A Life*, vol. 1 (Baltimore: Johns Hopkins University Press, 2008).

4. J. David Greenstone, *The Lincoln Persuasion: Remaking American Liberalism* (Princeton, NJ: Princeton University Press, 1993), 59.

5. See Hannah Arendt, *The Human Condition* (Chicago: University of Chicago Press, 1958). My citation here is meant to be polemical; there is a received view that what Arendt calls "action" amounts to mere speechifying and posturing, particularly if it occurs in a political sphere that is hermetically sealed against social concerns. That view seriously misconceives Arendt's distinction between the political and the social, and it seriously underreads the meaning of action. Whatever else it is, action involves the acknowledgment and support of the agency of others. Action does not happen if one is so driven by urgent social necessities that one tramples the persuasive and deliberative machinery of democratic rule (which is, I think, what Arendt meant when, in *On Revolution* [Harmondsworth, UK: Penguin Books, 1962], she highlights the separation of the political and the social). But it cannot help but have some concrete beneficial effect on how people actually live their social lives.

6. That said, only John Channing Briggs develops the connection between Milton and Lincoln.

7. *Abraham Lincoln: Speeches and Writings*, 2 vols., ed. Don E. Fehrenbacher (New

York: Library of America, 1989), 1:34; hereafter cited as *Speeches and Writings.*

8. Edmund Wilson, *Patriotic Gore* (New York: Oxford University Press, 1962).

9. For this view, see George Forgie, *Patricide in the House Divided* (New York: W. W. Norton, 1979); Dwight G. Anderson, *Abraham Lincoln: The Quest for Immortality* (New York: Alfred A. Knopf, 1982); Charles B. Strozier, *Lincoln's Quest for Union: Public and Private Meanings* (New York: Basic Books, 1982). For a critique of this view, see Richard Current, "Lincoln after 175 Years: The Myth of the Jealous Son," *Papers of the Abraham Lincoln Association* 6 (1984): 15–24; John Simon, "Commentary at 10th Annual Lincoln Symposium," *Papers of the Abraham Lincoln Association* 6 (1984): 25–27; Herman Belz, "Abraham Lincoln and American Constitutionalism," *Review of Politics* 50, 2 (1988): 169–197; Gabor Boritt, *The Historian's Lincoln: Pseudohistory, Psychohistory, and History* (Urbana: University of Illinois Press, 1988).

10. As noted earlier, Briggs is almost alone among commentators in hearing Miltonic and Shakespearean echoes in the speech.

11. This reading of Milton's Satan character is akin to the views developed by William Flesch in *Generosity and the Limits of Authority* (Ithaca, NY: Cornell University Press, 1992). My own sense of Milton's relevance to this speech owes something to the in-class comments of my student Sharon Astyk, who took an undergraduate independent study course on Milton in 1994.

12. See Eric Foner, *Free Soil, Free Labor, Free Men: The Ideology of the Republican Party before the Civil War* (New York: Oxford University Press, 1970).

13. *Speeches and Writings,* 1:28.

14. Ibid., 29.

15. Ibid., 35.

16. See Martin Diamond, "Ethics and Politics: The American Way," in *The Moral Foundations of the American Republic,* ed. Robert H. Horwitz (Charlottesville: University Press of Virginia, 1979).

17. Alexis de Tocqueville, *Democracy in America,* ed. J. P. Mayer (Garden City, NY: Doubleday, 1969), 436.

18. Ibid., 444.

19. Ibid., 533, 538.

20. Henry David Thoreau, *Walden* (New Haven, CT: Yale University Press, 2004), 7.

21. *Speeches and Writings,* 1:33.

22. Ibid.

23. This is obviously not what Douglas had in mind, and it was not what happened in Kansas—but it was certainly what the supporters of the squalid Lecompton Constitution fraud had in mind.

24. Harry Jaffa puts it very elegantly in *Crisis of the House Divided* (Garden City, NY: Doubleday, 1959), 223:

> The Caesarian danger is an inner danger, arising mainly from the coincidence of vaulting ambition and mob violence. But mob violence is peculiarly dangerous to popular government when it is—as Lincoln clearly believed it

was—an expression of the impatience of the people, intoxicated with the idea that they are the source of all legitimate power. For intoxication with their own supremacy may lead to the conviction that the constitutional forms erected to secure their rights are barriers to their rights. The people, in short, tend to identify their rights with their passions and to oppose obstacles to their passions as if they were obstacles to their rights.

25. By noting these things about the will—that it is full of inner contradictions, that it exists at different time scales that contest one another, and that only the long-reflected-upon upshot of the will counts as an expression of the will—I seek to reconcile two opposing strains of legal interpretation. Ronald Dworkin, following H. L. A. Hart, sees in law an inevitable and unresolvable tension between the underlying value the law seeks to embody and its concrete expression under particular social and political circumstances, between what he calls its *concept* and its *conception*. The former is morally deeper than the latter, but it is impossible to articulate it completely, and it is a source of as many questions as answers. Bruce Ackerman distinguishes between ordinary lawmaking and higher lawmaking by arguing that the former is delegated to lawmakers by voters who pay (imperfect) attention to public affairs; these voters are private citizens but not mere consumers, or what Ackerman calls "pure privatists." Moments of higher lawmaking, in contrast, involve some direct appeal to the people, emerge at moments of political crisis, and follow a traditional set of procedural rules. (Ackerman describes the 1787–1788 ratification struggle, the adoption of the three Reconstruction amendments, and the aftermath of the judicial revolution of 1937 as instances of higher lawmaking.) Ackerman's proposal is attractive, but it risks severing the connection between the higher law and abstract principle that is such an important feature of Dworkin's theory; under Ackerman's conditions, higher lawmaking might become ordinary lawmaking with a louder voice. I intend this analysis of popular will to reconcile Ackerman's and Dworkin's views. See Bruce Ackerman, *We the People I: Foundations* (Cambridge, MA: Harvard University Press, 1991); Bruce Ackerman, *We the People II: Transformations* (Cambridge, MA: Harvard University Press, 1998); Ronald Dworkin, *Law's Empire* (Cambridge, MA: Harvard University Press, 1986).

26. This account of willing owes a great deal to Hannah Arendt's description of the unending strife in our spirits between "willing" and "nilling" in *The Life of the Mind* (New York: Harcourt Brace, 1978). Help me to want, Augustine prays, what I want to want, and not what I do want.

27. Quoted in Briggs, *Lincoln's Speeches Reconsidered*, 46–47. Briggs cites even stronger connections, such as Lovejoy's own public wondering whether he was about to be treated as the burned McIntosh had been. Further, Briggs's careful analysis of Edward Beecher's contemporary account of Lovejoy's murder makes it clear that the issue was not merely the behavior of an antiabolitionist mob; it was the behavior of a passive population that had no particular desire for the confrontation to happen but was drawn into it anyway. After his expulsion from St. Louis, Lovejoy

had relocated to Alton, where mobs threw his press into the Mississippi River more than once. At a public meeting, the citizens of Alton had considered whether to defend Lovejoy's freedom of expression and the rule of law, but they ultimately decided, like their counterparts during a similar confrontation at Nauvoo, to ask Lovejoy to leave town. This essentially left it to the antiabolitionist mobs to settle the question. When the confrontation happened, a member of the mob was killed by one of Lovejoy's defenders, and then Lovejoy himself was killed. Like the battle of Lexington, the violence seems to have been precipitated by an accident, although it was an accident waiting to happen. See ibid., 44–45. For another view of the relationship between the Lovejoy and McIntosh cases, see Neil Schmitz, "Murdered McIntosh, Murdered Lovejoy: Abraham Lincoln and the Problem of Jacksonian Address," *Arizona Quarterly* 44, 3 (1988): 15–39.

28. *Speeches and Writings*, 1:30.

29. For details, see Paul Simon's biography of Lovejoy, *Freedom's Champion: Elijah Lovejoy* (Carbondale: Southern Illinois University Press, 1994), 45–48, cited in John C. Waugh, *One Man Great Enough: Abraham Lincoln's Road to Civil War* (New York: Harcourt, 2007), 54. Judge Luke Lawless persuaded the grand jury convened to look into the burning of McIntosh not to indict anyone, and he blamed McIntosh's killing of Sheriff Hammond on abolitionist troublemaking. Lawless's charge to the grand jury singled out Lovejoy's criticism of the lynching, combined with his rather moderate opposition to slavery, as an instance of the abolitionist fanaticism that had motivated McIntosh: "The negro then kills and burns for the love of God and in the name of the Divine Redeemer, and rushes on to crime and carnage under the influence of what appears to him a holy impulse and aspiration." Lovejoy, responding to Lawless's incendiary attack, claimed that the judge's Catholicism and his support for slavery were linked, finding "the cloven feet of jesuitism, peeping out from under the veil of almost every paragraph of the judge's instructions to the jury." Lovejoy's anti-Catholic rhetoric here contrasts with the way he (like Lawless himself) linked the burning of McIntosh with the destruction of the Ursuline convent in Charlestown, Massachusetts, by anti-Catholic mobs in August 1834. Lovejoy had already set in motion the train of events that culminated in his own murder. For details, see the account in Louis Gerteis, *Civil War St. Louis* (Lawrence: University Press of Kansas, 2001).

30. *Speeches and Writings*, 1:30.

31. Ibid., 31.

32. Ibid.

33. Ibid., 29.

34. There is a detailed account of both the slave hysteria case and the lynching of the gamblers in David Grimsted, *American Mobbing* (New York: Oxford University Press, 2003), 11–12.

35. I have supplemented Freehling's account, and the accounts in the historical literature, with the description in Henry Foote's memoir, which is the basis for much of the historians' accounts anyway. Foote, who was later an important south-

ern unionist (although a member of the Confederate Congress) and still later a campaigner for the Reconstruction amendments to the Constitution, is most famous for drawing a pistol on the Senate floor during the debates over the Compromise of 1850 and for boring President Taylor to death (literally) with a long Fourth of July oration that same year.

36. The number is from Grimsted, *American Mobbing*, 12. In addition, four gamblers were hung, and four were beaten and set adrift on the Mississippi, three of whom probably died.

37. Grimsted (*American Mobbing*, 12) notes that southerners tried to blame the 1835 hysteria on abolitionist propaganda—first, they claimed that abolitionists had been in on the conspiracy, and then they claimed that abolitionist agitation had panicked the Mississippians into madness. But Lewis Tappan's campaign to send abolitionist pamphlets through the mails did not reach Livingston County until well after the event.

38. *Speeches and Writings*, 1:32–33.

39. George Orwell makes this point in his famous essay "Shooting an Elephant."

40. *Speeches and Writings*, 1:31.

41. Ibid., 36.

42. In fact, the only US president to ever appear in a military uniform was George W. Bush, when he flew to the USS *Abraham Lincoln* to give the notorious "Mission Accomplished" speech.

43. *Speeches and Writings*, 2:359.

CHAPTER TWO

Providentialism and Politics: Lincoln's Second Inaugural Address and the Problem of Democracy

Michael Zuckert

Lincoln's Second Inaugural address is usually seen as the culminating document in his extraordinary career as a public rhetorician. A recent book on the address is titled *Lincoln's Greatest Speech*, and there are few who disagree with that judgment. That book—and most of the others that pay special attention to the Second Inaugural—focuses on the manifest theological content of the speech. Although the theology must be taken seriously, my focus is on the politics of the speech. I do not mean to impugn Lincoln's sincerity in the Second Inaugural, and I do not mean to make a statement on Lincoln's inner or true beliefs. As Glen Thurow said many years ago, "Lincoln's speeches were political speeches, not personal confessions. Religion is present in Lincoln's speeches because of its relevance to political problems."[1] And, I might add, because of its relevance to Lincoln's political agenda of the moment. In a more recent statement Lucas Morel endorses and extends Thurow's point: "Lincoln's personal beliefs and their relation to his public speeches and actions remain veiled. Speculation along these lines, therefore, has distracted scholars from a more rigorous examination of the ends for which he used religious imagery and appealed to religious sentiment as a statesman."[2] Whatever Lincoln's personal beliefs were, he speaks of religion in public, that is to say political, contexts.

THE SECOND INAUGURAL AS A POLITICAL ACT

It is relatively easy to demonstrate the political aims of the Second Inaugural. The speech was delivered on March 4, 1865, as provided for in the Constitution. Nearly four months had passed between the voting for president in early November and the inauguration of the winner in early March. Lincoln obtrusively but allusively calls attention to the context of the Second Inaugural in its opening paragraph: "The progress of arms, on which all else chiefly depends, is as well-known to the public as to myself; and it is, I trust, reasonably satisfactory and encouraging to all." After four years of horrendous war, the end was in view. Indeed, one month later, Lee would surrender to Grant, effectively ending the war. On the day before he delivered the Second Inaugural, Lincoln (through Stanton) wrote to Grant about the terms for Lee's surrender.[3] Very soon after that surrender, Lincoln delivered his last major speech, a statement outlining his policy for Reconstruction.[4]

The details of Lincoln's plans for the postwar reconstitution of the union are not essential for our purposes, but the general character of what he hoped to do and the political situation he faced are necessary for an understanding of the immediate point of the Second Inaugural. Both the general direction of Lincoln's thinking and the political situation can be readily gleaned from the contrast between the plan outlined in his Proclamation on Amnesty and Reconstruction of December 1863 and confirmed in his last speech, delivered just about one month after the Second Inaugural, and the plan adopted by Congress in the Wade-Davis bill of July 1864.

Well before the war was won, Lincoln was thinking hard about the terms for the "resumption of the national authority within the States wherein that authority has been suspended" and for the "reconstruction" of the rebel state governments themselves.[5] Lincoln's plan had three chief elements: amnesty for (some of) the rebels, reconstitution of the state governments, and provisions for the newly freed slaves within the rebel states.

Lincoln offered a full pardon for the crime of treason, with the restoration of all rights of person and property (except for property in slaves) to those who subscribed to a specified oath (with the exception of certain groups of rebels named in the proclamation). The prescribed oath was completely prospective and made no reference to any rebel acts performed in the past. The oath required a commitment to support the Constitution and the Union in the future and to accept and obey the congressional laws and executive orders (the Emancipation Proclamation) providing for the freedom of the slaves. Participants in the rebellion who were not offered the oath included those who had held high offices in the civil or military forces of the rebel states or the Confederacy and those who had resigned civil or military offices in the government of the United States to join the rebellion. These exceptions were relatively few. All those below the rank of colonel in the Confederate armed forces would be eligible to take the oath.

The states could form new governments when the oath takers amounted to one-tenth of the number of voters in the 1860 presidential election. The oath takers who had adhered to the terms of the oath and were otherwise qualified voters under state law were authorized to reestablish a republican government that, if it recognized the freedom of the slaves, would be recognized by the US government as the legitimate government of the state.

In addition to requiring recognition of the freedom of the slaves, Lincoln's plan required that the states provide for their education. However, it gave the states some legislative leeway to deal with the situation in ways "consistent as a temporary arrangement, with [the former slaves'] present condition as a laboring, landless, and homeless class."[6] That is, the former slave states in "this vital matter [were to] be left to themselves."[7] Lincoln did not insist on full equal rights and liberty for the freedmen immediately. In part, he hoped that giving citizens of the states some autonomy in this matter would make them "somewhat more ready to give up the cause" of slavery, as well as ameliorate the immense disruption involved in the transition from one system of labor to another.[8]

The radicals and many others in Congress were not happy with Lincoln's terms, which seemed to them far too lenient. In response, Congress passed the Wade-Davis bill in July 1864. Congressional terms were much harsher. The Wade-Davis bill covered most of the same topics, but it began with a provision different from anything in Lincoln's plan: the president shall appoint, with the consent of the Senate, a provisional governor for each of the rebel states "who shall be charged with the civil administration of such state until a state government therein shall be recognized." Since achieving an acceptable state government would be much more difficult under the terms set by Congress, the office of provisional governor was essential to the Wade-Davis scheme and was, for a time, the central instrument of Reconstruction contained in the bill.

Whereas Lincoln prescribed a forward-looking oath as a condition for receiving an executive pardon and required only 10 percent of prewar voters to take the oath to qualify the state for Reconstruction, Congress demanded that 50 percent take a so-called ironclad test oath. The terms of the ironclad oath were both prospective and retrospective. One had to pledge not only future loyalty to the Constitution and laws of the United States but also past loyalty—that is, oath takers had to pledge that they had not participated in the rebellion in any way. Even "voluntary support" of any of the rebel state governments disqualified one from taking the oath. Lincoln's oath aimed to reincorporate the seceders back into the political life of the union as rapidly as possible. The congressional oath aimed to exclude and punish all those who had taken part in the rebellion. The Wade-Davis bill was also more stringent in extending legal protections and rights to the freedmen than Lincoln's plan was, going so far as to provide for something like equal protection of the laws (section 10) and emancipation in all the affected states.

Lincoln pocket vetoed the bill, leading sponsors Benjamin Wade and Henry Winter Davis, two of the most intense of the radical Lincoln haters, to issue a "manifesto" in newspapers around the nation. Lincoln's veto message was relatively mild, hardly indicating the depth of disagreement between his views on the proper way to restore the union and Congress's. He particularly objected to the bill's undoing of what he had already done by way of recognizing the rehabilitated governments of Louisiana and Arkansas, and to the presumption that Congress had the power to abolish slavery in the states. He did acknowledge that the Wade-Davis procedures would be an acceptable path to restoration and recognition of any rebel state that opted to follow those terms rather than his. Wade and Davis were not mollified. In August 1864, just months before the presidential election, they launched a highly personal attack on Lincoln, charging that he had opposed their bill to further his electoral chances. At this time, General John Frémont was still a candidate for the presidency, and he was much favored over Lincoln by many radicals like Wade and Davis.

As head of the executive branch and commander in chief, Lincoln had certain immediate advantages over his congressional opponents in the struggle to control Reconstruction, but Congress had potent resources as well, and these were likely to become even more potent as the war drew to a close and the president's war powers diminished. In particular, as Lincoln conceded, each house of Congress had the sole right to judge the credentials of its members; thus, the House and Senate could refuse to seat delegates from states reconstructed according to Lincoln's plan. And it did. Likewise, Congress possessed the legislative power, which, in the long run, would surely be a major factor in setting Reconstruction policy.

The struggle between Lincoln and Congress over Reconstruction policy provides the first and most immediate context for the Second Inaugural address. Lincoln's terms were mild, even lenient. His aim was to reintegrate the seceded states into the Union as quickly as possible and to minimize the punitive measures against the rebels, even those at the highest leadership stratum. As biographer David Donald told it:

> Certainly Lincoln was not in favor of punishing the confederates. As he said . . . it was "his firm resolution to stand for clemency against all opposition." He had no wish to capture and try even the leaders of the Confederacy. "He hoped there would be no persecution, no bloody work, after the war was over," he told the cabinet. . . . "Frighten them out of the country, open the gates, let down the bars, scare them off."[9]

As the Wade-Davis bill and the history that unfolded after Lincoln's assassination demonstrate, there was far from universal support for the president's policy of eschewing retribution. Donald recounts another cabinet meeting shortly after Lee's surrender where Lincoln pronounced:

> It was providential . . . that the administration could settle on a plan for reconstruction without interference from "the disturbing elements of Congress," which was in recess. "If we were wise and discreet," the President told his cabinet, "we should reanimate the States and get their governments in successful operation, with order prevailing and the Union reestablished, before Congress came together in December. "We could do better," he assured his advisors; "accomplish more without them."[10]

Lincoln knew that his Reconstruction policy would run afoul of the anger, desire for vengeance, and sense of self-righteous vindication that the war's successful outcome was promoting. His Second Inaugural was intended to generate support for his approach to postwar policy by blunting the feelings and sentiments that stood so strongly against it. No matter how beautiful or theologically provocative the Second Inaugural may be, it is first and foremost a political speech meant to further a specific political agenda, for which Lincoln had many reasons quite independent of the address's theological content.

The speech's final paragraph is memorable:

> With malice toward none; with charity for all; with firmness in the right as God gives us to see the right, let us strive on to finish the work we are in; to bind up the nation's wounds; to care for him who shall have borne the battle, and his orphan—to do all that may achieve and cherish a just and lasting peace, among ourselves, and with all nations.

Realizing that concluding the war is the first task in "finish[ing] the work we are in," but that implementing Reconstruction policy, over which there is already serious controversy, is the second, helps us see what Lincoln is calling for in this wonderful conclusion to his speech. His recent reelection victory, in which the radicals finally rallied to his side, put him in a much stronger position than he had been at the time of the Wade-Davis manifesto. Lincoln is taking the opportunity of his Second Inaugural address to develop support for his lenient or charitable Reconstruction policy, as opposed to the harsher policy that "malice" would commend.

As Ronald White, author of a book-length study of the speech, observes, the final paragraph is implicitly headed with a "therefore."[11] All that has come before is meant as the basis or premise for the conciliatory conclusion. The preceding paragraph sets forth the major premises from which Lincoln draws the exhortation for his favored Reconstruction policy. The first premise concerns the *cause* of the war: that is, that slavery "somehow" caused it. One side sought "to strengthen, perpetuate, and extend the institution," while the other side sought only "to restrict the territorial enlargement of it." The former would "rend the union" and make war rather than accede to the limited policy aim of the latter, which would accept war rather than allow the union to "perish." The war as such was thus a joint product of both sides.

And so was slavery itself. As White points out, Lincoln refers to it as "American"—not southern—"slavery." "Both North and South" justly suffered in this war, for it was both "by whom this offence came." Lincoln does not dwell on the specifics, but these were well known. The North too profited from the institution: in the old days by being part of the slave trade, and more recently by serving as carriers of slave-produced goods to Europe and as consumers of slave-produced products at home, among many other intertwinings of the two sections in the practice of slavery.

Both sides share in the guilt of slavery. Lincoln does not allow the North to wink away its participation; nor does he allow northerners to feel self-righteously justified and morally superior, or at least not superior enough to justify treating southerners as hopeless sinners and themselves as innocent and virtuous. In speaking against the natural pretensions to moral superiority already prevalent in the North, Lincoln is acting like the New Reformers he had spoken of in his Temperance address more than twenty years earlier. The northerners he is chiding are like the Old Reformers, who pretend to care for the victims of drink but actually care most for their own moral superiority, and from that fortress they end up denouncing and rejecting those they claim to help. Common to the Old Reformers and the present-day northerners is a sense of self-righteousness that serves as a prod for cruelty and harshness.[12] By insisting on shared guilt, Lincoln is seeking to remove the sense of moral superiority from his northern listeners and thus to remove, or at least temper, a sense of justified reprisal.

Lincoln's northern listeners also feel aggrieved because they have suffered so much. The war lasted almost four years to the day, from the firing on Fort Sumter to the surrender at Appomattox, and the cost in men and money was immense. Death or maiming affected nearly every family in the North. That a strong desire for reparations and revenge should thrive is no surprise. Yet Lincoln works to tame these passions as well. He reminds his audience that the war has had a similar "magnitude" and "duration" for both parties. The South too has suffered greatly. On another occasion he might have expatiated on how the South had suffered even more, losing a much larger proportion of its young men and living through the devastation caused by the war's battles being fought mostly on southern territory.

Even more than shared suffering, Lincoln emphasizes a novel theory of the cause of that suffering: it is not so much the parties to the war but God who brought it. He gave to both North and South this "terrible war." He caused it to last this long and could rightly cause it to last much longer and produce even greater suffering. Not only is the guilt of slavery shared but also God's judgment on the guilty. The suffering experienced in the North is not the fault of the rebels, as Lincoln determinedly refrains from calling them in this context, but of God. Is God then to be blamed? Surely not, for it is a judgment on the sins of both sections, and even if the suffering were much worse, it would conform to the biblical saying that "the judgments of the Lord are true and righteous altogether." Shared penance before a just God, not vengeance against the losers in the war, is called for.

The sins of the Americans are but illustrative of the gospel: "Woe unto the world because of offences! For it must be that offences come; but woe to that man by whom the offences cometh!" (quoting Matthew 18:7). The offenses came from all, and the woe, in the form of the war, came to all as well. In the larger scheme of things, North and South are not enemies but brothers: they share the suffering, the guilt, the judgment. Both are subject to God's wrathful action in history. Vis-à-vis the God who brings the woe, they are one and united, sharing in all that is essential. Both being sinners, the gospel saying "judge not that ye be not judge" perfectly suits the occasion.

Therefore, malice toward the "enemy" is not appropriate; charity is. It follows from Lincoln's analysis of the war and the combatants that punishment and vengeance are not to be meted out. The task of the day is "to bind up the nation's wounds," not the wounds of the northerners. All through the crisis, Lincoln had insisted that secession was impossible—that the southerners, contrary to their aim, always remained part of the union, part of the nation. The wounds suffered in the South also require binding. Lincoln's kind of mild reunification follows from his interpretation of the meaning of the war and its violence. The concluding paragraph, with its appeal to the Christian virtue of charity and its Christian turn against malice, vengeance, and related negative actions, supports the same policy. In a sense, Lincoln does something very similar to what he advocated in his Perpetuation address—he appeals to the people's already existing religious sentiments to shore up a policy (law abidingness there, mild Reconstruction here) that he believes is necessary for the political health of the nation in the face of powerful temptations for the American people to act differently.

THE SECOND INAUGURAL AND THE GETTYSBURG ADDRESS

Lincoln is using his "bully pulpit" to gain support for his Reconstruction policy. He does so by providing an interpretation of the war—not merely its causes but its meaning as well. His task here is thus parallel to what he attempted in the Gettysburg Address. In that 1863 speech he interpreted the war as a "test" of the nation "dedicated to the proposition that all men are created equal"—or, better put, as a test of that proposition itself as a foundation for a viable political community. The Gettysburg Address is thus, in a sense, the culmination of his public stance since at least 1854, when he used the principles of the Declaration of Independence to oppose Stephen Douglas's "don't care" policy about slavery and the even more objectionable emerging consensus that slavery was a positive good. At Gettysburg, Lincoln confidently projects that if the nation can undergo a "new birth of freedom," it will pass its test, at least for the time being.

The task of the Second Inaugural is the same—or at least very similar: to find the meaning of the war in such a way that points forward to what needs to be done after the war. The task for the future has shifted somewhat, although it is clear that Lincoln understands the task of Reconstruction to incorporate Gettysburg's "new birth of freedom." The interpretation of the meaning of the war has shifted to a much greater extent. In 1863 the war was a test of the American principles of equal rights, consent, and democracy. In 1865 it is a product of God's dealing with America in history. In a word, the Gettysburg Address appears to concern the problems of political philosophy; the Second Inaugural concerns the problems of political theology.

At Gettysburg, Lincoln indicates that passing the test requires a rededication to the founding principle. This rededication requires more than just a reverential affirmation of the founding; it must be an extension of the founding—a *new* birth of freedom, just as the first birth was a birth of liberty. What would issue from this new birth is a nation rid of the blight of slavery, which, from the start, was a denial of the proposition to which the nation was originally dedicated and by which it was defined. So, according to Lincoln at Gettysburg, the meaning of the war is this: a test of the proposition that all men are created equal. Given that meaning, the task of those in the midst of the war is to renew and extend the original dedication in line with the nature of the modern equality-liberty-rights principle as developed in his earlier Temperance address.

In the Second Inaugural, the meaning and the task appear to differ quite substantially from those identified at Gettysburg. The war, he now tells the nation, is not a test but a "woe" justly inflicted by God on the entire nation for "the offence" of slavery. That is to say, it is a punishment. The task that follows is "charity for all," to be concretely expressed in a wound-healing, nonretributive, conciliatory policy toward all who suffered God's punishment. The underlying connection between the meaning of the war as divine punishment and the nation's task of charity for all appears to be the idea that God has punished America already. It is not up to us fellow offenders to pile on. Or, as the Bible says in a passage that Lincoln does not quote but that underlies the theology of the speech: "'Judgment [punishment, vengeance] is mine' saith the Lord."[13]

At Gettysburg, the chief actors in the drama of the nation are "our fathers" and "we the living." In the Second Inaugural, the chief actors are God and we the living who are about to win this war. But this formulation understates the role of "we the living" in the 1863 speech and the role of God in 1865. The main, decisive difference between these two efforts to interpret the war lies in the greatly enhanced role of God. We can understand Lincoln's appeal to God in the latter speech as an attempt to complete the thought contained in the former speech. At Gettysburg, Lincoln traces the moral character of the nation back to "our fathers." The nation is what it is because of their dedication to the proposition that all men are created equal. The task now lying before the nation is to vindicate the work of our fathers by rededicating ourselves to that same proposition in the form of the new birth of freedom. But a skeptic or an inquiring mind might ask: Why should we remain dedicated to that proposition? It is ours, but is it good? What gives it its normative force?

The Second Inaugural provides an answer that Lincoln's audience can readily understand: since the war is a punishment visited on us by God for the offense of slavery, God, not only "our fathers," must endorse the equality principle. There can be no higher source for the moral imperative of equality. The Second Inaugural thus completes the Gettysburg Address by providing a grounding for the nation's defining commitment: we should remain dedicated to the equality principle because it is God's will that we do so. As an extension or completion of the task of the Gettysburg Address, the Second Inaugural not only puts the trial of the Civil War in the context of the entire sweep of the secular history of America but also locates it in the much larger narrative of divine history and of God's dealings with man.

VOX POPULI, VOX DEI: THE SECOND INAUGURAL AND POPULAR SOVEREIGNTY

To complete the thought and the attempt at rededication in the Gettysburg Address, Lincoln ascends all the way to the divine and to Providence in his Second Inaugural. His career as a statesman attempting to come to terms with the nature and possibilities of his native land led him to this point, which was the necessary response to a growing and deepening sense of the dangers to which American republicanism was most likely to succumb. Lincoln's later, deeper public religiosity may or may not have been a reflection of a deeper religiosity resulting from personal ordeals such as the death of his son Willie or the terrible burdens of public office to which he willingly but painfully subjected himself. But there was definitely a political dimension to his turn to public religion. This can be demonstrated only through a brief review of Lincoln's public reflections on America and on Providence.

All scholars who consider Lincoln's religion are forced to take note of the evolution of his stance toward religion and God. As a young man he developed a reputation as a "freethinker," as some sort of skeptic. He apparently read and was influenced by rationalist writers such as Thomas Paine and Constantin Volney, two Enlightenment religious skeptics. Yet in 1865 he delivered a speech that many qualified observers, including the great American theologian Reinhold Niebuhr, considered the greatest religious statement by an American public figure, or perhaps by any American. Consider the judgment of religious historian Mark Noll:

> The simple truth is that none of America's great religious leaders—as defined by contemporaries or later critics—mustered the theological power so economically expressed in Lincoln's second inaugural. None

provoked so profoundly the ways of god or the response of the human to the divine constitution of the world. None penetrated as deeply into the nature of Providence. And none described the fate of humanity before God with the humility or sagacity of the President.[14]

While Lincoln was running for Congress in 1846, a competitor spread rumors among the voters about his early religious skepticism. In self-defense, he was forced to issue a handbill, denying the accusations against him. Even here, when Lincoln has every incentive to play up whatever religious attachments and beliefs he possesses, he is remarkably restrained. Key to Lincoln's position is the way he formulates the charge against him: "A charge having gotten into circulation in some of the neighborhoods of this [congressional] district, *in substance* that I am an open scoffer at Christianity, I have by the advice of some friends concluded to notice the subject *in this form.*"[15] The "form" of the charge to which he is responding is the "substance" of the rumors circulating. It is a form given to the charges by Lincoln himself. According to Donald, however, the charge was that "he was an infidel," which is quite a different thing, and he chose not to reply to that more serious accusation.[16]

Lincoln concedes at the outset that there is some fire producing all this smoke. He does not belong to any Christian church, and "in early life" he had inclined to the view "that the human mind is impelled to action, or held in rest by some power, over which the mind itself has no control."[17] But he denies ever denying "the truth of Scriptures," nor has he spoken with "intentional disrespect of religion in general or of any denomination of Christians in particular."[18] That is, he forcefully denies the charge as he formulates it: he is not "an open scoffer at Christianity." But this denial still leaves two relevant possibilities. First, he is a scoffer but not an open one, for he seems to distinguish between open or public advocacy and advocacy per se. He has defended the necessitarian doctrine, he tells us, before "one, two, or three, but never publicly."[19] Moreover, he does not deny or address the second, more significant possibility: that he is an infidel. One can easily be an infidel and not an "open scoffer."

He does not tell us that he is a believer in Christianity. He says only that, at one time, he was a closet defender of "the Doctrine of Necessity," a doctrine he understands "to be held by several of the Christian denominations." Indeed, the denial of free will—the other side of the doctrine of necessity—was a belief held by many Christian sects and defended by some of the most prominent Christian theologians, especially those of the Reformation. To go no further, both Luther and Calvin were prominent defenders of the doctrine of necessity. But in their development of the doctrine, the force "over which the mind has no control" is the omnipotence of God. If this is the doctrine to which Lincoln subscribes, it is remarkable that he does not say so, for there are other, less orthodox versions of the doctrine of necessity, versions that find the causal forces of human action and thought not in the will and mind of God but in blind nature. Hobbes and Spinoza, Helvetius and La Mettrie come to mind as Enlightenment-era thinkers who defended such a position. Given what Lincoln says—and does not say—it seems that in his youth he accepted something close to the latter view.

By 1846, Lincoln intimates that he has outgrown necessitarianism, but he does not say what, if anything, has replaced it.[20] What he does do—and what must have been most reassuring to the voters in his district—is state that he, personally, could never vote for "an open enemy of, and scoffer at, religion."[21] He does not tell us where he stands on secret enemies and scoffers, however. The main reason for his inability to support open enemies of religion is that he does "not think any man has the right to insult the feelings, and injure the morals, of the community in which he may live."[22] Neither of these reasons commits him to accepting the truth of the Christian religion, although the second does commit him to the view that Christianity is morally salutary for the community. However, this is not to say—and certainly he does not say—that he has replaced his belief in the old doctrine with a new belief in Christianity. The most one can conclude is that Lincoln is respectful of Christianity, indeed, of "religion in general," but not that he is clearly a believer.

What Lincoln says in his handbill coheres quite well with—or at least does not contradict—one of the most striking aspects of his Temperance address. In that address Lincoln anticipates one of the major themes of the Second Inaugural, as he argues in favor of a charitable rather than a denunciatory attitude toward drinkers and their enablers. As he emphasizes, as little as twenty years ago, the consensus was that drinking and commerce in alcohol were very respectable pursuits, and when drink led to harm, it was universally thought that "the injury arose from *abuse* of a *very good thing*" rather than "from the *use* of a *bad* thing."[23] The old consensus favoring drink leads Lincoln to some reflections on the claims of consensus itself: "The universal sense of mankind, on any subject, is an argument or at least an *influence* not easily overcome."[24] He proceeds to illustrate his point in a way that jars greatly with the Second Inaugural: "The success of the argument in favor of the existence of an overruling Providence mainly depends on that sense"—that is, on the universal consensus among humanity. David Lowenthal is one of the few Lincoln scholars to note this explosive claim:

By saying that the argument for a providential God "mainly" depends for its success on its being the universal sense of mankind, Lincoln weakens rather than strengthens that argument. For the sense that such a God exists may derive from a hope and need for divine protection, universally felt, and in this case would hardly constitute proof for the existence of such a being. What all men believe is not really an argument, though it may well be what Lincoln calls an "influence," for it leaves unanswered the question as to what grounds there are for thinking the belief true.[25]

Although the argument based on universal consent is problematic as evidence of the correctness of the belief in Providence, according to Lincoln, the belief "mainly" rests on that consensus. Men believe it because other men believe it. Lowenthal draws what appears to be the just conclusion: if the argument for consensus is the main argument for "overruling Providence," then in Lincoln's opinion, "all other arguments for it are weaker still."[26]

We need not go as far as Lowenthal does to note the immense gulf between the message of the Second Inaugural and that of the Temperance address. In 1842 Lincoln took great pains to stand apart from the universal opinion in favor of Providence; in 1865 he took equally great pains to align himself with the providential view he implicitly challenged earlier. The apparent distance between the younger and the more mature Lincoln, or between Lincoln as a private man and Lincoln as a very public man, is even clearer in his "Meditation on the Divine Will." There, Lincoln straightforwardly affirms that "the will of God prevails," a sentiment almost identical to that expressed later in his Second Inaugural address.[27]

The Lincoln of the Temperance address attributes a far different role to God compared with that in the "Meditation" and the Second Inaugural. In 1842 he speaks of human nature as "God's decree" that "never can be reversed."[28] Human behavior, Lincoln says here, is determined by this human nature, not by divine Providence, as the later statement claims. Indeed, the determination of human behavior by human nature seems much more akin to the doctrine of necessity of Lincoln's earlier days than to the attribution of human action and outcome to Providence. Over time, Lincoln comes to attribute more to divine will. Thus, in the "Eulogy on Henry Clay" delivered in 1852, Lincoln described Clay as "such a man the times have demanded, and such, in the providence of God, was given us."[29]

Providentialism makes its first emphatic appearance in Lincoln's writings in his farewell address delivered in Springfield in February 1861, as he departed for Washington. As John Channing Briggs observantly notes, "Lincoln hardly used the word 'Providence' in the antebellum period, avoiding it as he avoided joining a church."[30] That avoidance changes with the farewell address. In taking leave of his friends and neighbors in Springfield, he presciently wonders whether he will ever return. He did not, except to be buried. But he also conveys a sense that he faces "a task . . . greater than that which rested upon Washington."[31] Greater than Washington! It is impossible not to hear echoes of the Perpetuation and Temperance addresses, with their elevation of Washington. It is hard, also, not to think of the problematic Lincoln posed in the Perpetuation address: Can the latecomers match the glory of the founders? Is there an outlet for men of the highest ambition within the political order bequeathed to them by "the fathers"? Lincoln seems to be thinking back to this question with ambition and fame before his eyes. Lincoln, if not Clay or Webster, has access to a field of glory comparable to or greater than that of the founders.

In this highly significant context, Lincoln begins to speak of Providence in terms that would become familiar in his later statements. "Without the assistance of that Divine Being, who ever attended [Washington], I cannot succeed. With that assistance I cannot fail. Trusting in Him, who can go with me, and remain with you and be everywhere for good, let us confidently hope that all will yet be well."[32] Any hesitation the younger Lincoln may have had with respect to the doctrine of providential care for mankind is completely absent here. Whatever skeptical doubts about religion the younger Lincoln may have had give way to expressions of complete trust "in Him." It is surely striking that Lincoln suddenly speaks so differently from his wonted past. Perhaps his appreciation of the task he faces —greater than Washington's—has given him a new awareness of the need to rely on divine aid.

This is also, one might say, the first moment of Lincoln's presidency. He will not be inaugurated for almost a month, but here he sets out on a meandering journey across the country to Washington, with many stops along the way. Given the conventions of the day, which forbade active campaigning by presidential contenders, this will be the first time most Americans outside of Illinois will get a look at him. And he will be traveling as president-elect, not as merely a party man or an attorney. He will be seen as president. He initiates this journey by living up to the part.

What might have led President-elect Lincoln to begin to speak in this new way? Recall the context of his career. He was recently elected in a complicated three-way contest, but in some significant sense, that election was mostly a continuation of his long debate with Stephen A. Douglas. But the fuller context goes much further back to the 1838 Perpetuation address, in which Lincoln was especially concerned about the outbreak of lawlessness in the form of mob violence. He was not concerned, however, with ordinary mob action or rioting; rather, he was concerned with mobs that substitute direct extralegal action for the action of the law. To Lincoln, it was no accident that the regime based on the idea of popular sovereignty should eventuate in this sort of direct action, for in this type of regime, the people are the source and the ultimate beneficiaries of political power. As Lincoln later put it: government of, by, and for the *people*. But his analysis in the Perpetuation speech is meant to reveal that this kind of direct exercise of the people's sovereign power is a great threat to the perpetuation of the regime of popular sovereignty. That is to say, from a fairly early age, Lincoln was aware of the steep downside of the rule of popular sovereignty, an inference from the even more fundamental principle that "all men are created equal."[33] Early on, he recognized the question posed by this regime: can the principle that liberates all and produces self-government remain disciplined and restrained enough in practice to retain self-government?

The events that occurred before the Perpetuation address were far from the only threats to actual popular sovereignty that Lincoln saw inhering in the principle of popular sovereignty. Stephen Douglas was *the* great champion of popular sovereignty, and what had it come to mean in his hands? Perhaps Lincoln's most succinct statement on the truth versus the Douglas position on popular sovereignty came in his speech in Columbus, Ohio, in September 1859. There he asked, "What is Judge Douglas' Popular Sovereignty? It is, as a principle, no other than that, if one man chooses to make a slave of another man, neither that other man nor anybody else has a right to object."[34] As Lincoln understands it, Douglas's idea of popular sovereignty comes to the claim that there is no right outside the people's decision on right. The decision of the people is the highest right, and there is no substantive principle of right that can stand against it.

Popular sovereignty, in Douglas's rendition, floats above all substantive moral principle. Thus, Lincoln regularly says that Douglas's popular sovereignty principle would make perfect sense as a solution to the problem of slavery in the territories if slavery were not wrong. But because slavery is itself wrong, the people do not have a right to pronounce it right. So far as popular sovereignty is a correct principle of political morality, it is so because of the truth that all men are created equal.[35] But for that very reason, popular sovereignty cannot rightly decide against the very equality principle that grounds it. So far as it attempts to do so, it undercuts its own ground.

And yet there is a constant temptation and tendency for the principle of popular sovereignty to overstep its rightful realm and claim the entire space of moral and political right. Douglas's popular sovereignty doctrine is a gussied-up version of the tendencies to lawless popular rule that Lincoln made visible in the Perpetuation address. It is a routinized and "legalized" version. Popular sovereignty is in constant danger of taking too literally the old saying *vox populi, vox dei*. Traditionally, this means that God's will makes itself known through the voice of the people. In the Douglas version, it means something quite different: the voice of the people *is* the voice of God, or the people replace God or any other suprahuman source of right. Popular sovereignty is readily corrupted into something we might call human sovereignty, and in this view, there is no source of right other than human will, a view sometimes called conventionalism.[36] That is the position Lincoln is intent on opposing, for it is this very doctrine that puts justice at risk for all and threatens both the liberty and the equality of rights on which self-government rests.

In the Gettysburg Address and in his prepresidential rhetoric, Lincoln appeals to "our fathers" and to their Declaration of Independence as the source of right beyond the will of the present generation. It is tempting to conclude that as Lincoln reflected on his analysis and on his experience dealing with Douglas and popular sovereignty, he concluded that faith in the fathers would not suffice. Faith, as its historic associations attest, must be rooted in something more ultimate—and what can be more ultimate than a providential God who cares for the affairs of the nation and its citizens? Whatever Lincoln's personal beliefs may have been, he had reason to appeal to the God of history, who judged nations. Such a God stands guard against a Douglas-like embrace of the sole sovereignty of human will.

In the midst of the Civil War, at Gettysburg in 1863, Lincoln returns to many of the same themes he had developed in his prepresidential years. As we have seen, he presents the war as a *test* of whether this nation or any nation grounded on and dedicated to the equality of men can endure, precisely because this doctrine can easily degenerate into the anarchic dissolution of authority and ultimately of society, as implicit in the doctrine of secession. The idea of secession is merely the idea of popular sovereignty disaggregated. If human will is the sole or at least the most authoritative source of right, why should the will of the whole collectivity rule? Why not the will of the separate parts? Why not the will of the individual? That is to say, the dissolution of government and community that Lincoln reduced secession to in his First Inaugural address is a major part of the test the Civil War poses to a government based on the equality principle.

The providentialism of the Second Inaugural is thus the solution to several dimensions of the problem of popular sovereignty that Lincoln confronted in his earlier ruminations on republican governance and modern freedom. On the one side, it guards against the descent into the affirmation of mere human will as the source of right, as opposed to the rational will as developed in Lincoln's own arguments on justice. On the other side, it guards against the descent into anarchy threatened by the same grounding of right in will. The ultimate result of both is the same: despotism, in which the promise of freedom and equality is lost. If America fails the test, then the watching world might well conclude that the proposition "all men are created equal" is no fit basis for a political society. It is in this sense that Lincoln speaks of America as the world's "last best hope."

PROVIDENTIALISM AND THE SECOND INAUGURAL

God as sovereign posits God's will as the legislative will that gives humanity the norms of right by which it should govern itself. But in his presidential years, Lincoln goes further: God not only gives us the "oughts" of existence but rules in more active ways as well. As Lincoln said in his "Meditation": "the will of God prevails."[37] God's will rules in history and determines outcomes. Lincoln's is a very strong form of providentialism.

As Noll makes clear in his *Civil War as a Theological Crisis*, this kind of providentialism was very widespread in Civil War America, but it most often took forms that were quite different from the Second Inaugural.[38] Consider, for instance, "The Battle Hymn of the Republic," a poem by Julia Ward Howe written in the early days of the war. It is worth pausing to note the similarities and, even more importantly, the differences between it and the Second Inaugural. Like the Gettysburg Address and even more like the Second Inaugural, "Battle Hymn" is an attempt to find the meaning of the Civil War. Like the Second Inaugural, it finds that meaning in God acting in history. The Union is doing God's work on earth. God is "in the watch fires" of the camped soldiers; the swords of the army are "His truth"; his "fearful lightning" strikes down those against whom He is wrathful. The army is doing something parallel to what Jesus did: "As He died to make men holy let us die to make men free." The Union forces, the army of God, having made the slaves free, will, as an instrument of God, make "the soul of wrong"—that is, the slaveholding South—"his slave." The enslavers will be slaves—metaphorically, to be sure. But the spirit of "Battle Hymn" is not the spirit of the Second Inaugural. In the former, the war and the northern armies are "the coming of the Lord." God is on our side; right is with us alone. God seeks to punish the slaveholders; He most definitely does not approach in a spirit of charity.

Howe's poem girds politics with the divine, but it produces what John Burt has called "crusader politics" or, in a spirit of evenhandedness, "jihadi politics."[39] This is far from the spirit of Lincoln's Second Inaugural and thus far from his political theology. What Howe and Wade and Davis saw as righteous justice, as doing God's work, Lincoln labels "malice."

The two most significant differences between the political theologies of "Battle Hymn" and the Second Inaugural are the aforementioned shared guilt and shared punishment for the crime of slavery and the greater opacity of God's purposes in Lincoln's version. Little more needs to be said about the first point. In this particular instance, Lincoln reminds the self-righteous of the North that they too have been implicated in slavery, and their judgment of others must always be tempered by a skeptical eye toward their own purity. "Let he who is without sin cast the first stone."

The second point requires more attention. The Howe poem takes for granted that the purpose of the war and God's intent in it is "to make men free," to end slavery. Lincoln, writing four years later and with his own experience of both the start of the war and its course, sees things slightly but significantly differently. His account emphasizes the difference between the aims of the men who made the war and those of God, who controlled its outcome. Neither side sought war. Both sought peace, and to that degree, they had a common interest and aim. But they also had divergent interests that revolved around the issue of slavery, which "all knew ... was somehow the cause of the war." Lincoln says "somehow" because slavery as such was not the direct and immediate cause of the war. The North was not fighting to end slavery where it existed; the South was not fighting to impose slavery where it did not exist. Each side had more limited policy aims. The one side sought "to strengthen, perpetuate, and extend slavery." The "insurgents" could not get their way while members of the union, or so it appeared with the election of Lincoln and the growth of the Republican Party. They therefore sought to separate from the union or "to *destroy* it without war." Yet "they would make war rather than let the nation survive." The Lincoln administration was "devoted altogether to *saving* the union without war," but it "would *accept* war rather than let it perish." Neither side sought the war, but both preferred war to the other side's achievement of its aim.

This is an excellent example of how political actions often have unintended consequences. The coming of the Civil War was not the result of the will of either party alone; it was the result of the interaction of the aims and intentions of the two. Lincoln concludes his account of the origin of the war with this luminous sentence: "And the war came." It is a beautiful sentence because it captures the deep ambiguity of history. The grammar of the sentence suggests that not the parties but the war itself is the agent of its coming. And so it appears to the human agents caught up in this war—and in so many other wars in human history, including World War I. It seems that some impersonal agent or some superhuman agent brought the war. But Lincoln shows that this is an illusion. Neither side willed the war, but both willed things that conjointly produced the war.

Likewise, neither side willed "the magnitude or the duration" the war "attained." The war's magnitude and duration were a function of neither side's ability to achieve its chief aims in the face of the other's opposition. Had either side given up its aims short of victory, the war would have been briefer and smaller. Again, the result was not what any of the parties sought, but it was the consequence of what both sought.

Finally, and most importantly, the end result was quite different from what either side sought. "Neither anticipated that the *cause* of the conflict might cease with or even before, the conflict should cease." The result of the war has been "fundamental and astounding." Lincoln is referring, of course, to the ending of slavery via his Emancipation Proclamation and the pending Thirteenth Amendment. A war that nobody sought, provoked by a somewhat peripheral aspect of the institution of slavery, a war in which one side sought only to leave the union and the other only to preserve the union, produced a result that was unexpected by all.

Since nobody expected or aimed for this outcome, Lincoln posits a supervening hand at work. The war was long and harsh for both sides, as punishment for the shared sin of slavery. The war ended as it did, contrary to the aims and prayers of both sides, because "the Almighty has His own purposes." Only in the outcome can we discern His purpose. Since the Almighty's purposes are not the purposes of any of us mere humans, we can never be certain, as Howe was certain, that we know what His purposes are or that we are on His side. Howe turned out to be correct that the war would "make men free," but she was very much mistaken about the character of the war and surely about God's unequivocal partisanship for her team.

If God's hand is visible in accomplishing the otherwise unintended consequence of ending slavery in America, then it behooves us all—North and especially South—to accept that outcome. "Not I, Abraham Lincoln, with my perhaps questionably legal Emancipation Proclamation, not my sectional party, but God Himself has brought an end to slavery." Just as one major thrust of the speech is addressed to the victorious North to remind the winners that they too have been judged and found wanting, with the implication that "charity for all" is the only suitable guide for postwar policy, so God's verdict on slavery reminds the defeated South that the "peculiar institution" has run its course, and southerners should accept the liberation of the slaves as God's will. Lincoln's theology of God as supreme judge, punishing the guilt of both sides, and God as supreme executive, determining the course of history, supports the twin poles of his policy for the future: to secure the liberty of the freed and to reintegrate "the erring sisters" into the family of the union on favorable and charitable terms, to the extent this comports with his goal of securing the rights of the freedmen.

The strong providentialism of Lincoln's political theology—that is, the affirmation that God's inscrutable or near-inscrutable will prevails in history—does indeed forfend the temptations to "crusader" or "jihadi" politics. We can never be quite sure that we are in God's army. But this same political theology seems to point to an equally problematic political stance of fatalism and passivity. If God's will is visible only in the outcomes that we cannot foretell, must we not wait on God's action? If God acts as decisively in history as Lincoln seems to be saying, are we not thrown back on a kind of de factoism—whatever is, is right, since it embodies the will of God in history? Do we see evidence here for Donald's emphasis on "a basic trait evident throughout Lincoln's life: the essential passivity of his nature"?[40] In his early days, Lincoln accepted the doctrine of necessity, most likely a doctrine of natural causal necessity. In his later days, he endorsed a doctrine of providential necessity. Both have in common a depreciation of human agency. And yet all these doctrines of necessity are incompatible with Lincoln's emphasis on human liberty from the Temperance address forward. The fatalism implied by these various necessitarianisms is incompatible with Lincoln's emphasis on enterprise, hard work, and advancement in life though effort, as evident in his Wisconsin State Fair address and his "Inventions and Discoveries" lecture, among other places. The emphasis on Lincoln's personal passivity is incompatible with his oft-noted "little machine" of ambition, a trait noted by Donald himself on the very same page as his statement about Lincoln's "essential passivity."

Fatalist providentialism thus seems greatly at odds with Lincoln's general thinking and acting. Is this what he is really saying? It does not seem so. If he is committed to a form of providentialism indistinguishable from de factoism, is not God responsible for slavery's thriving for so long? Lincoln seems to affirm something like this when he speculates that "if American slavery is one of those offences which, *in the Providence of God*, must needs come, but which, having continued through His appointed time, He now wills to remove, and that He gives to both North and South, this terrible war, as the woe due to those by whom the offence came, shall we discern therein any departure from those divine attributes which the believers in a living God always ascribe to Him?"(emphasis added). Speaking for the claims of logic, if we understand this passage in de facto providentialist terms, one might well "discern [a] departure" from one divine attribute—justice. If slavery exists by divine Providence, and if God wills its existence and in His power causes it to thrive, then it seems unjust to punish "those by whom the offence came."

That Lincoln casts this, his most providentialist passage, as a hypothetical might tempt the less pious among us, or those who suspect Lincoln's piety, to wonder whether Lincoln is not, in this very solemn place, injecting some of his old freethinking ways, encouraging his thinking readers to answer his question in this distinctly unorthodox way. Such a maneuver makes little sense in a speech of this sort, so Lincoln must have had something else in mind. Most likely he is signaling that he does not mean fatalism-inspiring de factoist providentialism. Traditional theology has long recognized a distinction between God's Providence as permissive and His will as determinative. Lincoln must mean that God *permitted* slavery to exist and even thrive, but now He no longer wills it to survive. Why he permitted it for 250 years is beyond our power to know. Despite His permissive will that slavery survive, the human beings who engaged in the practice are still blamable, for as Lincoln affirms, we can know that slavery is unjust despite the fact that it exists and is thus part of the historical action of the providential God. Lincoln comments that "it may seem strange that any men should dare to ask *a just God's assistance* in wringing their bread from the sweat of other men's faces" (emphasis added). Since a just God would not approve of the peculiar institution, it must be unjust and known to be or knowable as unjust. Justice and injustice are knowable to us as commands of scripture or deliverances of reason, as Lincoln maintained regularly throughout his career. Since men knew or could know the "ought" independently of the "is," it comports with the justice of God to punish them, despite His permissive will allowing slavery.

So, Lincoln's providentialism read in this weaker way can work to redeem God's justice in bringing punishment for slavery. But can we read Lincoln's providentialism in this weaker way? It seems not, for he says, "American slavery is one of those offences which, in the Providence of God, *must needs* come, but which, having continued through His appointed time, He now wills to remove" (emphasis added). It is not a weak or permissive providentialism that Lincoln affirms but a strong, active, determinative Providence that necessitated both slavery *and* its removal. In what sense can Lincoln say that the "offence" came from men?

Lincoln's dual doctrine on Providence may not make perfect sense as a logical account of slavery in America, but it does make sense as a political theology, albeit one specially framed for the present moment. A God that condemns both North and South for the crime of slavery undergirds Lincoln's generous, even magnanimous plans for Reconstruction. God as cause of the outcome of the war undergirds Lincoln's resolve to make freedom for all the lasting meaning of the war. Is Lincoln's God or Providence contradictory? So be it.

The theology of the Second Inaugural serves the needs of the moment, but does it serve the future as well? Can it be a political theology for the nation going forward? What does it accomplish, if accepted? To the first two questions, we must answer with a qualified no. On the one side, it affirms that God cares, that He holds us to standards of right not just in the next life but in this one as well. Much more like the Hebrew Bible than the New Testament, Lincoln envisages God's meting out of judgment as this-worldly and communal, not otherworldly and personal. As a nation, we are subject to judgment and are surely not the highest force in the whole. We are a nation "under God."

But God's purposes in history are not clear to any of us. We must not proceed as if we possess perfect clarity about God's will, yet we must have faith that His will is just. But we cannot merely worship success or the status quo as an embodiment of the justice we are mandated to seek, for we have access to knowledge of right independent of history. It is not for us to bow indiscriminately to the verdict of history, for God's purposes are opaque, and our task is to "remain firm in the right as God gives us to see the right." Our view of the right may be partial, and it may be subject to correction and revision, but it is what we have, and it must serve as our star and compass. Thus we must not merely surrender to the judgments of history as though they are the judgments of God—they *are* the judgments of God, but our business is to follow the right as we see it. In *this* case, Lincoln can discern a perfect conjunction of the right as we can independently judge it and God's Providence as visible in history. In this case, history has clear normative force.

What are we to make of the hypothetical character of Lincoln's most theological passages? The political religion Lincoln preaches is perfectly intelligible in term of both his long- and short-term analyses of American political needs. This conclusion, of course, by no means compels the view that Lincoln disbelieved or was anything but perfectly sincere in his profession of this religion.

I do believe that we can make a little headway if we return to the theme of the hypothetical character of Lincoln's main claims in the Second Inaugural. There is a deep link between this hypothetical character and the speech's providentialism. As we have seen, Lincoln is particularly eloquent at elucidating how the coming of the war, its character, and its outcome were not what any of the parties sought or expected. There are several ways to understand this fact, one of which is purely rational. As already discussed, political events rarely turn out as any one party intends because politics is a conflictual activity in which parties with different and more or less opposing aims face each other. The outcome is a result of the various forces in play, and it can seldom be exactly predicted because these forces are usually not exactly known, nor is the skill with which they are deployed. Outcomes (almost) always transcend the actors. Given that outcomes escape the actors' control, it is impossible to attribute the outcomes in any direct way to the actors. Lincoln's hypotheticals are one response to this situation: one can, but one need not, attribute outcomes to a higher power, to an intelligence that is not identical to that of any of the human actors. It is surely not rationally demonstrable that a higher intelligence has produced the result, but neither is it demonstrable that Providence has not done so. To interpret events in this way is hypothetical, in the sense that one can choose to do so and to have faith that it is so. But this is only to say what is almost commonsensical: providentialism is a matter of faith, not demonstration. By speaking in hypotheticals, Lincoln shows that he is uncommonly aware of this fact.

The beautiful Second Inaugural, with its complex political theology, was a rhetorical sally in Lincoln's efforts to accomplish a postwar policy of reconciliation and lasting harmony between the sections and the races. Perhaps it could be called "The Peace Hymn of the Republic," for its aim was to counter the triumphalist spirit of "The Battle Hymn of the Republic," which joined with the vengeful and angry spirit in the North to threaten the nation with a very different kind of reconstruction that would elevate black over white and North over South, reinforcing preexisting resentments and setting them in stone, so to speak. Thus, the political theology of the Second Inaugural was meant to counter the political theology represented in "Battle Human."

In Lincoln's version, God's intent is more opaque. It is justice, yes, but human beings must humbly recognize the limits of their knowledge of justice and hesitate to align God too closely with their own particular projects.

God's partisanship is less clear, because in His infinite wisdom and power, He transcends the finitude of mere mortals. We human partisans should be less hasty to claim that God is on our side and therefore less quick to believe that we are justified in our most extreme actions because God is with us—and against "them." We must be careful not to confuse our "wrath" with His.

Howe sang of a transparent Providence; Lincoln of an opaque Providence or, perhaps better, of a Providence "seen through a glass darkly." The dangers of transparent Providence are the "divine-right-makes-everything-right" mentality of the Inquisition, of the John Brown raid, and of related religion-inspired crimes. The danger of opaque Providence is passivity and a kind of distancing from moral and political commitments that looks much like relativism. That is not where Lincoln wanted to end up, however. His "glass darkly" providentialism led, in part, to "charity for all," but it also led to "firmness in the right as God gives us to see the right." We have the power to see right—some of it, at least. This too is part of the providential order. We must take our bearings by right as we are given to see it, because right is ultimately what God seeks and that by which we are judged. In staying in this right as God gives us to see it, we must remember our limited powers to see the whole of right and resist with all our might the self-righteousness that comes with unwarranted certainty and moral conviction. We must, Lincoln mandates, somehow live the tension between the firmness of a commitment to right as we see it and the distance from those commitments entailed by our finitude and self-serving self-interest. But how do we live that tension? Lincoln has an answer: firmly to stand by the right—not in a spirit of malice, but with charity for all. At the moment Lincoln delivered his address, charity was called for. But what of other moments? What of the moment when the South seceded and he faced the choice of defending the union or "letting our errant sisters go," as some counseled? It is not so easy to say what Lincoln's political theology mandated then.

Lincoln's mature political theology is thus a complex and tension-ridden thing. He sought to use political theology to construct a public philosophy that could not only undergird his sought-after policy of Reconstruction but also support a broad, healthy democratic politics by countering the three main pathologies to which democracy and the doctrine of popular sovereignty can lead. First, his affirmation of the divine governance of history counters the temptation to embrace the idea of human moral sovereignty and self-sufficiency—that is, the idea that human will is the only source of value. Second, the idea of "through a glass darkly" providentialism is also meant to guard against what Machiavelli called "pious cruelty"—that is, indulgence in a kind of harsh and repressive politics based on the firm confidence that one is doing God's work. Finally, the idea that we must firmly persevere in and pursue the right as God gives us to see it (i.e., as we see it) is meant to counter the tendency toward passivity posed by the other two aspects of Lincoln's political theology. By giving us the ability to see the right, to have standards of right as a basis and mandate for action, God indicates that the proper human stance is not passive obeisance to history but a free yet not sovereign stand within history.

It is in many ways a beautiful doctrine, and one of its merits is that it speaks in one aspect or another to the great dangers Lincoln saw in the modern democratic experiment. But one cannot call it a success in every way. Like other forms of providentialism, it leaves us with tension-filled and even contradictory mandates for action. No doubt, subtle theologians might work out satisfying ways of resolving these tensions, but recall that Lincoln was presenting an interpretation of the public meaning of the war and, even more, a public philosophy to undergird American democracy. In this context, the subtleties of the theologians and the philosophers cannot suffice—the people as a whole are unlikely to be able to navigate through the Scylla and Charybdis that Lincoln's doctrine requires.

Lincoln brought the American tendency to (somehow) amalgamate politics and religion to a kind of culmination, but what he actually demonstrated is the great difficulty of doing so. The teaching of the Second Inaugural failed to shape Reconstruction as Lincoln hoped it would, and it passed from the scene along with its author. No president after Lincoln, and no public figure of any sort, has reached the depths of the Second Inaugural or matched its beauty of language and sentiment. This suggests that whatever truth and other merit it possesses, it has not succeeded in becoming part of the public philosophy of the American people. After Lincoln, American political leaders engaged in only the most glib and empty attempts to bring religion and politics together. The best they have been able to achieve is the now standard phrase that ends nearly every presidential speech—"God bless America."

NOTES

1. Glen Thurow, "Abraham Lincoln and American Political Religion," in *The Historian's Lincoln: Pseudohistory, Psychohistory, and History*, ed. G. S. Boritt and Norman O. Forness (Urbana: University of Illinois Press, 1988), 129.

2. Lucas E. Morel, *Lincoln's Sacred Effort: Defining Religion's Role in American Self-Government* (Lanham, MD: Lexington Books, 2000), 12.

3. *Abraham Lincoln: Speeches and Writings*, 2 vols., ed. Don E. Fehrenbacher (New York: Library of America, 1989), 2:685; hereafter cited as *Speeches and Writings*.

4. Ibid., 697–701.

5. Annual Message to Congress, December 8, 1863, ibid., 551.

6. *Speeches and Writings*, 2:557.

7. Ibid., 553.

8. Ibid.

9. David Herbert Donald, *Lincoln* (New York: Simon & Schuster, 1995), 582–583.

10. Ibid., 591–592.

11. Ronald C. White, *Lincoln's Greatest Speech: The Second Inaugural* (New York: Simon & Schuster, 2002), 166.

12. John Burt, *Lincoln's Tragic Pragmatism: Lincoln, Douglas, and Moral Conflict* (Cambridge, MA: Belknap Press of Harvard University Press, 2013), 693.

13. Romans 12:19–21.

14. Mark A. Noll, "'Both . . . Pray to the Same God': The Singularity of Lincoln's Faith in the Era of the Civil War," *Journal of the Abraham Lincoln Association* 18, 1 (January 1997): 4; cf. Reinhold Niebuhr, "The Religion of Abraham Lincoln," in *Lincoln and the Gettysburg Address: Commemorative Papers*, ed. John Dos Passos and Allan Nevins (Urbana: University of Illinois Press, 1964), 72–87; Joseph R. Fornieri, *Abraham Lincoln's Political Faith* (De Kalb: Northern Illinois University Press, 2003), 39.

15. *Speeches and Writings*, 1:139, emphasis added.

16. Donald, *Lincoln*, 114.

17. *Speeches and Writings*, 1:139.

18. Ibid.

19. Ibid.

20. See David Lowenthal, *The Mind and Art of Abraham Lincoln, Philosopher Statesman: Texts and Interpretations of Twenty Great Speeches* (Lanham, MD: Lexington Books, 2012), 54.

21. *Speeches and Writings*, 1:140.

22. Ibid.

23. Ibid., 84.

24. Ibid., 85.

25. Lowenthal, *Mind and Art of Lincoln*, 43.

26. Ibid.

27. *Speeches and Writings*, 2:359.

28. Ibid., 1:83.

29. Ibid., 272.

30. John Channing Briggs, *Lincoln's Speeches Reconsidered* (Baltimore: Johns Hopkins University Press, 2005), 275.

31. *Speeches and Writings*, 2:199.

32. Ibid.

33. See ibid., 1:583.

34. Ibid., 2:36.

35. Harry V. Jaffa, *Crisis of the House Divided: An Interpretation of the Issues in the Lincoln-Douglas Debates* (Chicago: University of Chicago Press, 2009).

36. See Leo Strauss, *Natural Right and History* (Chicago: University of Chicago Press, 1953), chap. 3.

37. *Speeches and Writings*, 2:359.

38. Mark A. Noll, *The Civil War as a Theological Crisis* (Chapel Hill: University of North Carolina Press, 2006).

39. Burt, *Lincoln's Tragic Pragmatism*, 18.

40. Donald, *Lincoln*, 14.

PART TWO

Lincoln and Liberty

CHAPTER THREE

Lincoln and the Ethics of Emancipation: Universalism, Nationalism, Exceptionalism

Dorothy Ross

In the history of emancipation, the ethical dimension of the story is always prominent, and since the 1960s, it has been influentially portrayed as the gradual, halting, but growing triumph of universalist liberal and Christian principles, a key moment in a progressive national narrative of growing freedom. The abolitionists stand astride the story as prophetic and ultimately triumphant voices of principle. We have good reasons to accept that account; universalist ethical principles and abolitionist determination were essential to emancipation. Inspired by the civil rights movement and the ongoing struggle for racial equality, the recovery of the importance of universal principles of human rights is a major achievement of historiography over the last half century. Important as that recovery is, however, the history of emancipation and its implications are skewed if we do not take sufficient account of the complex ethical role played by the nation in the process leading to emancipation. As Edward L. Ayers suggests, the current narrative too easily "reassures Americans by reconciling the great anomaly of slavery

---

I would like to thank Ira Berlin, Francois Furstenberg, Michael Johnson, and Caleb McDaniel for their helpful and challenging comments on this essay in various stages of its preparation. It was originally published in *Journal of American History* 96 (September 2009): 379–399. I am grateful to Oxford University Press for granting permission to reprint it here. I have added to it a postscript that addresses some relevant new work on Lincoln published after 2009.

with an overarching story of a people devoted to liberty." It distorts our understanding of both emancipation and the nation at a crucial moment of their intertwined history.[1]

The nation, of course, has never been absent from consideration of the Civil War era during which slavery was abolished. The nation can hardly be removed from the war to save the union, and the war is always seen as an enabling condition for emancipation and the Reconstruction amendments. But the nation has not always or fully been considered as an ethical factor in its own right. This essay is an effort to bring the nation back into the ethics of emancipation. Human rights were always weighed in a moving context not only of interests and fears but also of other values, and the foremost other value at work in the abolition of slavery in the United States was the nation. If we reconsider emancipation with that value in view, allegiance to the nation becomes a decisive ethical factor in the abolition of slavery and an ambiguous one, responsible for both blocking and advancing emancipation, expanding and limiting the commitment to human rights. In that story, Abraham Lincoln stands as both an important actor and a revealing figure of the conflicting ethical implications of American nationalism.

David Brion Davis's magisterial work is the primary source in contemporary historiography for the century-long rise of antislavery sentiment as the central factor in the abolition of slavery in the United States and the Atlantic West.[2] As Davis shows, at its core, the moral argument against slavery was about the character of humanity—what enlightened thinkers called, using the generic masculine, the true nature of man. In the Anglo-American world, the Protestant and Enlightenment shift toward humanistic values endowed human nature with new dignity; new capacity for reason, benevolence, and moral choice; and inherent rights.[3] The Anglo-American shift in moral consciousness began to occur just as the North American colonies turned to universal natural rights to declare their independence from Britain, energizing the ideals of human equality and self-determination. Liberal and evangelical Christianity called individuals to action, fueling the rise of abolition. Humanity's common, categorical right to liberty undermined the justification of slavery in the eighteenth century and culminated in the egalitarian thrust of the Civil War and Reconstruction.

As all historians have recognized, the argument for human rights faced formidable obstacles. The combination of material advantage, class authority, and political power that can be summed up in the term "interest" was probably the most challenging, but close behind was the widespread fear that emancipation would let loose a bloodbath, as whites imagined the violence they were inflicting on blacks being turned back against themselves.

Moreover, as Davis emphasizes, Christian and Enlightenment principle left ample room for qualifying judgments. The continuing hierarchical understanding of the Christian cosmos, of natural qualities, and of social organization allowed the abridgment of common humanity. Many Americans North as well as South rejected the argument against slavery altogether on moral grounds, relying instead on biblical authority and racial science. Many argued that liberal rights applied only to persons who demanded and were capable of exercising them and that Africans lacked the capacity for freedom. In the democratizing antebellum decades, the more powerful the language of equal rights became, the more racial differences were amplified.[4] Given these barriers to the recognition of universal human rights, it is not surprising that historians have put their ultimate triumph in the Civil War and Reconstruction at the ethical center of emancipation history.

Historians' understanding of Lincoln has been brought into conformity with this story of emancipation. Although some popular traditions, particularly those of African Americans, had long regarded Lincoln as the Great Emancipator, early-twentieth-century historians had placed his greatness elsewhere—in saving the union, elevating the common man, or moderating the fanaticism of radicals and secessionists alike. During the twentieth century's Second Reconstruction, historians began to emphasize instead Lincoln's human rights credentials. Lincoln claimed a long-standing revulsion against the inhumanity of slavery, and during the 1850s he outspokenly declared it morally wrong. In an 1854 speech in Peoria, Illinois, that laid out the basic position he would take on slavery until 1863, he grounded his ethical stance in classically liberal doctrine: "The proposition that each man should do precisely as he pleases with all which is exclusively his own, lies at the foundation of the sense of justice there is in me," he declared. "The doctrine of self government is right—absolutely and eternally right." Whether the principle of self-government applied to the Negro depended simply on "whether a negro is *not* or is a man," a question whose answer he never doubted.[5]

Lincoln's historical reputation suffered, however, when his racial views came under closer scrutiny. During the 1850s Lincoln had made it clear that for all their equal humanity, he could not imagine blacks as equal citizens of the republic: If we free them, he asked, shall we "make them politically and socially, our equals? My own feelings will not admit of this; and if they would, we well know that those of the great mass of white people will not." He did not indulge in the flagrant race-baiting of his political opponents, but he had no problem repeatedly denying the Democrats' charges that he favored Negro equality. Until he issued the wartime Emancipation

Proclamation, Lincoln believed that the only long-term solution to slavery was colonization. George Fredrickson aptly summed up the new racially conscious view of Lincoln as someone who believed the Negro to be "a man but not a brother."[6]

Despite this historiographical turn, an effort to rehabilitate Lincoln as the Great Emancipator has worked to regain lost ground. Historians called on not only Lincoln's moral condemnation of slavery during the 1850s but also the change in his position on emancipation and civil rights during the Civil War, although how far and at what speed he changed has continued to be disputed. These historians emphasize the boldness of Lincoln's moves against slavery and explain his racist remarks as necessary, if regrettable, political rhetoric on the road to emancipation. Even if tarnished by racist politics, Lincoln's advancing liberal principles annexed his story to the larger emancipation narrative.[7]

That view has not altogether dominated Lincoln historiography. A number of Lincoln biographers, like many earlier historians, believe that Lincoln "always regarded the perpetuation of the Union as more important than the abolition of slavery." The recent efforts to emphasize Lincoln's emancipationist credentials, Fredrickson asserts—and I agree—"have not been able to reverse the priorities."[8] Historians and political theorists, meanwhile, have brought renewed attention to nationalism, providing new insights with which to address the historiographical divide. In order to understand Lincoln's changing moral stance toward slavery and emancipation, it is necessary to examine it in the context of his allegiance to the nation. My purpose is not to weigh his political calculations against his moral principles, as most recent studies have done—he was adept at combining both—but rather to clarify the ethical consequences of his adherence to two values—the American nation and universal liberty—to which he was sincerely but unequally devoted.

In placing universal moral principles, rather than nationality, at the center of the history of emancipation, historians are reflecting not only the contemporary interest in human rights but also the way ethical issues are understood in modern America's liberal culture. For liberals, universal principles generated by reason are what moral argument is about. Liberals define persons by their universal capacity for reason and moral will and ground ethical obligations in those qualities. In contrast, particularist ethical theories, which center obligation on social relationships, carry less weight. Particularist theories consider individuals not as abstract bearers of reason or will but as persons whose identities are embedded in particular social groups and who therefore have moral commitments that range as narrowly or widely as communal identification.⁹

Nationality, like membership in a family, local community, or ethnos, is a social relationship that enters into one's identity and is a source of moral obligation. Unlike the face-to-face communities of family or neighborhood, the nation is an "imagined community," but one that is deeply implanted in identity by ideology and shared culture. Rogers Smith has located the source of ideology's power to construct nationality in "ethically constitutive stories." Such stories create "potent moral affirmations of particular identities," so much so that the obligations imposed by nations "legitimately trump many of the demands made on its members in the name of other associations."¹⁰

According to liberal principles, however, the duties that emerge from social relationships must be subordinate to the demands of universal reason. Allegiance to a nation is suspect precisely because it is a particular ethical community and gives special moral consideration to the life of the community and its members.

Given the strength of liberal premises in modern American culture, it is not surprising that the nation is not taken sufficiently into account in discussions of the ethics of emancipation. Yet during the nineteenth century, a still powerful republican heritage and newer currents of nationalism made the American nation into a high and particular moral good. The "nation" in nineteenth-century America, as in Europe, was understood as a group of people that constituted a political, cultural, and territorial community. In the United States, "republic" and "union," each with its own distinctive meanings, also conveyed the sense of nationhood. First and foremost, Americans understood themselves as a political community, created by the historical event of the Revolution and the political institutions of "republic" and "constitution" around which the nation had formed. By the 1830s, 1840s, and 1850s, a period of both sectional conflict and nation building, the term "union" was commonly employed to express both the nation's unity and its careful structure of decentralized power. Whether defined as a polity and people united by common language, laws, and ancestry or as a political union bound together by historical affiliation, fraternal feeling, and the principle of states' rights, the union was invested with the sentiments of nationality.¹¹

The United States, like other modern nations, was created by deliberate cultural construction, the work of elites whose political, cultural, and economic interests were advanced by nation building. Hoping to link liberty and order, postcolonial elites launched campaigns to instill love of country, loyalty to republican principles and institutions, and fraternal feeling—sentiments that were inscribed in the patriotic rhetoric of literature, schoolbooks, political speech, and public ritual. National government in the antebellum United States was notoriously weak, but nationalist ideology was strong.[12]

Although nationalist rhetoric varied by party, class, region, ethnicity, and religion and was put to various strategic purposes, it nonetheless expressed common themes that joined elite interests to those of wide segments of the citizenry. The "ethically constitutive story" it told located the nation in a particular historical American people, the liberal republican political institutions they established, and the democratic opportunity those institutions fostered, drawing the expanding white male electorate and its economic ambitions into alliance with the nation. As a community, its unity and mutual obligation were often expressed in the language of family—the founding generation as "fathers," linking the generations across time, and "fraternal" sentiment as the glue holding the country together in the face of partisan, class, and sectional conflict. The nation, like the family, formed its members' identities and anchored their ethical world.[13]

Nationalist ideology cast the principles of liberty and republican government as both particular to the American nation and universal. By the authority of God, nature, and history, liberty was grounded in universal principle and specially seated in the United States. Repudiating the political and social oppression of Europe—the American story went—the Revolution and Constitution made America the first modern republic, governed by the free consent of the people, specially constructed and specially favored by nature to escape the fatal tendency of all previous republics to decline into corruption, class conflict, and tyranny. Its republican structure and individual liberty placed it at the forefront of the worldwide movement toward liberty; the nation thus occupied a unique place in history, one of universal significance, and one that grew in importance as liberal revolutions rose and then faltered in Europe. Historians have often called this "ethically constitutive story" American exceptionalism because America, more than any other country, was said to exemplify the universal ideals toward which world history was moving. The narrative gained additional power when it was lifted out of the uncertainties of history and invested with divine assurance. For most nineteenth-century Americans, history was enacted under the guidance of Providence or an active personal God, and nationalist ideology regularly attributed the American narrative to those divine sources. Some orthodox Christians and some skeptics, declining to claim knowledge of God's will in history, distanced themselves from the national ideology. Where it held sway, however, America was at once a real nation and the ideal one toward which history moved.[14]

When nationalism is taken into account in historical discussions of emancipation, the particular American nation has tended to disappear from view in favor of the universal ethical principles attached to it.[15] Yet the nation carried its own particular moral value and force that must be taken into account. Linking universal principle to national identity is a problematic alliance. The country's particular historical existence and liberal principles energized each other—and were also made hostage to each other.

Fused in ideology, America's principles and its historical existence were hardly seamless in practice. Despite the gradual rise of antislavery sentiment during the Revolution, the founders had placed crucial supports for slavery within the Constitution and omitted the natural law language of the Declaration of Independence, for the inalienable rights useful in starting a revolution were deemed disruptive in framing a stable social order, certainly if that social order included slavery. Even as northern states gradually abolished slavery and white men gained new kinds of freedom, slavery deepened its hold in the South, and northern jurists retreated from the human rights claims of natural law for the limits imposed by positive law. The Union was understood in both North and South to be a compact between free and slave societies, a hybrid slaveholding republic. To call that duality into question was to threaten the existence of the nation.[16] Allegiance to the actual nation was thus an obstacle to emancipation from the formation of the Constitution. For most northerners, universalist arguments for emancipation were immobilized by the nation's fundamental political and legal framework.

Nationalist ideology, however, had the capacity both to confirm the dual slaveholding republic and to challenge its contradictions. As the historiography of emancipation has emphasized, nationalist ideology exposed the contradiction of slavery and served as a source and stimulant of human rights principles in the United States, as it did elsewhere in the Western world. Abolitionists unreservedly adopted the universalist logic of American nationalism and reshaped their particularist allegiance to fit. Few pushed universalism as far as William Lloyd Garrison, who denied any moral weight to nationality if it abridged universal benevolence. Yet even for Garrison, the motto "our country is the world" expressed a two-pronged allegiance, one that he and other abolitionists owned when civil war broke out. For African American spokesmen, as for most abolitionists, the nationalist language of liberty remained throughout the antebellum decades a major resource for universal principle. Hosea Easton in the 1820s and 1830s, like Frederick Douglass in the 1850s, declared blacks and whites, slaves and freemen, to be members of the American nation and entitled to all the "Civil, Religious, and Social Privileges of the Country." In the light of the Declaration's assertion of natural rights, Douglass interpreted the Constitution as an antislavery document and the nation as a *potential* exemplar to the world.[17]

For most white people in the United States, however, conditioned by the existence of slavery, the inalienable rights conferred by the nation could be claimed only by whites. Although America's ethically constitutive story bound its adherents to respect the human rights of all people, most white Americans denied blacks the common humanity and national membership that entitled them to equal respect. In the popular ethnoracial strain of nationalism, the Anglo-Saxon or more broadly Caucasian race that had founded the nation was considered uniquely capable of republican liberty both in America and in the world and was thus an essential basis of national identity. As the expansionist Senator William H. Seward expressed it in 1850, Americans were one "homogeneous" Caucasian people, while "the African race, slave and free," was incapable of "assimilation and absorption," an "inferior" mass and "disturbing" factor in the project of building a free continental country. For Seward and his "ruling homogenous family," race removed blacks from the nation and its exceptionalist destiny of extending liberty.[18]

Yet Seward was against slavery, and in this same speech in which he defined the nation by race, he went on to declare that there was a "higher law"—a universal law of nature and God—that condemned slavery.[19] For Seward, as for many antebellum Americans, if nationalist ideology aroused universalist antislavery ideals, it did not lead them to reconstitute the nation on universalist principles. One function of nationalist ideology is to cover over the contradictions between ideals and practice, to bathe the darker shades of national reality in the glow of the ideal. In the glow of American exceptionalism, black slavery could disappear from the identity of the nation. White consciences could be assured that despite the nation's structural incorporation of slavery, its proclamation of universal principle made it a bastion of liberty.

The federal structure of the nation facilitated this strategy and was jealously guarded by the South's robust version of states' rights. Slavery could be considered a domestic institution under the control of the states, virtually outside the domain of national power and identity.[20] It is probably fair to say that for most whites, during much of the antebellum period, the exceptionalist link between nation and liberal principle obscured, rather than exposed, the profoundly contradictory values embedded in America's national self-conception.

Lincoln shared in this antebellum history of the nation and its uneasy complicity in slavery. He is a prime example of how universal principle and particular nation worked together—and against each other—toward emancipation.

As many historians have concluded, there is no better place to begin understanding Lincoln than one of his first public speeches, to the Young Men's Lyceum of Springfield, Illinois, in 1838. His topic was "The Perpetuation of Our Political Institutions," a topic synonymous for Lincoln with the perpetuation of the nation.[21] He defined the nation in accord with nineteenth-century nationalism as a particular historical people ("we, the American People") and as an entity with its own territory ("the fairest portion of the earth") and a government that embodied universal values ("a political edifice of liberty and equal rights"). Using the language of exceptionalism, he described America's republican institutions as more conducive to liberty "than any of which the history of former times tells us." The duty of his generation was to bequeath the nation "undecayed by the lapse of time and untorn by usurpation to the last generation." Like most Americans—but more consciously than most—Lincoln located the sources of that moral obligation in both the particular and universal meanings of the nation: "gratitude to our fathers, justice to ourselves, duty to posterity, and love for our species in general."[22]

Lincoln characterized this historical nation throughout the essay—and for the remainder of his life—as an intergenerational family. "Hardy, brave, and patriotic . . . ancestors" made the nation; we are their "inheritors." The task of his own generation was a problem for him because he had absorbed the fear of the republic's fragility in a time that shadowed the exceptionalist narrative. In classical republican discourse, time is the enemy of the life of the republic, the bearer of decay and usurpation. Lincoln feared that historical circumstances now made maintenance of the American republic more difficult for the heirs than founding had been for the fathers. Lincoln saw around him increasing "disregard for law" and mob violence; in time, he feared, violence would make the people lose faith in their political institutions and succumb to a tyrant. Notably, the examples of violence he chose were caused by abolitionist agitation or by slavery. Against this threat Lincoln urged that "reverence for the laws" become "the *political religion* of the nation.... Let every man remember that to violate the law, is to trample on the blood of his father, and to tear the character of his own, and his children's liberty." In other words, if the republic is to fulfill its exceptionalist destiny and live forever, later generations must cling to first principles, the structure of law the fathers put in place.[23]

There were undoubtedly personal reasons why Lincoln, from the outset of his career, believed so deeply in the nation as a moral good and felt so deeply the task of preserving it. To a poor, ambitious young man who became a successful lawyer and Whig politician, the nation meant the principles of liberal individualism, democratic equality, and national development that fueled his own rise in life. But he was not alone in this attachment. His generation had been educated in a language of nationalism that stressed familial ties, reverence for the Constitution, the exceptionalist mission of the American republic in world history, and the danger of republican decline. "As a nation of freemen, we must live through all time or die by suicide," he said. Come what may, Lincoln was not going to be the son that allowed the nation to "die by suicide."[24]

The American nation and the universal principles it embodied in world history remained Lincoln's central values for the rest of his life. If he was aware of a conflict between nation and principle as he began his career, he accepted the exceptionalist claim of the slaveholding republic as a bastion of liberty. By 1838, when he delivered his Lyceum speech, abolitionists were beginning to loosen the ideological glue that held nation and principle together, but Lincoln inveighed against the violence that threatened the nation, set off by abolition and slavery both, rather than against slavery itself. Historians always credit Lincoln's reverence for the law and the Constitution, but Lincoln invoked it here specifically in the service of maintaining the nation. As Fredrickson notes, his "constitutionalism and legalism as impediments to anti-slavery activism were ... part and parcel of his reverence for the Union," and his constitutional scruples remained corollary to his nationalism throughout his political career.[25] For Lincoln especially, as for northerners generally, allegiance to the nation added powerful moral weight to the interest, fear, and racism that contained the emancipationist argument.

What began to change the balance of forces was the prospect of the extension of slavery into the trans-Mississippi territories in the mid-1840s. The territorial conflict mobilized for the first time a powerful northern interest against slavery, demanding "free soil" in the West while promising not to interfere with slavery where it already existed. As Lincoln said, "We want [these territories] for the homes of free white people . . . Slave states are places for poor white people to remove FROM; not to remove TO. New free States are the places for poor people to go to and better their condition." More slave states would also compound the disadvantage in "control of the government" that northern voters already faced.[26] For Americans North and South, the territorial debate involved economic and political interests that also brought into play their national self-conception as a free nation, and the world's increasingly hostile judgment of slavery raised the stakes of the debate still further. Slavery in the South and free labor in the North were defended as moral goods necessary to the free identity of the white republic and its exceptionalist promise. As William R. Brock argued some years ago, "the relation of slavery to national character" was "the essential point of debate."[27]

The moral weight of national allegiance thus began to count *against* slavery in the North, although not necessarily *for* emancipation. Many free-soil advocates expressed as much dislike of blacks as of slavery. Still, the relation of slavery to the nation's character reopened the question of the morality of slavery. As John L. O'Sullivan complained, "What has become of the Southern doctrine—what, of the Northern Democratic position—that the institution of slavery, whether good or evil, was a local and not a federal institution—with which the Free States had nothing to do—for which they were in no wise responsible, either to their own conscience or to the judgment of the world?"[28] The identification with the nation roused by the free-soil debate could apparently bring home to individual conscience what the abstract commands of reason had not and force a fresh consideration of nationalist claims.

Certainly that appears to be true for Lincoln. In his free-soil statement of 1845—while urging that the northern states leave slavery alone where it already existed—Lincoln registered for the first time a recognition that slavery put American nationality and universal liberty at odds: "I hold it to be a paramount duty of us in the free states, due to the Union of the states, and perhaps to liberty itself (paradox though it may seem) to let the slavery of the other states alone."[29] In 1845, as in 1838, Lincoln's "paramount" value remained the nation, and that meant preserving the slaveholding republic.

The conflict between nation and principle was now visible, however, in Lincoln's "paradox," and he worked to erase it. As moral theorists have noted, the conflict between universalist principle and the partial obligations arising from particular social relations is one of the most vexing of modern life, for their claims are incommensurable.[30] Lincoln saw the possibility that the nation's exceptionalist character might bridge the competing obligations to nation and liberty. Maintaining the slaveholding republic preserved the exceptionalist nation and thus, "perhaps . . . (paradox though it may seem)," fulfilled the "duty of us in the free states" to "liberty itself." The conditional "perhaps" and the seeming "paradox" would soon disappear from his speeches. In the free-soil debate, allegiance to the exceptionalist nation allowed escape from the obligation to universal freedom, even as it awakened universalist moral principles against slavery.

Lincoln's equation between the real and the ideal nation carried the stipulation, however, that slavery not be allowed to grow: "I hold it to be equally clear, that we should never knowingly lend ourselves directly or indirectly, to prevent that slavery from dying a natural death—to find new places for it to live in, when it can no longer exist in the old."[31] For Lincoln, as for the free-soil movement generally, the underlying premise was that slavery in time would die "a natural death" if deprived of new lands. Whether Lincoln ever looked into that premise is doubtful; as Don Fehrenbacher concludes, it appears in his writings as a vague "hope," an assumption rather than an argument. The logic had plausibility, although slavery was proving increasingly adaptable in the old southeastern states, and some southern writers mounted plausible arguments against the assumption of "natural death."[32] It was a convenient belief for southerners interested in expansion and for northerners hopeful that slavery would eventually disappear.

During the 1850s, when free soil moved to the center of the national political agenda, Lincoln moved into free-soil politics. When he eulogized his Whig hero Henry Clay in 1852, he still argued that the threat to the nation came from abolitionist extremists who would fragment the union in the name of immediate emancipation. But now he also denounced the southern militants who would undermine the nation's freedom. When an increasing number of southern spokesmen, in an effort to defend slavery as a positive good, began to attack the Declaration, Lincoln was truly alarmed. He viewed with "astonishment," he said, those who "are beginning to assail and to ridicule the white-man's charter of freedom—the declaration that 'all men are created free and equal.'" Beware, he warned, lest "in our greedy chase to make profit of the negro," we destroy "even the white man's charter of freedom."[33]

Spurred by this threat to the nation's and the white man's principled liberty, Lincoln spelled out in his Peoria speech in 1854 his categorical liberal defense of human rights for all, black and white: "The doctrine of self-government is right—absolutely and eternally right." The Declaration's universalistic language of equality and inalienable natural rights, as the foundation of American liberty, was the foundation for the slave's right to self-government as well as the white man's. Only a firm moral position against slavery, Lincoln argued, not the popular sovereignty doctrine of his political rival, Stephen A. Douglas, could prevent the expansion of slavery and save the nation's exceptionalist character. America's world-historical mission was crucial to Lincoln, as he quoted criticism from "the liberal party of the world" and declared that "Our Republican robe is soiled."[34]

Still, republican liberty required the nation that bore it, and that nation was still a slaveholding republic. The human rights that Lincoln offered were thus of limited scope. Lincoln's absolute principle of "self-government" was evidently embedded in civil society alone, centered on the natural right of every man to the fruit of his own labor. He often followed up his declaration that blacks could not be the political and social equals of whites with a ringing affirmation of equal labor rights: "The Negro may not be my equal, but in the right to eat the bread, which his own hand earns, *he is my equal and . . . the equal of every living man.*"[35] That line garnered much applause from free-soil audiences, for it not only struck a sympathetic chord; it conveniently shunted human equality away from political and social relations to the more circumscribed realm of work.

While theorists had long distinguished between natural and political rights, the increasing democracy of the antebellum decades had blurred the distinction. Under the regime of white manhood suffrage, "equal rights" was popularly understood to encompass both the natural rights of the Declaration and the political rights by which they were safeguarded. "Self-government" was at once a moral and political ideal.[36] Twice during his 1854 speech Lincoln himself admitted that the two were linked in principle.[37] The free-soil movement firmed up the difference to avoid equal citizenship for blacks. Equal political and social rights would make Africans into African Americans, members of the nation as well as the human race. Although Fredrickson was thinking of race when he concluded that for Lincoln the Negro was "a man but not a brother," the phrase fits exactly the distinction between membership in humanity and membership in the nation that Lincoln and the free-soil Republicans drew.

In addition to narrowing the definition of human rights, allegiance to the nation continued to present a basic structural obstacle to universal liberty. As Lincoln wrote to a southern friend, although slavery had always violated his moral sense, "I bite my lip, and keep quiet," like most northerners, "in order to [remain loyal] to the constitution and the Union." Lincoln was concerned that Douglas had reopened the slavery controversy—"the great Behemoth of danger"—that threatened to topple the nation. The way to restore peace, Lincoln said, was to restore the first principles that defined the nation's character. The founding generation had brought slavery into the union and protected it by law only because of necessity, he argued; they *believed* that slavery was morally wrong and expected it to disappear in the future. Lincoln wanted to restore both prongs of the fathers' original compromise: "Let us turn slavery from its claims of 'moral right,' back upon its existing legal rights, and its arguments of 'necessity.' Let us return it to the position our fathers gave it; and there let it rest in peace." As he repeated through the decade, including at Cooper Union in 1860, when he made his most ringing appeal for moral principle, "If you would have the peace of the old times, re-adopt the precepts and policy of the old times."[38]

Even as he pronounced free soil essential to liberty, then, the nation required compromise. "Much as I hate slavery," Lincoln admitted, "I would consent to the extension of it rather than see the Union dissolved, just as I would consent to any GREAT evil, to avoid a GREATER one."[39] Throughout the decade, Lincoln tried to avoid having to choose between these two moral goods by tightening the identification of nation with liberty, but if forced into a conflict between saving the nation and ensuring an end to slavery, he was clear where his priority lay.

While Lincoln placed his hopes in the original principles of the founders, time was moving rapidly forward. In 1857 the *Dred Scott* decision relied on original intent to declare that blacks had not been included in the Declaration's and Constitution's rights, that they could never be citizens, and that Congress had no power to prevent slavery in the territories. The decision's reasoning apparently forced Lincoln to try to justify the founding generation as men of principle in the face of their—and his own—compromise with "necessity." When the fathers declared all men equal in "certain inalienable rights," they did not mean to confer such rights on all men immediately, he said. "They meant simply to declare the *right*, so that the *enforcement* of it might follow as fast as circumstances should permit. They meant to set up a standard maxim for free society . . . and even though never perfectly attained, constantly approximated, and thereby constantly spreading and deepening its influence, and augmenting the happiness and value of life to all people of all colors everywhere."[40] Lincoln's progressive reading of the Declaration's principles allowed him to couple a ringing future idealism with the postponement of emancipation.

The maxim authorized present action to keep slavery from spreading, but not to overturn the fathers' compromise. It conferred "no right . . . to enter into the slave States, and interfere with the question of slavery at all," nor should the North have any "inclination" to do so. Here he differed sharply from the radical free-soilers, who believed there were a number of constitutionally valid ways to undermine southern slavery and who planned to avail themselves of them. Lincoln, in contrast, in order to maintain the union, declared allegiance to both the slaveholding republic of the past and the liberal republic of the future.[41]

It is ironic that Lincoln grounded his progressive maxim in the founders' feeble hope for a future end to slavery. If in 1790 the founding generation had hoped with some degree of realism that progress would bring an end to slavery, by the 1820s, emancipation had become a distant futurity. As John Adams admitted to Thomas Jefferson, it was a hope left passively to "God . . . and his agents in posterity." The irony became plainer the following year, when Lincoln challenged Douglas by provocatively declaring that "a house divided against itself cannot stand," a declaration that, on its face, suggested not just free soil but an attack on southern slavery. "I believe this government cannot endure, permanently half *slave* and half *free*." When Douglas accused him of demagoguery and pointed out that the union had in fact endured for eighty-two years half slave and half free, Lincoln did not answer that the future would be different from the past. On the contrary, he made it clear that he was saying no more now than he had always said, that he wished to place slavery "where the founders of this Government originally placed it." Ever since the founding, "the public mind did rest, all that time, in the belief that slavery was in course of ultimate extinction. That was what gave us the rest that we had through that period of eighty-two years." Well, eighty-two years of rest from agitation over slavery is a gross exaggeration. But to consider the eighty-two years since the founding as running a course toward the extinction of slavery—the very period when slavery had become ever more entrenched—a veritable "Behemoth of danger"— exposes the contradiction between ideal and reality that Lincoln's exceptionalist nationalism blurred.[42]

So too does his timetable for emancipation. The founding generation's original embrace of progress had frozen slavery into the distant future. Lincoln's "ultimate extinction" was threatened with the same fate. At one point in 1858 he explained that extinction of slavery might take "a hundred years, if it should live so long"; at another point he said it would be "a hundred years at the least; but that it will occur in the best way for both races in God's own good time, I have no doubt."[43] If this passive stance represented an effort to pander to his racist audience, the more active stance Lincoln took in Chicago in 1859 could equally be attributed to political motives, this time to the desire to shore up his antislavery Republican base against a last-minute takeover by Stephen Douglas:

> I suppose [slavery] may long exist, and perhaps the best way for it to come to an end peaceably is for it to exist for a length of time. But I say that the spread and strengthening and perpetuation of it is an entirely different proposition. There we should in every way resist it as a wrong, treating it as a wrong, with the fixed idea that it must and will come to an end.[44]

However one parses Lincoln's mix of political calculation and moral principle, ending slavery, either passively or actively asserted, was going to be left to the uncertainties of an extended future. Lincoln is rightfully remembered for his valorization of the Declaration's principles of universal liberty and equality as central to the nation's identity—his signature stamp on the political culture of the era. But the linkage between nation and freedom he enacted in principle cut both ways. As Lincoln interpreted the link during the 1850s, its condemnation of slavery came at the cost of timely emancipation. It made up in eloquent moral principle what it surrendered in reality.

Lincoln's fervent support of both universal liberty and a particular historical nationality, his attachment to a fixed past and a progressive future, gave him a set of free-soil views that straddled the political spectrum from abolitionist fervor against slavery to conservative unionism. It is no accident that abolitionists distrusted him, nor that he emerged as the Republican candidate for president in 1860 who was most acceptable to all wings of the party.[45]

The victory of the Republican Party and the secession of the Deep South states put both the nation and the principles attached to it in danger. Lincoln's response was entirely in keeping with his dual values and chief priority: he vowed to maintain the union and the principle of ultimate freedom it embodied. Lincoln thus drew a firm line as tentative compromise efforts multiplied: on "the question of extending slavery under the national auspices,—I am inflexible." But he would accommodate the South on "whatever springs of necessity from the fact that the institution is amongst us." Unlike Republican radicals, he was willing to shore up the slave system with a strong fugitive slave law, continuation of the internal slave trade and of slavery in the District of Columbia, and an irrevocable constitutional amendment guaranteeing slavery in the states where it already existed.[46]

When compromise failed, Lincoln did not blanch at war. He had justified the right of secession under the principle of self-government when Texas had seceded from Mexico, but when the United States was to be dismembered, he declared that "in contemplation of universal law, and of the Constitution, the union of these states is perpetual." Secession put the Confederate leaders in the role of tyrants who were forcing the American nation to suicide. Their rebellion must be put down.[47]

Secession and the war that followed gave over the nation to the North and its free-labor nationalism. If the debate over territorial expansion had raised fears for the character of the nation, secession aroused primordial fears for the existence of the nation itself as a political, territorial, familial unity. The nation became an object of more passionate attachment and self-conscious reflection. Public discourse of all sorts linked the nation and the nation-state in new ways to individual consciousness and community identity. The proliferation of familial tropes during secession and war signaled both the aspiration for organic unity and the heightened sense of national belonging. Divine support of the American nation and its world-historical mission gained new prominence as clergy and laymen attributed spiritual meaning to the nation's existence and purposes.[48]

Emancipation emerged piecemeal through the war years in the context of—and specifically for the purpose of—saving the sanctified nation. In the political debates of the war years, as Adam I. P. Smith has convincingly shown, the nation occupied the moral high ground. If, since the 1790s, electoral politics had been "on some level . . . always about nationhood—then the Civil War raised the stakes even higher: electoral politics in wartime became more than ever a battle over who constituted the legitimate nation." As groups across the political spectrum vied for the honor of transcending partial interests in service of the nation, it became clear that "a radical political agenda could only be advanced within the ambit of a nationalist political discourse that rhetorically transcended partisanship."[49]

The first measures against slavery—the Confiscation Acts and Lincoln's partial, compensated emancipation proposals—were thus war measures designed to weaken the Confederacy and encourage it to end the war. Between July and September 1862, in response to faltering Union armies, Lincoln came to believe that the North could not win on the battlefield without bringing the Confederacy's slave population over to the Union side. As war eroded the institution of slavery, the massive defection of slaves to Union lines set the emancipation process in motion. The outcome was still uncertain, however, and required the exercise of white as well as black popular sovereignty to effect. Lincoln set these forces in motion by issuing the

Emancipation Proclamation on January 1, 1863. Again he carefully framed it as a war measure with its operation limited to the areas in rebellion. For Lincoln and the northern public whose opinion he carefully watched, emancipation could be justified only to save the nation.[50]

The August before, when he was thinking about the necessity of such a proclamation and antislavery spokesmen were impatiently urging him forward, Lincoln wrote a public letter to Horace Greeley to clarify his motives for delay: "My paramount object in this struggle *is* to save the Union, and is *not* either to save or to destroy slavery. If I could save the Union without freeing *any* slave I would do it, and if I could save it by freeing all the slaves I would do it; and if I could save it by freeing some and leaving others alone I would also do that."[51] Recent historians who have emphasized only the human rights side of Lincoln's ethical purpose have been anxious to explain away this statement as mere political maneuver—Lincoln the shrewd politician staking out his power to act and shoring up his conservative flank as he is about to move toward emancipation.[52] But this account is seriously incomplete. If Lincoln had to convince the public that his preeminent aim was to save the nation, it was because experience had shown him that the great majority of the public valued the nation above liberty for the slaves. Nor was he personally dissembling. He was saying exactly what all his previous statements would lead us to expect. Lincoln surely welcomed the opportunity to strike a blow at the institution of slavery when "necessity" permitted. But keeping the nation intact had always been his paramount moral concern, toward which freeing the slaves at any point in time might, or might not, contribute.

Once convinced that emancipation was necessary to save the union, Lincoln issued the proclamation and resisted efforts to reverse course. The war could now be dedicated to emancipation as well as saving the union, and the nation hallowed by the universal moral purpose that nationalist ideology had always claimed for it. In the Gettysburg Address, as Harry Jaffa pointed out long ago, "What was called a self-evident truth by Jefferson becomes in Lincoln's rhetoric an inheritance from 'our fathers' . . . Lincoln transforms a truth open to each man as man into something he shares by virtue of his partnership in the nation." Lincoln made the nation into the moral source of universalist liberal principle and a living center of spiritual force.[53]

Some recent liberal interpreters of Lincoln have been uneasy about this romantic nationalism and have tried to absolve him of belief in American exceptionalism. His reading of American exceptionalism certainly lacked the arrogance of patriots who unquestioningly claimed Americans as the chosen people of God and their own version of national purpose as God's. Lincoln had begun his career as a fatalist who rejected the need for a deity, but by the 1850s, he increasingly ascribed the chain of historical cause and effect to divine Providence. For Lincoln, America's exceptionalism was the product of a providential history in which God's ultimate purposes could not be known; America's vanguard role was part of a progressive worldwide stream of liberal principle whose outcome could not be certain. But so far as he could know it, the story Lincoln told about the United States was an exceptionalist one.[54]

As his duties mounted and the casualties multiplied beyond all expectation, he called increasingly on Providence and, with it, on exceptionalist tropes. During the secession crisis on his way to Washington, he humbly placed himself "in the hands of the Almighty, and of this, his almost chosen people." In his First Inaugural, he put the country in the hands of "Him, who has never yet forsaken this favored land." By his Second Inaugural, he required the Calvinist God of vengeance to account for the terrible war visited on the nation for its sin of slavery. Lincoln, as ever, was circumspect in his claims: note his "*almost* chosen people" and "never *yet* forsaken." And in the Second Inaugural he began, "*If we shall suppose*" that American slavery is an offense God wishes to punish. Exploring the borderlands between history and divine dispensation, Lincoln never claimed fully to know God's will, but he did believe that God had given America a world-historical role to play in the progress of universal liberty. The nation had been given special responsibility for the principle of liberty; if the American republic failed, free government could perish forever from the earth. As one historian wryly notes, "One looks in vain for any admission on Lincoln's part that God might manage without a unified United States."[55]

After the Emancipation Proclamation, public support widened in the North for a permanent end to slavery. The absence of an exodus of freed slaves to the North, the transformation of runaway slaves into Union laborers, and the bravery of the newly commissioned black soldiers all partially eased northern fears and encouraged moral arguments for liberty. For the Republican majority in the North, slavery came into focus as the cause of the war and emancipation as necessary to end it and prevent future hostilities. The National Union Party that formed in 1864 to reelect Lincoln included in its platform the promise to pass a constitutional amendment that forever ended slavery. As Smith has shown, "The Unionists . . . implicitly transformed emancipation into an aspect of nation-building: slavery must die because it threatened the life of the nation." To say that emancipation required the force of nationalist purpose is to say that for all the growing sentiment for justice for the slave, the nation remained the North's higher and most widely accepted ideal.[56]

With Lincoln's support, Congress voted for full and permanent emancipation in the Thirteenth Amendment. Much of the congressional debate occurred in the midst of Lincoln's still doubtful campaign for reelection. While the amendment passed easily in the Senate, the House approved it in a lame-duck session only after his convincing electoral victory. The major reasons for urging the amendment—as in the larger political discourse of the war years—were directly linked to preserving the nation.[57] Virtually every supporter in the Senate, and most in the House, argued that permanent emancipation would speed Union victory, prevent future civil wars, and secure the nation. Nationalism allowed the radical Senator Charles Sumner to escape the odium of "philanthropy" by urging passage of the amendment "to save the country from peril . . . to save the national life." Nationalism likewise allowed a reluctant Kentucky unionist in the House to accept emancipation: "If I must choose between secession and slavery on the one hand and universal emancipation and nationality on the other, I would embrace and cling to and defend our nationality."[58]

When saving the nation necessitated emancipation, the principles of enlightened and Christian humanity could do their work. Although a few defenders of slavery still claimed divine authority, Lyman Trumbell opened the Senate debate with the disclaimer, "It is now very generally conceded that slavery is not a divine institution." Most supporters of the amendment went much further, claiming God's law on their side and declaring slavery a sin. Virtually all supporters urged emancipation as a matter of "right" or "justice." Reverdy Johnson, a Maryland unionist, asserted that blacks themselves, by escaping at the first opportunity and flocking to Union camps, had demonstrated "in the very effort the inextinguishable right to liberty." Many other speakers justified freedom as the deserved reward for the bravery of black soldiers. All three sources of moral conviction—Christianity, justice, and nation—were often linked, as speakers referred to "this great and Christian nation" or declared that "Liberty exalted in this proud capital will exert its proper sway over the whole world and for all time."[59]

While arguments remained much the same over the course of the full year of debates, one change is noteworthy. During the lame-duck session of the House, most of the Democrats who had opposed the amendment—even if they still opposed it—now proclaimed that they and their party had always thought slavery morally wrong; they gave principled support to states' rights and national peace, they said, not slavery.[60] Lincoln's decisive victory obviously made these partisans anxious to put the Democratic Party on the side of the majority of voters. What is noteworthy is that they believed majority opinion now required them to object to slavery on moral grounds. Under the aegis of the nation, the moral revolution against slavery of the mid-eighteenth century had finally come to fruition.

The fulfillment of human rights has had longer to wait. The Thirteenth Amendment deliberately abolished slavery rather than explicitly conferring civil or political rights. At the time of passage, Congress and the state ratifying conventions were uncertain how far beyond the right to free labor the new black freedom would extend. Shortly before his death, Lincoln quietly urged the governor of Louisiana to grant black soldiers and "the more intelligent" Negroes the vote, but anxious to restore the national union, he did so only in private communications and left the decision to the returning states themselves. The war had deepened Lincoln's egalitarian instincts, but his nationalism and its corollary constitutionalism still worked against the full extension of the principle of liberty, as it had before the war.[61]

The debates over emancipation to which Lincoln was a party, as many historians have asserted, revitalized the Declaration's principles of human rights and, by planting their roots in law and political culture, kept them alive for later use. Both the doctrine of equal rights that widened modern American democracy and the sense of human solidarity that helped construct the welfare state had sources in the emancipation effort. Still, many of the freedoms gained in the Reconstruction amendments were soon circumscribed. I have argued that the moral power of allegiance to the nation played a crucial role in both instantiating human rights and limiting them. Concern for the nation had been a critical factor over the long course of the emancipation debate. In the antebellum decades, fear for the nation helped stymie abolition. It was only in the nationalist context inaugurated by the free-soil debate that antislavery principles gained an articulate spokesman in Lincoln, and only in the heightened nationalist context of civil war, when the ideals of nation and human rights were fighting on the same side, that emancipation gained widespread northern support. Allegiance to the nation provided the crucial moral force for the political enactment of emancipation, and it was Lincoln's sensitivity to the nation's claim for survival that gave him an important role in the outcome. Given that reality, it is not surprising to find that after the war, reuniting the nation took precedence over justice for the freed people. The preeminent allegiance to the nation that is implied in David Blight's story of reunion was not just a postwar phenomenon; it had governed the country's response to slavery since the founding of the republic.[62]

The emancipation debates—with considerable help from Lincoln—revived and strengthened the exceptionalist ideology that linked universal principles of liberty and equality to the American nation. That tie produced mixed results, for the moral implications of exceptionalism depended on the context of nationalism within which it operated. Before the war, exceptionalist rhetoric had likely obscured more often than it revealed the country's dereliction, as it initially did for Lincoln. Only when sectional conflict and the Civil War joined liberty to national survival did exceptionalist ideology become a powerful force for emancipation. Even then, Lincoln's willingness to subsume universal human rights in allegiance to the nation solved the moral conflict he faced between principled liberty and national survival, but it placed limits on his actions and narrowed his moral vision. When the egalitarian sentiments aroused by wartime nationalism receded, Americans were once again tempted to rely on the rhetoric of national freedom rather than the practice. The familial nation that emerged from the war encouraged Americans over the next few decades—and well into the twentieth century—to define the nation by race. As powerful a support of liberty and equality as exceptionalist ideology can be, the nationalist core of American identity retains the power to vitiate universal principle.

POSTSCRIPT

Neglect of the role the nation played in Lincoln's thought and the effort to place Lincoln within—and emphasize his commitment to—the process of emancipation have continued apace since my original article was published in 2009.[63] Here, I would like to call attention to how some of the new work done since then has refined my understanding of Lincoln as both nationalist and emancipator.

Historians' efforts to present Lincoln as a bold emancipator have required them to show when and how he changed. He began his political career as an opponent of both slavery and abolition and remained, through much of his presidency, a conventional racist who could not quite imagine blacks as equal citizens of the republic. By the end of his career, however, he had issued the Emancipation Proclamation, helped secure passage of the Thirteenth Amendment, and broached the possibility of suffrage for at least some of the freedmen. My effort has been to put that process of change within the context of Lincoln's nationalism, to show that his egalitarian, universalist principles were hampered not only by racial stereotypes and political caution but also by his fundamental devotion to two values—the American nation and universal liberty. Throughout his life and career, those values were in tension—or even conflict—with each other, and his changing views can best be understood as a product of his struggle to reconcile them.[64]

Historians who emphasize Lincoln's move to emancipation often quote Frederick Douglass's retrospective praise: compared with most of his countrymen, Douglass said, Lincoln was a bold emancipator. Historians often omit or ignore, however, the sentence with which Douglass began his praise, the sentence that defines Lincoln's purposes: "His great mission was to accomplish two things: first, to save his country from dismemberment and ruin; and, second, to free his country from the great crime of slavery." Note Douglass's wording: Lincoln's two aims were to "save his country" and to "free his country from . . . slavery." Douglass implicitly recognized that Lincoln's devotion to the nation grounded both purposes.[65]

Many historians have attributed a third fundamental value to Lincoln. Later in this volume, Manisha Sinha locates the source of Lincoln's caution, before and after the war began, in his attachment to the Constitution and the framework of laws it supported. Lincoln's determination to uphold the Constitution and to conform his actions to its constraints cannot be doubted. I have argued, however, that for Lincoln, the more basic attachment, and the value to which constitutionalism was corollary, was the nation. As Lincoln himself said in 1864, when he took his presidential oath to uphold the Constitution, it "imposed upon me the duty of preserving, by every indispensable means, that government—that nation—of which that constitution was the organic law. Was it possible to lose the nation, and yet preserve the constitution? By general law life *and* limb must be protected; yet often a limb must be amputated to save a life; but a life is never wisely given to save a limb."[66] He was willing to issue his Emancipation Proclamation and risk his constitutional scruples in order to win the war and save the nation. In accord with that priority, Lincoln discovered a Constitution that allowed him to save the national life.

Lincoln's 1838 Lyceum speech, also known as the Perpetuation address, continues to be an important starting point for interpreters of Lincoln, as John Burt's essay in this volume attests. The idea of the nation Lincoln expressed there derived from his liberal republican view of the nation as "a political edifice of liberty and equal rights," from the nationalist ideology of American exceptionalism that seated universal liberty and its providential historical destiny in the United States, and from his romantic nationalist understanding of the nation as a particular historical people inhabiting a particular territory and joined by organic, familial bonds. Although Lincoln's nationalist rhetoric was commonplace in 1838, it was vital to Lincoln and had wide public appeal. The nation was the ground on which he chose to locate himself and his political ideals.[67] Like the great majority of his countrymen, he accepted the exceptionalist claim of the slaveholding republic as a bastion of liberty.[68]

When the free-soil debates of the mid-1840s forced Lincoln to recognize the conflict between his two values, he used his exceptionalist vision of the nation to try to mend the breach. Duty to the exceptionalist nation could satisfy the duty to liberty itself. In 1854, as the territorial controversy intensified, he imagined a moment when he would have to choose between his two values, and he firmly chose the nation as the greater good. As a rule, however, and increasingly through the 1850s, Lincoln tried to avoid making a choice by grounding universal liberty in a nation whose founding principles promised, in the course of time, the "ultimate extinction" of slavery.

James Oakes accepts Lincoln's primary aim to maintain the union but regards his fusion of the recalcitrant nation with liberal principle as unproblematic. In *Freedom National* and *The Scorpion's Sting*, he argues that Lincoln's commitment to "ultimate extinction" during the 1850s already carried a full commitment to emancipation.[69] Oakes is right, I think, to emphasize that the controversy over slavery during the 1850s involved national jurisdiction. He draws from that issue, however, a logic that moved the entire antislavery coalition and controlled antislavery thinking throughout the period. At every point over that critical period, he says, Lincoln's intentions and policies, like those of the Republicans generally, grew out of, echoed, or amounted to much the same thing as those of the abolitionists. Oakes thus radicalizes the antislavery camp and minimizes the differences in principle and purpose within it—differences that Lincoln's double values allowed him to straddle.[70]

According to Oakes, the Republicans "never had to move from Union to emancipation because the two issues—liberty *and* union—were never separate for them."[71] If we pay attention to Lincoln's nationalism, however, we can see that beneath his exceptionalist conception of the nation, he was deeply aware of the conflict between his two ideals, and in 1860 he hoped only that they might ultimately be brought together. Oakes argues that by 1860, the Republicans had formulated a deliberate plan to use the national government to attack the federal supports of southern slavery and erode its borders, thus encircling it and forcing voluntary emancipation. But that scenario of the southern scorpion's self-inflicted death, even based on

Oakes's evidence, was less a plan than a vaguely and disparately imagined hope. Once they were in power, the radical Republicans intended to withdraw federal aid to slavery, but it was only after the South forced secession and war that moderates like Lincoln were willing to attack the ramparts of the slaveholding republic. As Ira Berlin suggests, when Lincoln claimed he had not controlled events but had been controlled by them, the power of those events to move him to emancipation could have been what he had in mind.[72] If not for those contingent events, Lincoln and the nation likely would have remained mired in the limbo of "ultimate extinction" for some time to come.

The relative importance of contingency is a factor in every historical analysis, and few historians today wish to argue for inevitability. Even David Brion Davis, who established the long timescale of moral transformation that made the Reconstruction amendments "the culmination of the Age of Emancipation," concludes that the outcome was perhaps "foreseeable" after British emancipation in 1833 but by no means "inevitable," depending in the end on the contingencies of war. Events still shaped intentions and consequences.[73] Oakes denies the inevitability of consequences: "The Republicans hated slavery and intended to destroy it, but intentions don't make outcomes inevitable." Contingency was not a factor in Lincoln's thinking, however, from the mid-1850s onward. In this view, Lincoln was already a bold emancipator.[74]

Viewed in the context of Lincoln's nationalism, his acceptance of slavery's "ultimate extinction" abridged the natural rights he offered black Americans and left emancipation an uncertain prospect, whereas the nation was an unyielding presence. In his resort to "necessity," Lincoln recognized that his formula compromised the demands of liberal justice for the sake of maintaining the nation. His egalitarian principles deepened during the 1850s as he recognized that any invidious distinctions threatened the liberty of all. An exceptionalist nation, he came to realize, could not remain *permanently* half slave and half free. But his nationalism remained firm, and secession amplified it. A man with southern family roots who consistently overestimated the strength of southern unionism, Lincoln was attached to the whole union. A proud nationalist with world-historical ambition, he insisted on preserving a powerful, continental nation respected in Europe and of consequence in the world.

Some historians have looked for a moment when Lincoln's commitment to equal liberty trumped his commitment to the nation. As Rogers Smith points out, Lincoln said at Philadelphia, on the way to his inauguration, that "he was about to say" he would rather be assassinated than see the nation salvaged on a basis other than the promise that "in due time the burden shall be lifted from the shoulders of all men." Smith reads that statement as an indication that Lincoln had come to value liberty above the nation; I read it as a statement of his reluctance to sacrifice the hope that slavery would be eliminated "in due time"—a hope that allowed him to join liberty to nation.[75] Eric Foner concludes that, before his inauguration, Lincoln had no political choice but to maintain the free-soil position on which he had been elected, and he still expected to be able to defuse the crisis and avoid war.[76]

When compromise efforts collapsed, Lincoln had no choice but to go to war to save the nation, and the war created opportunities to attack the institution of slavery. Historians like Oakes who portray Lincoln as the emancipator have emphasized the extent to which he seized those opportunities. Here is where Lincoln began to lay claim to that title, although he moved, I believe, with more caution and more reservations than they acknowledge. Foner's *The Fiery Trial* is alone among important recent texts in recognizing the complexity of Lincoln's intentions and his slow movement toward emancipation. Foner credits Lincoln with grasping the opportunities presented by the war and Congress, but he also lays out in convincing detail how Lincoln worked—before he declared emancipation and even after—to promote colonization schemes that would encourage the voluntary exit of blacks from the United States.

The communal dimension of nationality that Lincoln expressed—his flesh-and-blood view of the nation as an intergenerational family—fundamentally impeded his thinking. When he recalled how the historical nation had incorporated white immigrants in 1858, the bodily, familial basis of nationality came to the fore. Praising the "iron men" who had founded the nation—"the race of men whom we claim as our fathers and grandfathers"—Lincoln went on to note: "We have besides these men—descended by blood from our ancestors—among us perhaps half our people who . . . have come from Europe—German, Irish, French, and Scandinavian . . . [and here found] themselves our equals in all things." When these individuals look back to the founders, they find no connection "by blood." But when they read the Declaration of Independence, "then they feel that that moral sentiment taught in that day . . . is the father of all moral principle in them, and that they have a right to claim it as though they were blood of the blood, and flesh of the flesh of the men who wrote the Declaration, and so they are."[77] Lincoln outlined here the basis for a civic community formed by universal principle and universally shared flesh and blood, one that could be interpreted to grant black Africans, as it had granted white Europeans, equal membership in the historical nation. But a multiracial national family was difficult for him to imagine. He was careful to stipulate that the white Europeans who had come to the United States had found themselves "our equal in all things." It is unclear whether Lincoln meant equal in capacity, equal in treatment, or both.

Racial slavery had nonetheless made blacks a different case. Lincoln always pointed to physical difference as the root of invidious racial distinction; he seemed less certain about mental or moral inequalities. When he tried to convert a group of black ministers to colonization during the war, it was apparently the color difference that made him call black and white the most opposite of all the races. As his efforts at colonization attest, he was unable to fully embrace the national future that emancipation created, so he moved cautiously and kept his options open.

According to Foner, it was not until August 1864, with military victory still in doubt, that Lincoln fully committed to emancipation. When he refused to consider a peace deal that would allow slavery to continue, he made emancipation "an end in itself, a position Lincoln would not abandon even if it meant risking his own reelection."[78] Because military victory was not yet achieved and a Democratic president might agree to Confederate independence, Foner implies that Lincoln was risking a unified nation: emancipation was now the absolute; if worse came to worst, the union was expendable. I agree that by August 1864, if not somewhat before, with the Emancipation Proclamation and the Gettysburg Address behind him and the bravery of black Union soldiers proven, Lincoln had fully committed to emancipation. But he still wanted to join nation and liberty. His refusal at that late moment to make a peace deal that sacrificed emancipation reflected his calculation of both ideal commitments and the risks they faced. He took a chance on saving both nation and liberty, and he won.

Lincoln's willingness to struggle with his joint commitment to nation and liberty, his willingness to finally put his familial nation to the test of universal liberty, was surely the major part of his greatness. Still, we cannot know how he would have balanced national reunion and African American liberties in the years that followed. The exceptionalist nation he envisioned remained and remains an unstable formation of reality and ideal. The particularities of national history, as well as the communal dimension of nationality, do not easily mesh with universalist aspirations. The history that preceded the Civil War and that which followed it tells us that America's exceptionalist nationalism is as likely to obscure as it is to inspire the universal values it claims.

NOTES

1. An influential source of the narrative of growing liberty, in which emancipation is spearheaded by abolitionist principle and realized in civil war, is James McPherson's work over a lifetime of scholarship, chiefly *The Struggle for Equality: Abolitionists and the Negro in the Civil War and Reconstruction* (Princeton, NJ: Princeton University Press, 1995), *The Abolitionist Legacy: From Reconstruction to the NAACP* (Princeton, NJ: Princeton University Press, 1975), and *Battle Cry of Freedom: The Civil War Era* (New York: Oxford University Press, 1988). For astute reviews of that national narrative, see Edward L. Ayers, "Worrying about the Civil War," in *Moral Problems in American Life*, ed. Karen Halttunen and Lewis Perry (Ithaca, NY: Cornell University Press, 1998), 145–166, esp. 156; and Michael Johnson, "Battle Cry of Freedom?" *Reviews in American History* 17 (June 1989): 214–218.

2. David Brion Davis, *The Problem of Slavery in Western Culture* (Ithaca, NY: Cornell University Press, 1966); David Brion Davis, *The Problem of Slavery in the Age of Revolution 1770–1823* (Ithaca, NY: Cornell University Press, 1975). For the completion of his account of emancipation in the United States as the product of contingent events and "a century's moral achievement," see David Brion Davis, *Inhuman Bondage: The Rise and Fall of Slavery in the New World* (New York: Oxford University Press, 2006), esp. 330–331. On the special contribution of antebellum Christianity to the result, see Elizabeth B. Clark, "'The Sacred Rights of the Weak': Pain, Sympathy, and the Culture of Individual Rights in Antebellum America," *Journal of American History* 82 (September 1995): 463–493.

3. On universalist principles of human rights, see Davis, *Problem of Slavery in the Age of Revolution*, chaps. 1, 6, 7; Knud Haakonssen, "From Natural Law to the Rights of Man: A European Perspective on American Debates," in *A Culture of Rights*, ed. Michael J. Lacey and Knud Haakonssen (Cambridge: Cambridge University Press, 1991), 19–61; Lynn Hunt, *Inventing Human Rights* (New York: W.W. Norton, 2007); and Jerome J. Shestack, "The Philosophic Foundations of Human Rights," *Human Rights Quarterly* 20 (1998): 201–234.

4. Davis, *Problem of Slavery in the Age of Revolution*, chaps. 6–7. On the rise of racial theory and racism, see Bruce Dain, *A Hideous Monster of the Mind: American Race Theory in the Early Republic* (Cambridge, MA: Harvard University Press, 2002); George M. Fredrickson, *The Black Image in the White Mind: The Debate on Afro-American Character and Destiny, 1817–1914* (Middletown, CT: Wesleyan University Press, 1971); Reginald Horsman, *Race and Manifest Destiny: The Origins of American Racial Anglo-Saxonism* (Cambridge, MA: Harvard University Press, 1981); Joanne Pope Melish, *Disowning Slavery: Gradual Emancipation and "Race" in New England, 1780–1860* (Ithaca, NY: Cornell University Press, 1998); and James Brewer Stewart, "The Emergence of Racial Modernity and the Rise of the White North, 1790–1840," *Journal of the Early Republic* 18 (Summer 1998): 181–217. On liberal argument in defense of black slavery, see Francois Furstenberg, *In the Name of the Father: Washington's Legacy, Slavery, and the Making of a Nation* (New York: Penguin, 2006), chap. 5. On defenses

of the morality of slavery, see Drew Faust, *A Sacred Circle: The Dilemma of the Intellectual in the Old South* (Baltimore: Johns Hopkins University Press, 1977), and Mark A. Noll, *America's God: From Jonathan Edwards to Abraham Lincoln* (New York: Oxford University Press, 2002), chap. 19.

5. Merrill D. Peterson, *Lincoln in American Memory* (New York: Oxford University Press, 1994); Lincoln to Joshua F. Speed, August 24, 1855, in *The Collected Works of Abraham Lincoln*, 9 vols., ed. Roy P. Basler (New Brunswick, NJ: Rutgers University Press, 1953), 2:320–323 (hereafter cited as *Collected Works*); Lincoln, "Speech at Peoria," October 16, 1854, ibid., 265–266, 271; George M. Fredrickson, *Big Enough to Be Inconsistent: Abraham Lincoln Confronts Slavery and Race* (Cambridge, MA: Harvard University Press, 2008), 46–48. Throughout this essay, I attribute to Lincoln only his written words or speeches directly recorded at the time.

6. Lincoln, "Speech at Peoria," in *Collected Works*, 2:256; George M. Fredrickson, "A Man but Not a Brother: Abraham Lincoln and Racial Equality," *Journal of Southern History* 41 (February 1975): 39–58. When Fredrickson returned to the subject, he expanded his account but largely reaffirmed his earlier judgment; see Fredrickson, *Big Enough to Be Inconsistent*. On historians' views of Lincoln with regard to race, see Fredrickson, *Big Enough to Be Inconsistent*, 9–28, and Peterson, *Lincoln in American Memory*, 350–358, 384.

7. Perhaps the most influential account of Lincoln's single-minded fight for emancipation and racial equality is La Wanda Cox, *Lincoln and Black Freedom: A Study in Presidential Leadership* (Columbia: University of South Carolina Press, 1981). Cox attributes evidence against that view to Lincoln's style of leadership, which she characterizes "as often devious as forthright" (43). Other works that emphasize Lincoln's emancipationist and egalitarian motives also apply political analysis asymmetrically and ignore the political motives that fueled Lincoln's antislavery actions, among them James Oakes, *The Radical and the Republican: Frederick Douglass, Abraham Lincoln, and the Triumph of Antislavery Politics* (New York: W. W. Norton, 2007), and Richard Striner, *Father Abraham: Lincoln's Relentless Struggle to End Slavery* (New York: Oxford University Press, 2006). For a contrasting view that attributes Lincoln's antislavery leadership to both Christian principles and "shrewd political pragmatism," see Richard J. Carwardine, *Lincoln: A Life of Purpose and Power* (New York: Vintage, 2003), 81. For works that emphasize Lincoln's moral leadership toward emancipation and his political skill but regard his cautious leadership style as the virtuous exercise of prudence, see William Lee Miller, *Lincoln's Virtues: An Ethical Biography* (New York: Vintage, 2002), and Allen C. Guelzo, *Lincoln's Emancipation Proclamation* (New York: Simon & Schuster, 2004). See also Peterson, *Lincoln in American Memory*, 298–310, 327–340, 348–358, 382–384.

8. David Potter (first quote) cited in Fredrickson, *Big Enough to Be Inconsistent*, 79–85, 117, chap. 3. For works that give due weight to Lincoln's unionism and deny, in the words of Mark E. Neely Jr., "any easy characterization of Abraham Lincoln as a consistent and crusading emancipationist," see Neely, *The Last Best Hope of Earth: Abraham Lincoln and the Promise of America* (Cambridge, MA: Harvard University

Press, 1993), 100; William E. Gienapp, *Abraham Lincoln and Civil War America* (New York: Oxford University Press, 2002), chap. 5; and David Donald's classic contemporary biography, *Lincoln* (New York: Simon & Schuster, 1995), 15, 133–137, 362–369.

9. The disjunction between these two starting points for moral theory has been central to the liberal communitarian debates of the past decades. See David Miller, *On Nationality* (New York: Oxford University Press, 1995); Shlomo Avineri and Avner de-Shalit, eds., *Communitarianism and Individualism* (New York: Oxford University Press, 1992); Nancy L. Rosenblum, ed., *Liberalism and the Moral Life* (Cambridge, MA: Harvard University Press, 1989); Philip Selznick, *The Moral Commonwealth* (Berkeley: University of California Press, 1992); George P. Fletcher, *Loyalty: An Essay on the Morality of Relationships* (New York: Oxford University Press, 1993), chap. 1.

10. Miller, *On Nationality*; Benedict Anderson, *Imagined Communities* (London: Verso, 1991); Avishai Margalit, "The Moral Psychology of Nationalism," in *The Morality of Nationalism*, ed. Robert McKim and Jeffrey McMahan (New York: Oxford University Press, 1997), chap. 6; Rogers M. Smith, *Stories of Peoplehood: The Politics and Morals of Political Membership* (New York: Cambridge University Press, 2003), 20, 102.

11. On the modern nation as a project of cultural construction, see Smith, *Stories of Peoplehood*, 32–42; David A. Bell, *The Cult of the Nation in France: Inventing Nationalism, 1680–1800* (Cambridge, MA: Harvard University Press, 2001), 1–22; Anthony D. Smith, *National Identity* (Reno: University of Nevada Press, 1991), chap. 1.

12. On unionism as the commonest antebellum form of American nationalism, see Rogan Kersh, *Dreams of a More Perfect Union* (Ithaca, NY: Cornell University Press, 2001), 2–17, chap. 3. For the importance of territorial unity in nineteenth-century nationalism, see Thomas Bender, *A Nation among Nations: America's Place in World History* (New York: Hill & Wang, 2006), chap. 3.

13. On the construction of American nationalism, see Furstenberg, *In the Name of the Father*; Merle Curti, *The Roots of American Loyalty* (New York: Atheneum, 1946); Rush Welter, *The Mind of America 1820–1860* (New York: Columbia University Press, 1975); Jean H. Baker, *Affairs of Party: The Political Culture of Northern Democrats in the Mid-Nineteenth Century* (Ithaca, NY: Cornell University Press, 1983), chap. 2; David Waldstreicher, *In the Midst of Perpetual Fetes: The Making of American Nationalism* (Chapel Hill: University of North Carolina Press, 1997); Cynthia M. Koch, "Teaching Patriotism: Private Virtue for the Public Good in the Early Republic," in *Bonds of Affection: Americans Define Their Patriotism*, ed. John Bodnar (Princeton, NJ: Princeton University Press, 1996), 19–52.

14. Dorothy Ross, "American Exceptionalism," in *A Companion to American Thought*, ed. Richard W. Fox and James T. Kloppenberg (New York: Oxford University Press, 1995), 22–23; Dorothy Ross, *The Origins of American Social Science* (New York: Cambridge University Press, 1991), 22–30; Noll, *America's God*, chaps. 4–5, 21; Sydney E. Ahlstrom, "Religion, Revolution and the Rise of Modern Nationalism: Reflections on the American Experience," *Church History* 44 (December 1975): 492–504; Mark Y. Hanley, *Beyond a Christian Commonwealth: The Protestant Quarrel with the American Republic 1830–1860* (Chapel Hill: University of North Carolina Press,

1994). For a more heterogeneous conception of American exceptionalism, see Michael Kammen, "The Problem of American Exceptionalism: A Reconsideration," *American Quarterly* 45 (March 1993): 1–43.

15. Bender, *Nation among Nations*, chap. 3; McPherson, *Battle Cry of Freedom*. But compare the more nuanced discussion of nationalism in Eric Foner, *The Story of American Freedom* (New York: W. W. Norton, 1998), chap. 5. On the inextricability of principle from particularity in liberal nationalism, see Smith, *Stories of Peoplehood*, 88–92, and Bernard Yack, "The Myth of the Civic Nation," *Critical Review* 10 (Spring 1996): 193–211.

16. Daniel T. Rodgers, *Contested Truths* (Cambridge, MA: Harvard University Press, 1987), chap. 2; Robert M. Cover, *Antislavery and the Judicial Process* (New Haven, CT: Yale University Press, 1976); Don Fehrenbacher, *The Slaveholding Republic* (New York: Oxford University Press, 2001); Paul Finkelman, *Slavery and the Founders* (Armonk, NY: Routledge, 1996). Although I use here Fehrenbacher's apt phrase, I reject his conclusion that the Constitution was "neutral" (x) on the issue of slavery, as well as Finkelman's conclusion that it was a "pro-slavery" document (31); neither term captures its mixed character, designed to protect both the free and the slaveholding elements of the compound nation.

17. Caleb McDaniel, "Our Country Is the World: Radical American Abolitionists Abroad" (Ph.D. diss., Johns Hopkins University, 2006); James Brewer Stewart, *Holy Warriors: The Abolitionists and American Slavery* (New York: Hill & Wang, 1996); Paul Goodman, *Of One Blood: Abolitionism and the Origins of Racial Equality* (Berkeley: University of California Press, 1998); Patrick Rael, *Black Identity and Black Protest in the Antebellum North* (Chapel Hill: University of North Carolina Press, 2002); George R. Price and James Brewer Stewart, eds., *To Heal the Scourge of Prejudice: The Life and Writings of Hosea Easton* (Amherst: University of Massachusetts Press, 1999), esp. 113; Frederick Douglass, "What to the Slave Is the Fourth of July?" in *The Frederick Douglass Papers*, 5 vols., ed. John W. Blassingame et al. (New Haven, CT: Yale University Press, 1979–1992), 2:359–388.

18. On ethnoracial nationalism, see Horsman, *Race and Manifest Destiny*; Kersh, *Dreams of a More Perfect Union*, 115–122; Thomas R. Hietala, *Manifest Design: Anxious Aggrandizement in Late Jacksonian America* (Ithaca, NY: Cornell University Press, 1985); Eric Kaufmann, "American Exceptionalism Reconsidered: Anglo-Saxon Ethnogenesis in the 'Universal' Nation, 1776–1850," *Journal of American Studies* 33 (1999): 437–457; George E. Baker, ed., *The Works of William H. Seward*, 4 vols. (Boston: Houghton Mifflin, 1872), 1:56. On the civic disabilities of free blacks, see Rogers M. Smith, *Civic Ideals: Conflicting Visions of Citizenship in U.S. History* (New Haven, CT: Yale University Press, 1997), 220–221, chap. 9.

19. Baker, *Works of Seward*, 1:66–67, 74–75.

20. Kersh, *Dreams of a More Perfect Union*, 134–135, 144–149; Andrew C. Lenner, *The Federal Principle in American Politics, 1790–1833* (Lanham, MD: Rowman & Littlefield, 2001), chap. 2, 124–145, 130, 140, 168.

21. Except when referring to the generic "country," Lincoln used the term "na-

tion" in this essay to refer to the United States. He often continued to do so thereafter, especially when emphasizing the whole people or the historic entity whose destiny hung in the balance. He first began to refer to the United States as the "Union" (in other than a generic sense of "country") in October 1845 when discussing territorial issues, with the term often carrying the connotation of a union of states. During the 1850s he used the term "Union" more frequently than "nation" and most often invested it with the connotations and sentiments of nationality. When secession turned to war, "the Union" became the name for the whole nation the North now claimed to represent and was fighting to preserve. See, for example, Lincoln to Albert G. Hodges, April 4, 1864, in *Collected Works*, 7:281.

22. Lincoln, "Address before the Young Men's Lyceum of Springfield," January 27, 1838, ibid., 1:108–115, esp. 108–109.

23. Ibid., esp. 109, 112.

24. Ibid. On Lincoln's and his generation's organic attachment to the nation understood as a bodily familial connection, see Paul W. Kahn, *Legitimacy and History: Self-Government in American Constitutional Theory* (New Haven, CT: Yale University Press, 1992), chap. 2. For the familial language of nationalism common in antebellum political discourse, but not for their flawed explanations, see Major L. Wilson, *Space, Time, and Freedom: The Quest for Nationality and the Irrepressible Conflict 1815–1861* (Westport, CT: Praeger, 1974), and George B. Forgie, *Patricide in the House Divided* (New York: W. W. Norton, 1979).

25. Fredrickson, *Big Enough to Be Inconsistent*, 52–53.

26. Lincoln, "Speech at Peoria," in *Collected Works*, 2:268.

27. Eric Foner, *Free Soil, Free Labor, Free Men* (New York: Oxford University Press, 1995), ix–xxxix, chaps. 1–2; Eugene D. Genovese and Elizabeth Fox-Genovese, *The Mind of the Master Class* (Cambridge: Cambridge University Press, 2005), chaps. 1, 2, 7; William R. Brock, *Parties and Political Conscience: American Dilemmas 1840–1850* (Millwood, NY: KTO Press, 1979), 139. Two recent works that locate the aggressor in South and North, respectively, point up the importance of national identity in the discourse of sectional conflict: Manisha Sinha, *The Counter-Revolution of Slavery: Politics and Ideology in Antebellum South Carolina* (Chapel Hill: University of North Carolina Press, 2000), and Susan-Mary Grant, *North over South: Northern Nationalism and American Identity in the Antebellum Era* (Lawrence: University Press of Kansas, 2000).

28. *Democratic Review* 16 (January 1845): 8–9, quoted in Brock, *Parties and Political Conscience*, 147.

29. Lincoln to Williamson Durley, October 3, 1845, in *Collected Works*, 1:347–348.

30. Steven Lukes, "Making Sense of Moral Conflict," in *Moral Conflict and Politics* (New York: Oxford University Press, 1991), 3–20.

31. Lincoln to Durley, in *Collected Works*, 1:347–348.

32. Don E. Fehrenbacher, *Prelude to Greatness: Lincoln in the 1850s* (Stanford, CA: Stanford University Press, 1962), chap. 4, esp. 76–77; Fredrickson, *Big Enough to Be Inconsistent*, 49; Jay R. Carlander and W. Elliot Brownlee. "Antebellum Southern Po-

litical Economists and the Problem of Slavery," *American Nineteenth Century History* 7 (September 2006): 389–416.

33. Lincoln, "Eulogy on Henry Clay," July 6, 1852, in *Collected Works*, 2:130; Lincoln, "Speech at Peoria," ibid., 276.

34. Lincoln, "Speech at Peoria," ibid., 265–266, 276. On the role his political rivalry with Douglas played in Lincoln's free-soil position, see Fehrenbacher, *Prelude to Greatness*, chaps. 1–2, 4, and Fredrickson, *Big Enough to Be Inconsistent*, 40–41. For Lincoln's acute awareness of his evangelical constituency's moral commitment to antislavery and its important role in his political strategy of the 1850s, see Carwardine, *Lincoln*, xiv, chap. 2.

35. Lincoln, "Speech at Springfield," June 26, 1857, in *Collected Works*, 2:405; "First Debate with Stephen A. Douglas at Ottawa," August 21, 1858, ibid., 3:16. On the centrality of the right to free labor for Lincoln, see Foner, *Free Soil, Free Labor, Free Men*, 296, and Fredrickson, *Big Enough to Be Inconsistent*, 48, 65–66.

36. Hunt, *Inventing Human Rights*, 22–29; Rodgers, *Contested Truths*, 74, 186–189; Sean Wilentz, *The Rise of American Democracy Jefferson to Lincoln* (New York: W. W. Norton, 2005); Gordon S. Wood, *The Radicalism of the American Revolution* (New York: Vintage, 1992), pt. 3.

37. Lincoln, "Speech at Peoria," in *Collected Works*, 2:266, 269. Cf. Fredrickson, *Big Enough to Be Inconsistent*, 63–64.

38. Lincoln to Speed, August 24, 1855, in *Collected Works*, 2:320; "Speech at Peoria," ibid., 270, 276; "Fourth Debate with Stephen A. Douglas at Charleston," September 18, 1858, ibid., 3:181; "Address at Cooper Institute, New York City," February 27, 1860, ibid., 538.

39. Lincoln, "Speech at Peoria," ibid., 2:270.

40. Lincoln, "Speech at Springfield," ibid., 2:406. Cf. Harry V. Jaffa, *Crisis of the House Divided* (Chicago: University of Chicago Press, 1959), 32–34, 61, 318, 325, 379–386. Jaffa does not regard Lincoln's failure to grant equal rights as "intrinsically unjust" and thus applauds him for consistent adherence to liberal principles.

41. Lincoln, "Speech at Chicago," July 10, 1858, in *Collected Works*, 2:492. On the radicals' constitutional program against slavery, see Foner, *Free Soil, Free Labor, Free Men*, 122, 208.

42. John Adams to Thomas Jefferson, 1821, quoted in Stewart Winger, *Lincoln, Religion, and Romantic Cultural Politics* (De Kalb: Northern Illinois University Press, 2003), 49–50; Lincoln, "'A House Divided': Speech at Springfield," June 16, 1858, in *Collected Works*, 2:461–462; "Speech at Chicago," July 10, 1858, ibid., 491–492. Cf. Oakes, *The Radical and the Republican*, 70: "There is something almost willfully naive in this vision of American history."

43. Lincoln, "First Debate . . . at Ottawa," in *Collected Works*, 3:18; "Fourth Debate . . . at Charleston," ibid., 181.

44. Lincoln, "Speech at Chicago," March 1, 1859, ibid., 370. On the political context, see ibid., n. 1, and Fehrenbacher, *Prelude to Greatness*, chap. 4.

45. McPherson, *Struggle for Equality*, chap. 1; Foner, *Free Soil, Free Labor, Free Men*, 131–132, 181–182, chap. 6.

46. Lincoln to William H. Seward, February 1, 1861, in *Collected Works*, 4:183; Lincoln, "Remarks Concerning Concessions to Secession," January 28, 1861, ibid., 175–176.

47. Lincoln, "Speech in United States House of Representatives: The War with Mexico," January 12, 1848, ibid., 1:438; "First Inaugural Address—Final Text, March 4, 1861," ibid., 4:262–271, esp. 264. See also Donald, *Lincoln*, 269, 293.

48. Melinda Lawson, *Patriot Fires: Forging a New American Nationalism in the Civil War North* (Lawrence: University Press of Kansas, 2002); Alice Fahs, *The Imagined Civil War: Popular Literature of the North and South 1861–1865* (Chapel Hill: University of North Carolina Press, 2001); Dorothy Ross, "'Are We a Nation?': The Conjuncture of Nationhood and Race in the United States, 1850–1876," *Modern Intellectual History* 2, 3 (2005): 327–360; James H. Moorhead, *American Apocalypse: Yankee Protestants and the Civil War 1860–1869* (New Haven, CT: Yale University Press, 1978); Adam I. P. Smith, *No Party Now: Politics in the Civil War North* (New York: Oxford University Press, 2006), chap. 4.

49. Smith, *No Party Now*, esp. 4, 66.

50. Neely, *Last Best Hope of Earth*, 106–107; Gienapp, *Abraham Lincoln and Civil War America*, 87–90, 105–106, 110–111; Ira Berlin, "Who Freed the Slaves? Emancipation and Its Meaning," in *Union and Emancipation: Essays on Politics and Race in the Civil War Era*, ed. David W. Blight and Brooks D. Simpson (Kent, OH: Kent State University Press, 1997), 105–121; Steven Hahn, *A Nation under Our Feet* (Cambridge, MA: Harvard University Press, 2003), 82, 89, 102.

51. Lincoln to Horace Greeley, August 22, 1862, in *Collected Works*, 5:388.

52. McPherson, *Battle Cry of Freedom*, 509–510; Striner, *Father Abraham*, 176; Cox, *Lincoln and Black Freedom*, 12; Guelzo, *Lincoln's Emancipation Proclamation*, 149–151; Oakes, *The Radical and the Republican*, 189.

53. Jaffa, *Crisis of the House Divided*, 227–228. For the rhetorical achievement of the Gettysburg Address, see Garry Wills, *Lincoln at Gettysburg: The Words That Remade America* (New York: Simon & Schuster, 1992), but compare Pauline Maier, *American Scripture: Making the Declaration of Independence* (New York: Vintage, 1997).

54. Lincoln was celebrated in the 1950s and 1960s for his powerful yet humble assertion of America's "civil religion." For a review and critique of this literature, see Melvin B. Endy Jr., "Abraham Lincoln and American Civil Religion: A Reinterpretation," *Church History* 44 (June 1975): 229–241. For recent authors who have exempted Lincoln from exceptionalist ideology, see James Kloppenberg, "Aspirational Nationalism in America," *Intellectual History Newsletter* 2 (2002): 64–65; Bender, *Nation among Nations*, chap. 3, esp. 124, 176; Winger, *Lincoln, Religion, and Romantic Cultural Politics*, 11, 75–76, 207; Noll, *America's God*, chap. 21. For an analysis of Lincoln's exceptionalist "tale of his nation" in somewhat different terms than presented here, see Jean H. Baker, "Lincoln's Narrative of American Exceptionalism," in *"We Cannot Escape History": Lincoln and the Last Best Hope of Earth*, ed. James

M. McPherson (Urbana: University of Illinois Press, 1995), 33–44. On Lincoln's fatalism and providentialism, see Allen C. Guelzo, *Abraham Lincoln: Redeemer President* (Grand Rapids, MI: William B. Eerdmans, 1999), chaps. 3–4.

55. Lincoln, "Address to the New Jersey State Senate," February 21, 1861, in *Collected Works*, 4:236; "First Inaugural Address," ibid., 271; "Second Inaugural Address," March 4, 1865, ibid., 8:332–333; Endy, "Abraham Lincoln and American Civil Religion," 240.

56. Smith, *No Party Now*, esp. 141–143.

57. Rogan Kersh came to this conclusion after taking a statistical sample of newspaper opinions and congressional debates on all three Reconstruction amendments. My reading of the congressional debates on the Thirteenth Amendment confirms that judgment. See Kersh, *Dreams of a More Perfect Union*, 216–218. For a discussion that attributes passage of the amendment to the universalist moral idealism embedded in American "ideological and institutional structures," see Herman Belz, *Emancipation and Equal Rights: Constitutionalism in the Civil War Era* (New York: W. W. Norton, 1978), xvii–xviii, 30–33. On the amendment as a product of contingent "political tactics, legal thought, and popular ideology," see Michael Vorenberg, *Final Freedom: The Civil War, the Abolition of Slavery, and the Thirteenth Amendment* (New York: Cambridge University Press, 2001), 3.

58. Smith, *No Party Now*, 56; Charles Sumner quoted in *Congressional Globe*, 38th Cong., 1st sess., February 9, 1864, 536; George H. Yeaman, ibid., 2nd sess., January 9, 1865, 170.

59. Lyman Trumbell quoted in *Congressional Globe*, 38th Cong., 1st sess., March 28, 1864, 1314; Reverdy Johnson, ibid., April 5, 1864, 1423; Isaac Arnold, ibid., March 19, 1864, 1197. See also John Farnsworth, ibid., June 15, 1864, 2980; Thomas Jenckes, ibid., 2nd sess., January 11, 1865, 225; Green Smith, ibid., January 12, 1865, 237; Cornelius Cole, ibid., January 28, 1865, 482.

60. William S. Holman quoted in *Congressional Globe*, 38th Cong., 2nd sess., January 11, 1865, 218; James A. Cravens, ibid., 219; Samuel S. Cox, ibid., January 12, 1865, 242; James S. Rollins, ibid., January 13, 1865, 258–259; Anson Herrick, ibid., January 31, 1865, 525–526; Martin Kalbfleisch, ibid., 530.

61. Vorenberg, *Final Freedom*, 212–230; Fredrickson, *Big Enough to Be Inconsistent*, 117–123.

62. David W. Blight, *Race and Reunion: The Civil War in American Memory* (New York: Cambridge University Press, 2001). See also Kersh, *Dreams of a More Perfect Union*, chap. 5.

63. This postscript was written in 2014.

64. Bender, *Nation among Nations*, chap. 3, is an exception to the recent neglect of Lincoln's nationalism. Using a transnational frame, however, Bender identifies Lincoln, the radical Republicans, and the liberal nationalists of 1848 Europe with universalist liberal principles and brackets or denies conflict between their two ideals.

65. "Oration by Frederick Douglass," in Blassingame et al., *Douglass Papers*, ser. 1, 4:427–440.

66. Lincoln to Albert G. Hodges, April 4, 1864, in *Collected Works*, 7:281.

67. Michael Burlingame shows that Lincoln's Lyceum address drew on common anti-Jackson rhetorical figures of the era. Lincoln nonetheless rose above his usual partisan satires and used the occasion to explore the logic of his nationalist republican principles. The two contemporary friends whom Burlingame cites as criticizing Lincoln's "spread-eagle" rhetoric did so after the war and in comparison with his mature eloquence. Michael Burlingame, *Abraham Lincoln: A Life*, 2 vols. (Baltimore: Johns Hopkins University Press, 2008), 1:140–141, 789 n. 49.

68. Nicholas Guyatt, *Providentialism and the Invention of the United States, 1607–1876* (Cambridge: Cambridge University Press, 2007), analyzes the nationalist ideology of American exceptionalism as a species of providentialism and also argues that it blinded most Americans to the existence of slavery and blacks' claim to equal citizenship.

69. In *Lincoln's Tragic Pragmatism: Lincoln, Douglas, and Moral Conflict* (Cambridge, MA: Harvard University Press, 2013), John Burt suggests that when Lincoln took the position that slavery was wrong in his 1858 debates with Stephen Douglas, both emancipation and racial equality were "within the penumbra of his intentions" (xii–xiii; see also 312, 649). Burt's focus, however, is on Lincoln's and Douglas's differing commitments to both liberty and democracy.

70. James Oakes, *Freedom National: The Destruction of Slavery in the United States, 1861–1865* (New York: W. W. Norton, 2013), esp. xxiii–xxiv; James Oakes, *The Scorpion's Sting: Antislavery and the Coming of the Civil War* (New York: W. W. Norton, 2014). For excellent critiques, see Manisha Sinha, "The Complicated Histories of Emancipation: State of the Field at 150," *Reviews in American History* 41 (2013): 665–671, and Ira Berlin, "Would Slavery Have Self-Destructed without the War?" review of Oakes, *The Scorpion's Sting*, in *Washington Post*, June 1, 2014, B7. Against Oakes's blanket formulation, note also Lincoln's private letter to William Seward during the secession crisis, in which he refused to compromise on the extension of slavery but added: "As to fugitive slaves, District of Columbia, slave trade among the slave states, and whatever of necessity springs from the fact that the institution is amongst us, I care but little, so that what is done be comely, and not altogether outrageous." Lincoln to Seward, February 1, 1861, in *Collected Works*, 4:183. These were precisely the issues that signaled, according to Oakes, the Republicans' ongoing determination to surround and destroy slavery when they took office.

71. Oakes, *Freedom National*, xxiv.

72. Berlin, "Would Slavery Have Self-Destructed?"

73. David Brion Davis, *The Problem of Slavery in the Age of Emancipation* (New York: Alfred A. Knopf, 2014), xvi–xvii, 336–337.

74. Oakes, *Scorpion's Sting*, 19, 21.

75. Rogers M. Smith, "Lincoln and Obama: Two Visions of American Civic Union," in *Representing Citizenship*, ed. Liette Gidlow (forthcoming, Wayne State University Press). Lincoln's conditional phrase, which Smith does not quote, further suggests that Lincoln is not here reversing his priorities. Cf. Lincoln, "Speech in In-

dependence Hall, Philadelphia, Pennsylvania," February 22, 1861, in *Collected Works*, 4:240.

76. Eric Foner, *The Fiery Trial: Abraham Lincoln and American Slavery* (New York: W. W. Norton, 2010), 152–156.

77. Lincoln, "Speech at Chicago," in *Collected Works*, July 10, 1858, 2:499–500.

78. Foner, *Fiery Trial*, 306–307. For the uncertainties involved in Lincoln's calculations at this point, see also McPherson, *Battle Cry of Freedom*, 769–773.

CHAPTER FOUR

What If Honest Abe Was Telling the Truth? Natural Rights, Race, and Legalism in the Political Thought of Lincoln

Nicholas Buccola

On August 21, 1858, Abraham Lincoln and Senator Stephen A. Douglas met in Ottawa, Illinois, to participate in the first of seven debates prior to the midterm election in November. In his opening speech at the debate, Lincoln declared that he had "no purpose directly or indirectly, to interfere with the institution of slavery in the states where it exists." He proceeded to say, "I believe I have no lawful right to do so, and I have no inclination to do so."[1] Just a few moments later, Lincoln added, "there is no reason at all furnished why the negro after all is not entitled to all that the declaration of independence holds out, which is, 'life, liberty, and the pursuit of happiness' [applause and loud cheers], and I hold that he is as much entitled to that as a white man."[2]

Passages such as these present contemporary scholars with a vexing question: how did Lincoln reconcile his commitment to natural rights with his rejection of abolitionism before the Civil War?[3] In other words, how was Lincoln able to square his commitment to the liberal doctrine of natural rights with his illiberal hostility to abolition?[4] Did he embrace this seemingly paradoxical view because he rejected the idea that slaves had natural rights, or did he accept it for reasons of political expediency? Or is there another, more compelling explanation for his resistance to abolition? In what follows, I consider and reject two responses to these questions: the racial contract thesis and the political expediency thesis. According to the racial contract thesis, Lincoln's resistance to abolition was rooted in his acceptance of white supremacy, which led him to exclude African Americans from the promise of natural rights. According to the political expediency thesis, Lincoln believed there was a moral obligation to abolish slavery, but he did not say so during the antebellum years because to do so would have been political suicide.

Both the racial contract thesis and the political expediency thesis suggest that Lincoln's antebellum political thought was fundamentally dishonest. If the racial contract thesis is true, Lincoln was being less than honest when he said he believed "the negro" was "entitled to all that the declaration of independence holds out." If the political expediency thesis is correct, Lincoln was concealing his true beliefs—that there was a moral obligation to abolish slavery—in order to secure political gain. In what follows, I argue that neither of these theses provides a sufficient explanation for Lincoln's resistance to abolition. Instead, I explain and defend what I call the Honest Abe thesis. I entertain the possibility that Lincoln was genuinely committed to the natural rights of African Americans (contra the racial contract thesis) *and* opposed to the idea that there was a moral obligation to abolish slavery (contra the political expediency thesis). According to the Honest Abe thesis, Lincoln genuinely believed he could embrace natural rights liberalism—which "looks to the constant fulfillment of an ideal pre-established normative order, be it nature's or God's whose principles have to be realized in the lives of individual citizens through public guarantees"—while at the same time rejecting abolitionism.[5] He did this by reformulating the duties required by natural rights–based political morality. Rather than requiring us to act to promote the *immediate* fulfillment of the naturally just normative order, Lincoln's liberalism required that we act in ways that would secure the *eventual* fulfillment of that normative order. My aim in this essay is to explain how he justified this position.

Lincoln's rationale for embracing this view had three major components. First, he had practical concerns about what could be done with the existing institution of slavery. As he put it several times throughout his political career, he "should not know what to do" about the existing institution even if "all earthly power" were given to him.[6] Second, he worried that public sentiment was too strongly against abolition to pursue such a policy. And third, Lincoln blended his commitment to natural rights with a legalist philosophy that could accommodate his rejection of abolitionism. Lincoln believed legalism provided the best strategy to keep the "public mind" at rest in the hope of slavery's ultimate extinction while the "public heart" continued to progress on the issue.

My focus in this essay is on Lincoln's legalism, which I contend was central to his antebellum political thought.[7] By "legalism," I have in mind political theorist Judith Shklar's definition of the doctrine as an "ethical attitude that holds moral conduct to be a matter of rule following, and moral relationships to consist of duties and rights determined by rules."[8] Legalism, Shklar wrote in her 1964 book on the subject, is "the personal morality of all those men and women who think of goodness as obedience to the rules that properly define their duties and rights."[9] In what follows, I argue that this dimension of Shklar's understanding of legalism—with its emphasis on how the law can function to redefine our moral relationships—can help us understand Lincoln's seemingly paradoxical political thought. I claim that legalism was the *key* set of ideas he relied on in his attempt to reconcile his belief that all human beings have natural rights with his rejection of an affirmative obligation to abolish slavery (even though he believed the institution violated natural rights). According to natural rights morality, all individuals have a duty to respect the rights of others, and the primary role of government is to protect rights. In Lincoln's legalist reformulation of natural rights doctrine, respecting and securing the rights of all people assumed the status of an ideal to be achieved in the future, but the nature of our moral obligations in the present took a decidedly different form. Rather than being obliged to respect the natural rights of others (in the case of ordinary citizens) or to protect the natural rights of all (in the case of the state), Lincoln argued that our "moral relationships" (between citizens and between citizens and the state) had been redefined by the law. Following the rules prescribed by law would, Lincoln acknowledged, often fail to advance (and in some cases undermine) the natural rights of some individuals. Lincoln believed, though, that the promotion of a legalist "cast of mind" and "social ethos" (to borrow Shklar's terms) was the best means available to honor the moral requirements of natural rights principles. If citizens and statesmen respected and revered the law, he argued, natural rights would be vindicated in the long run.

My argument proceeds in the following way. First, I explore Lincoln's commitment to natural rights to show that he was, fundamentally, a natural rights liberal. Second, I make the case that Lincoln's views of abolition were illiberal and explore the merits of the racial contract thesis and the political expediency thesis as possible explanations of his illiberalism. Third, I show how legalism blended with his natural rights liberalism prior to the Civil War before I offer my conclusions.

LINCOLN'S LIBERALISM: ON THE CENTRALITY OF NATURAL RIGHTS IN HIS THOUGHT

Prior to his famous debates with Douglas, Lincoln had established himself as a committed defender of the liberal doctrine of natural rights.[10] In his speech at Peoria, Illinois, on October 16, 1854, for example, he offered a decidedly liberal explanation of the "doctrine of self-government," which he declared to be "absolutely and eternally right." The "just application" of this doctrine to the issue of slavery, Lincoln argued, depends on "whether a negro is not or is a man." The question of rights, in other words, depends on the humanity of the subject. It is on the basis of human nature, Lincoln argued, that individuals have rights. "If he is not a man," Lincoln continued, "why in that case, he who is a man may, as a matter of self-government, do just as he pleases with him. But if the negro is a man, is it not, to that extent, a total destruction of self-government, to say that he too shall not govern himself?" Lincoln's response to this rhetorical question is telling:

> When the white man governs himself that is self-government; but when he governs himself, and also governs another man, that is more than self-government—that is despotism. If the negro is a man, why then my ancient faith teaches me that "all men are created equal"; and that there can be no moral right in connection with one man's making a slave of another. . . . No man is good enough to govern another man, without that other's consent.[11]

Lincoln then proceeded to cite the powerful language from the opening lines of the Declaration of Independence before concluding that "the relation of masters and slaves is, pro tanto, a total violation" of the Declaration's principles.[12]

Lincoln's commitment to the Declaration's principles is, of course, another piece of evidence in support of the claim that he was devoted to the idea of natural rights. "I have never had a feeling politically," Lincoln said in a speech in 1861, "that did not spring from the sentiments embodied in the Declaration of Independence."[13] As he had explained a few years earlier, during his great speech on the *Dred Scott* decision, natural rights principles are at the Declaration's core:

> I think the authors of [the Declaration] intended to include all men, but they did not intend to declare all men equal in all respects. They did not mean to say all were equal in color, size, intellect, moral

developments, or social capacity. They defined with tolerable distinctness, in what respects they did consider all men created equal—equal in "certain inalienable rights, among which are life, liberty, and the pursuit of happiness." This they said, and this they meant.[14]

Lincoln was not simply offering an explanation of what the authors of the Declaration believed. In addition, he had a clear normative aim. The Declaration's natural rights principles, Lincoln went on to argue, *ought* to guide us: "They meant to set up a standard maxim for free society, which could be familiar to all, and revered by all; constantly looked to, constantly labored for, and even though never perfectly attained, constantly approximated, and thereby constantly spreading and deepening its influence, and augmenting the happiness and value of life to all people of all colors everywhere."[15]

During his debates with Douglas, Lincoln reiterated his commitment to natural rights many times. As noted earlier, in the debate at Ottawa on August 21, 1858, he said, "there is no reason at all furnished why the negro after all is not entitled to all that the declaration of independence holds out," and "in the right to the bread which his own hand earns, he is my own equal and Judge Douglas' equal, and the equal of every living man."[16] In the debate with Douglas at Quincy, Illinois, on October 13, 1858, Lincoln made it clear that it was on the basis of natural rights principles that the Republican Party objected to the extension of the institution of slavery into the territories and, therefore, differentiated itself from the Democratic Party. "I suppose that is the whole thing. It is the difference between those who think [slavery] is wrong and those who do not think it is wrong. We, the Republican Party, think it wrong. We think it is a moral, a social and a political wrong."[17]

Based on what has been described so far, there seems to be little daylight between Lincoln's natural rights philosophy and what was espoused by leading abolitionists such as William Lloyd Garrison, Frederick Douglass, and Lydia Maria Child. And yet we know that Lincoln refused to join the abolitionist ranks and took pains to distance himself from their views. Time and again during their famous debates, Douglas accused Lincoln of being connected to "Black Republicans" such as "Fred. Douglass, Joshua Giddings, and Salmon Chase."[18] How are we to explain the distance between a natural rights abolitionist like Frederick Douglass, who believed there was an affirmative obligation to use all moral and political tools available to bring about the end of slavery, and Lincoln, who resisted this conclusion? Some scholars have suggested a rather simple answer: Lincoln was guided by political expediency.[19] Whereas reformers like Douglass were unconstrained by the demands of electoral politics, Lincoln was seeking elective office in a political culture that was inegalitarian and largely hostile to abolitionism. It would have been political suicide, therefore, for Lincoln to publicly commit himself to true abolitionist principles. In such a context, historian Richard Striner argues, Lincoln's only choice was to become a "political virtuoso" who used "deception" and "manipulation" to attain power and, once attained, use it in ethical ways.[20] Although I have little doubt that Lincoln's political ambition was an important factor in distancing his views from those of the abolitionists, I do not think this tells the whole story. What if, for the sake of argument, we take Lincoln at his word? What if we resist the temptation to see him as someone who agreed with the abolitionists in principle but could not follow them in practice? What if we accept that he thought his views of natural rights and abolition were fully consistent? If we take this step, we are left with the vexing question with which I began this essay: how was Lincoln able to reconcile his philosophy of natural rights with his rejection of abolition? One possibility is that his commitment to natural rights was "racialized" in the way suggested by the racial contract thesis. It is to this possibility that I now turn.

LINCOLN'S ILLIBERALISM: DID THE GREAT EMANCIPATOR REALLY BELIEVE IN UNIVERSAL NATURAL RIGHTS?

Lincoln's rejection of abolitionism was fundamentally illiberal, especially if we judge him through the lens provided by "the liberalism of natural rights."[21] It is appropriate to judge Lincoln through this lens because he claimed—as I demonstrated in the preceding section—that his commitment to natural rights was at the core of his political creed. The natural rights conception of liberalism—unlike, say, a utilitarian conception—imposes a strict obligation on the state to respect *and* protect the rights of all individuals.[22] The liberalism of natural rights, in sum, requires the state to make a good-faith effort to abolish slavery.[23]

How are we to explain, then, Lincoln's illiberal attitude toward abolition? One possibility is that Lincoln's views were shaped by what philosopher Charles Mills calls the "Racial Contract":

> The Racial Contract is that set of formal or informal agreements or meta-agreements (higher-level contracts about contracts, which set the limits of the contracts' validity) between the members of one subset of humans, henceforth designated by (shifting) "racial" (phenotypical/

genealogical/cultural) criteria C1, C2, C3 . . . as "white," and coextensive (making due allowance for gender differentiation) with the class of full persons, to categorize the remaining subset of humans as "nonwhite" and of a different and inferior moral status, subpersons, so that they have a subordinate civil standing.[24]

"The Racial Contract as a theory," Mills continues, "puts race where it belongs—at center stage—and demonstrates how the polity was in fact a racial one, a white-supremacist state, for which differential white racial entitlement and nonwhite racial subordination were defining, thus inevitably molding white moral psychology and moral theorizing."[25] If we apply the racial contract thesis to Lincoln's antebellum political thought, we might simply think of him as a would-be agent of a white-supremacist state whose liberal moral psychology and moral theorizing about natural rights were preceded—and dominated—by a theory of white racial entitlement and nonwhite racial subordination. In sum, the racial contract thesis holds that Lincoln's natural rights philosophy never included African Americans in a meaningful way.[26]

There is substantial evidence to support the racial contract explanation of Lincoln's illiberal attitude toward abolition. In the *Dred Scott* speech cited earlier, for example, Lincoln said, "Judge Douglas is especially horrified at the thought of the mixing of blood by the white and black races: agreed for once—a thousand times agreed."[27] In a speech in reply to Douglas at Springfield in July 1858, Lincoln said: "What I would most desire would be the separation of the white and black races."[28] Throughout his debates with Douglas, he repeated sentiments like these time and again. In his opening speech during the fourth debate, for example, Lincoln described being confronted by "an elderly gentleman" at his hotel who wanted to know if he was "really in favor of producing perfect equality between the negroes and the white people [great laughter]." Lincoln's response is worth quoting at length:

> I am not nor ever have been in favor of bringing about in any way, the social and political equality of the white and black races [applause], that I am not nor ever have been in favor of making voters of the negroes, or jurors, or qualifying them to hold office, or having them to marry with white people. I will say in addition, that there is a physical difference between the white and black races, which I suppose, will forever forbid the two races living together upon terms of social and political equality, and inasmuch, as they cannot so live, that while they

do remain together, there must be the position of superior and inferior, that I as much as any other man am in favor of the superior position being assigned to the white man.[29]

In addition, there were times during the debates when Lincoln explained his opposition to slavery in terms that were less focused on the rights of blacks than on the interests of whites. In the seventh and final debate at Alton, for example, Lincoln said: "I think that we have some interest as white men [in keeping slavery out of the territories]. Do we not wish that our surplus population may have some outlet to go to? Do we not have an interest, in going to that outlet that such institutions shall prevail as are pleasing to us?"[30] Comments like these might lead us to conclude that the roots of Lincoln's illiberal position on the abolition of slavery can be found in his acceptance of the racial contract. In other words, we might read these comments on race as indications that Lincoln did not really consider African Americans to be among those who possess natural rights. If this is true, then Lincoln's illiberal attitude toward abolition is rather easy to explain. According to this way of thinking, his view was not illiberal in the way I suggested above. If African Americans are "subpersons"—and hence do not possess natural rights—then one can reject abolition and remain a perfectly consistent liberal.

And yet, Lincoln's own language undermines this as the sole explanation of his illiberalism.[31] Indeed, the ideas he expressed just after his description of the encounter with the "elderly gentleman" indicate that the racial contract thesis does not tell the whole story. Lincoln continued:

> I say in this connection, that I do not perceive, however, that because the white man is to have the superior position, that it requires that the negro should be denied everything. I do not perceive because I do not court a negro woman for a wife, that I must necessarily want her for a slave [cheers and laughter]. My understanding is that I can just leave her alone. I am now in my fiftieth year, and certainly never have had a black woman for either a slave or wife, so that it seems to me that it is quite possible for us to get along without making either slaves or wives of negroes.[32]

Although these comments about interracial marriage further demonstrate Lincoln's unenlightened views of race, they also suggest that he believed, as a matter of principle, that African American men and women have natural rights that ought to be respected. In the three debates that followed, Lincoln returned again and again to the natural rights language of the Declaration of Independence to clarify his views of equality. While he continued to reject "political and social equality," he always did so with a reminder that he believed African Americans have equal natural rights: "there is no reason in the world," he said during the sixth debate, "why the negro is not entitled to all the natural rights enumerated in the Declaration of Independence—the right to life, liberty, and the pursuit of happiness. I hold that he is as much entitled to these as the white man."[33]

What is remarkable, then, is that Lincoln was simultaneously committed to the idea that slaves had natural rights *and* to the idea that there was no obligation to abolish the institution of slavery. On the one hand, Lincoln's recognition of the natural rights of African Americans indicates that he did not accept the racial contract idea in its entirety. There was room in his moral psychology and moral theorizing for the idea that nonwhites have natural rights that ought to be respected. On the other hand, the textual evidence introduced in this section does not allow us to completely reject the racial contract thesis. Lincoln's comments on race demonstrate that although he accepted a conception of natural rights that was universal, he was not a racial egalitarian. It seems evident that while he believed African Americans possessed dignity sufficient to be equal bearers of some rights, he did not believe they possessed moral worth equal to that of whites. This leaves us wondering whether Lincoln would have maintained illiberal views of abolition if the slaves in the South had been white. Would Lincoln's perception of the increased moral worth of white slaves have led him to believe that northerners had a duty to interfere with slavery? This is a counterfactual question we cannot answer, but it is worth keeping in mind.

The political expediency thesis provides us with an alternative explanation of Lincoln's illiberalism on abolition. According to this explanation, we might read Lincoln's antebellum views of race, rights, and abolition as evidence that he was the perfect embodiment of what political scientist Rogers Smith calls the "multiple traditions" interpretation of American political thought. According to this view, "American political actors have always promoted civic ideologies that blend liberal, democratic republican, and inegalitarian ascriptive elements in various combinations designed to be politically popular."[34] The political expediency thesis encourages us to consider the possibility that Lincoln's antebellum views were simply a "blend" of liberalism and inegalitarianism and that he privileged the latter over the former in order to be politically popular. After all, Lincoln was seeking political office in a society that was deeply racist and antiabolitionist.[35] Even if he did believe in his heart of hearts that there was a moral obligation to abolish slavery, admitting this to his audience would have been a sure path to political ruin.

Although each seems to capture part of the truth about Lincoln, neither the racial contract thesis nor the political expediency thesis (nor some combination of the two) is sufficient. Suppose we simply take Lincoln at his word—despite the fact that he was a politician. To return to the title of my essay, what if Honest Abe was telling the truth? Throughout his antebellum speeches, essays, and letters, he consistently defended the idea that African Americans *do* have natural rights while rejecting the idea that there is a moral obligation to protect those rights. How can we explain this? Despite his inegalitarian racial views and the constraints imposed by a racist political culture, Lincoln did not reject the idea that African Americans have natural rights. What remains to be discovered is how he reconciled his liberal commitment to natural rights with his illiberal rejection of abolitionism. To complete the picture, we must turn our attention to Lincoln's legalism, which gave him a way to redefine the requirements of natural rights morality. In a legalist framework, "moral relationships" are reconstituted "to consist of duties and rights determined by rules," and it was in this framework that Lincoln placed his faith.[36] Although he knew this framework failed to provide justice in the present, he believed it could put the public mind at rest and deliver justice in the future.

PUTTING THE PUBLIC MIND AT REST: LEGALISM IN THE POLITICAL THOUGHT OF LINCOLN

Lincoln was not a radical racial egalitarian, and, in the words of W. E. B. DuBois, he was "a politician down to his toes."[37] He did, however, believe that African Americans possessed dignity enough to be accorded natural rights, and as a politician, he was animated, at least in part, by his commitment to certain principles. So the puzzle remains: if Lincoln believed African Americans possessed natural rights, why was he hostile to abolitionism, a movement that was committed to protecting those rights?

In this section, I demonstrate how Lincoln used legalism to justify his illiberal attitude toward abolitionism while not completely abandoning his commitment to natural rights. Although legalism placed serious constraints on the ability of political actors to protect natural rights in the present, Lincoln believed it provided the best hope for protecting natural rights in the long run. Legalism allowed Lincoln to redefine the duties required by natural rights philosophy. Whereas he accepted the basic idea that "the right of one implies a duty on the part of others not to violate that right," he did not accept that there was any private or public obligation to intervene if individuals failed to observe this basic liberal duty.[38] Instead of requiring the immediate protection of basic natural rights in the present, Lincoln's legalist natural rights philosophy required everyone—citizens and statesmen alike—to do the thing most likely to vindicate natural rights in the long run: respect and revere the law. Lincoln recognized that there were many bad and even unjust laws, but he believed that faith in the law would deliver us from evil. In law he trusted.

Before proceeding to several expressions of legalism in Lincoln's antebellum thought, I must be more precise about the nature of my argument. As noted earlier, I am especially interested in how Lincoln used the legalist idea that the law redefines our "moral relationships." In other words, it redefines the precise nature of our rights and duties. I believe legalism was appealing to Lincoln because he thought it provided a means—both philosophically and politically—to reconcile his liberal commitment to natural rights with his illiberal hostility to abolition. I emphasize this point because there is so much in the literature on legalism that does *not* fit well with my interpretation of Lincoln. Shklar's explanation of legalism, for example, includes the claim that legalists have a "tendency to think of law as 'there' as a discrete entity, discernibly different from morals and politics."[39] I do not think Lincoln shared this tendency. As I demonstrate below, he saw the intimate connection between law and politics, and he recognized that a respect and reverence for the law was indeed a moral choice. In other words, Lincoln appreciated the political nature of law and the moral choice expressed in elevating it to sacred status. Furthermore, he was not a legalist in the sense described by Eric Posner, who characterizes the doctrine as one that "loses sight of the function of law and sees it as an end in itself."[40] Lincoln's commitment to legalism was conditional and instrumental. I say his commitment was *conditional* because he believed that the moral obligation to act in a way that perpetuated the legal order depended on whether that legal order was moving the society it governed closer to justice. Lincoln believed that the American constitutional order—though unjust in many particulars—was fundamentally just and, importantly, designed to achieve the vindication of natural rights in the long run. Lincoln's commitment to legalism was *instrumental* in the sense that he thought the "social ethos" promoted by the doctrine was the best means to keep the country at peace and on the road to universal liberty. On this point, Lincoln's distinction between the "public mind" and the "public heart" is crucial. Lincoln believed that the best way to put the public mind at rest was to have faith in the law. Meanwhile, the wrongness of slavery had to be addressed (in a measured tone) so that the public heart could continue to progress toward the acceptance of its ultimate extinction.[41] To make sense of precisely how this played out in Lincoln's political thought, we must turn our attention to several of his most important expressions of legalism.

An early and well-known manifestation of Lincoln's legalism can be found in his 1838 Lyceum address titled "The Perpetuation of Our Political Institutions." The Lyceum address is very complex, and I cannot do it justice here.[42] It is worth discussing, however, because it is such a powerful expression of Lincoln's legalism. He began the speech by crediting the founding generation with toiling to establish "a system of political institutions, conducing more essentially to the ends of civil and religious liberty, than any of which the history of former times tells us." As the "hardy, brave, and patriotic" founding generation passes away, it has fallen to us, Lincoln told his audience, to "transmit" these institutions to "the latest generation that fate shall permit the world to know." This task, he said, is not an easy one to perform. Its difficulty lies not in the threats to our institutions from foreign enemies but rather the dangers that "spring up amongst us." More specifically, the major threat to the perpetuation of our political institutions is "the increasing disregard for law which pervades the country."[43]

Lincoln then provided examples of disrespect for the law before informing his audience what he believed to be the key to the perpetuation of our political institutions. His arguments are worth quoting at length:

> The answer is simple. Let every American, every lover of liberty, every well wisher to his posterity, swear by the blood of the Revolution, never to violate in the least particular, the laws of our country; and never to tolerate their violation by others. As the patriots of seventy-six did to the support of the Declaration of Independence, so to the support of the Constitution and Laws, let every American pledge his life, his property, and his sacred honor;—let every man remember that to violate the law, is to trample on the blood of his father, and to tear the character of his own, and his children's liberty. Let reverence for the laws, be breathed by every American mother, to the lisping babe, that prattles in her lap—let it be taught in schools, in seminaries, and in colleges; let it be written in Primers, spelling books, and Almanacs;—let it be preached from the pulpit, proclaimed in legislative halls, and enforced in courts of justice. And, in short, let it become the political religion of the nation; and let the old and the young, the rich and the poor, the grave and the gay, of all sexes and tongues, and colors and conditions, sacrifice unceasingly upon its altars.[44]

It is difficult to imagine rhetoric that better captures what Shklar calls the legalist "cast of mind," "moral attitude," and "social ethos," all of which place rule following at the center of the moral universe.[45] Lincoln wanted his audience to follow the rules; indeed, even "bad" rules (or laws) "should be religiously observed." These bad laws "should be repealed as soon as possible," but while they are in force, they should be respected and, we can conclude from the above passage, revered.[46]

What are we to make of the relationship between the legalism Lincoln articulated in the Lyceum address and his commitment to natural rights? After all, Lincoln connected his arguments to the Declaration of Independence at the beginning of the speech, and he returned repeatedly to the idea that legalism is the appropriate moral attitude for lovers of liberty. But notice that the law trumps natural rights at every turn in the speech. To illustrate the difference between Lincoln's view of this relationship and other versions of natural rights liberalism, imagine that an abolitionist were delivering the speech.[47] In this imaginary speech, the abolitionist might say:

> Let every American, every lover of liberty, every well wisher to his posterity, swear by the blood of the Revolution, never to violate in the least particular, *the rights of other human beings*; and never to tolerate their violation by others. . . . Let every American pledge his life, his property, and his sacred honor;—let every man remember that to violate *the rights of another human being*, is to trample on the blood of his father, and to tear the character of his own, and his children's liberty. Let reverence *for natural rights*, be breathed by every American mother, to the lisping babe, that prattles in her lap—let it be taught in schools, in seminaries, and in colleges; let it be written in Primers, spelling books, and Almanacs;—let it be preached from the pulpit, proclaimed in legislative halls, and enforced in courts of justice. And, in short, let it become the political religion of the nation; and let the old and the young, the rich and the poor, the grave and the gay, of all sexes and tongues, and colors and conditions, sacrifice unceasingly upon its altars.[48]

Lincoln, unlike this imaginary abolitionist, believed that liberty is best promoted by reverence for the law, not natural rights. But how are we to make sense of this position in light of the fact that Lincoln did, indeed, care about natural rights? I suggest that the Lyceum address contains an early example of Lincoln's faith in legalism. He placed his faith in the idea that the law will, eventually, vindicate natural rights. His acknowledgment of "bad laws" is especially significant in this regard. Among these bad laws (indeed, the worst of them) are those that disrespect the natural rights of individuals. Lincoln asked his audience to place their faith in the law, even if such faith required them to disregard violations of natural rights in the present, because the supremacy of the law would promote liberty in the long run.

One of the most powerful examples of Lincoln's application of his legalist philosophy during the antebellum period is his attitude toward the Fugitive Slave Act of 1850. Among other things, this act forbade the states to interfere with the recapture of runaway slaves, and it "authorized federal marshals and specially-appointed commissioners to sign warrants for arrest and certificates for removal of suspected fugitives."[49] In sum, the Fugitive Slave Act was designed to facilitate the recapture of escaped slaves. During his debates with Douglas, Lincoln argued that although slavery was a violation of natural rights, the Fugitive Slave Act must be respected. The law should not only be *respected*, he argued; legalism requires even antislavery citizens and statesmen to *support* the law. At the third debate in Jonesboro, Illinois, he explained his position this way:

> How is it that many of us who are opposed to slavery give our adherence to the fugitive slave law? Why do we give our support to it in passing, and then abide by it when it is passed? The constitution gives the right to reclaim fugitive slaves. I don't quote the words, but that right is rather a barren right unless there be some legislation to enforce it. The mere words of the constitution enforce no right. Now, on what ground is it that members of Congress, who are themselves opposed to slavery in the abstract, vote for a fugitive slave law, as I do? On what ground? Because there is a constitutional right, and having sworn to support that constitution, I can not conceive that I do support it if I withhold necessary legislation to enforce the rights guaranteed by it. Is any one right any better guaranteed in the constitution than the other? Is there any argument why a member of Congress should give support to any one more than to any other?[50]

Lincoln's support for the fugitive slave law provides us with a good example of his legalism because he felt bound by the "rules" of the Constitution to support a law that was an obvious violation of natural rights. The positive law—the Constitution and the fugitive slave law enacted with its support—trumped Lincoln's understanding of what the "higher law" of universal natural rights required.[51]

In response to Lincoln's morally problematic position on the fugitive slave law, we might be tempted to simply write off his acquiescence to injustice as the product of political necessity.[52] While we must never forget that Lincoln was a politician, we ought to try to make sense of how he justified his views and at least entertain the possibility that his justifications were authentic. In other words, we should remain open to the idea that some combination of both politics and principle guided Lincoln when he was confronted with a problem like this one. Lincoln's blending of principle and pragmatism is on display in a set of letters he wrote to antislavery Ohio politician Salmon P. Chase in 1859 regarding the fugitive slave law. In a letter dated June 9, 1859, Lincoln tried to dissuade Chase from introducing a plank in the Republicans' 1860 national platform that would call for "a repeal of the atrocious Fugitive Slave Law" (modeled after a plank in the Republican platform in Ohio). In this letter, Lincoln warned Chase that such a plank would "explode" the Republican National Convention and possibly split the party. Lincoln refused to "enter upon" an argument as to the merits of different views of the fugitive slave law in this first letter. Instead, he simply told Chase: "I assure you the cause of Republicanism is hopeless in Illinois, if it be in any way made responsible for that plank. I hope you can, and will, contribute something to relieve us from it."[53] Chase wrote back on June 13 and requested Lincoln's views on the merits of the fugitive slave law. Lincoln's letter in response, dated June 20, provides a quintessentially legalist argument. Congress, he declared, has the "Constitutional authority to enact the Fugitive Slave Law" because the "U.S. Constitution says the fugitive slave 'shall be delivered up,'" and "whatever the Constitution says 'shall be done'. . . the government established by that Constitution . . . is vested with the power of doing."[54] To defend this view, Lincoln cited the "necessary and proper" clause of Article I. It is beyond the scope of this essay to assess the merits of Lincoln's argument; what matters for my purposes is that Lincoln's "ancient faith" in natural rights is nowhere to be found. In its place, we find his faith in the law.

Perhaps the most powerful expression of Lincoln's legalism was his steadfast commitment to the idea that there was an obligation to leave slavery alone where it existed. From his earliest days in politics to the outbreak of the Civil War, Lincoln insisted that slavery ought to be left undisturbed where it existed. Although Lincoln's position certainly had some roots in practical and political concerns about the "costs" of interfering with slavery, he also had principled reasons, and those reasons were often expressed in the moral vocabulary of legalism.

During the debate with Douglas at Ottawa, he put it this way: "I will say here, while upon this subject, that I have no purpose, directly or indirectly, to interfere with the institution of slavery in the States where it exists. I believe I have no lawful right to do so, and I have no inclination to do so."[55] These two sentences are remarkable. After stating his commitment to noninterference with existing slavery, Lincoln provided two explanations: first, he said he had "no lawful right" to interfere, and second, he said he had "no inclination to do so." The first explanation is, of course, a concise and straightforward manifestation of his legalism. One cannot have the "right" to do X, from a legalist perspective, if one does not have the "lawful" right to do X. It is again worth contrasting this position with the abolitionist view as expressed by Frederick Douglass. For Douglass, the question of "right" was determined not by the positive law but by the natural law. Because the laws supporting slavery were such blatant violations of natural rights—and hence of the natural law—they failed to qualify as binding laws in Douglass's mind. Although Douglass shared Lincoln's view that the rule of law could serve as an important support for natural rights, it could also undermine those rights.[56] One's obligation to obey the law is conditional, Douglass argued, not absolute. If the law's *proper* function is to protect the natural rights of individuals, then it ought to be respected (and perhaps even revered).[57] If, however, the law is being used to undermine natural rights, then it is being used *improperly* and is not entitled to respect, let alone reverence.

Lincoln saw this matter differently. The requirements of natural rights political morality, he argued, were binding only if they were required by positive law.[58] In an 1858 letter to J. N. Brown, Lincoln explained his view:

> I believe the declaration that "all men are created equal" is the great fundamental principle upon which our free institutions rest; that negro slavery is violative of that principle; but that, by our frame of government, that principle has not been made one of legal obligation; that by our frame of government, the states which have slavery are to retain it, or surrender it at their own pleasure; and that all others—individuals, free-states and national government—are constitutionally bound to leave them alone about it.[59]

Although slavery was clearly "violative" of the natural rights doctrine of the Declaration, Lincoln argued, there was no moral obligation to challenge it because not all natural rights principles have been enshrined in law. In sum, moral truth does not bind; only legal truth can do that.

Lincoln's second explanation of his commitment to noninterference with existing slavery—that he had "no inclination" to interfere with the institution—is, at first glance, a bit mysterious. Why wouldn't a devotee of natural rights like Lincoln at least be "inclined" to interfere with an institution that he believed violated natural rights? He offered many reflections on this noninterference principle throughout the debates. In the sixth debate, for example, Lincoln explained that although he believed slavery to be a "moral, social, and a political wrong," he had "due regard to the actual presence among us, to the difficulty of getting rid of it in any speedy and proper way, we have regard to all constitutional obligations thrown around it."[60] What "regard" did Lincoln believe was "due" to the existing institution, and more importantly, *why* did he believe it was due? Lincoln's reference to the "difficulty of getting rid of it" was clearly meant to remind his audience of the practical challenges of ending slavery. Lincoln's practical concerns about how to abolish slavery and what to do afterward definitely played a role in his reasoning, but these concerns do not fully explain why he was disinclined to interfere with slavery. Lincoln's use of the word "due" suggests that there were principles of justice at stake. If these principles of justice did not arise from natural rights, what was their source? Lincoln's own language in the passage indicates that the South was "due" noninterference, at least in part, as a matter of constitutional obligation. As he had explained in a speech at Chicago a few months earlier, there was a direct connection between his feeling of legal obligation and his disinclination to interfere with the institution where it already existed. "We agree," he said, "that, by the Constitution we assented to, in the States where it exists we have no right to interfere with it because it is in the Constitution and we are by both duty and inclination to stick by that Constitution in all its letter and spirit from beginning to end."[61] Lincoln's disinclination to interfere with slavery was, at least in part, rooted in his inclination to "stick by" the Constitution as he understood it.

In the final debate with Douglas, Lincoln returned to this issue as part of an ongoing exchange about how the Declaration of Independence applied to slavery. "I have never sought to apply" the principles of the Declaration, Lincoln said, "to those old States where slavery exists for the purpose of abolishing Slavery in those States. It is nothing but gross perversion to assume that I have brought forth the Declaration of Independence to ask that Missouri shall free her slaves." Instead, Lincoln insisted that the principles of the Declaration are essential "to laying the foundation of new societies."[62] For the existing society, Lincoln placed his faith in the Constitution. It was only by respecting and revering the Constitution, he argued, that the issue of slavery could be resolved. After leaving his discussion of the Declaration, Lincoln explained this view.

> But I have said that "the agitation [over slavery]," as I think "will not cease until a crisis shall have been reached and passed." I have said in what way I suppose that the crisis may be reached and passed. I have said that it may go one way or the other. I have said that it may be passed by arresting the further spread of it, and by bringing the public mind to rest in the belief that it is in course of ultimate extinction, and I have said, and I repeat, that my wish is that the further spread of it should be arrested, and that it should be placed where the public mind shall rest in the belief that it is in course of ultimate extinction.... I have a disposition to not have it believed by any honest man that I desire to go to war with Missouri. Not at all! I entertain the opinion upon the evidence sufficient to my mind, that the fathers of this government placed the institution of slavery among them when the public mind did rest in the belief that it was in course of ultimate extinction.[63]

Lincoln then proceeded to discuss how the Constitution had been designed to secure a gradual death for slavery if everyone would just "leave it alone." If Douglas and his allies on the one side and the abolitionists on the other side would just leave the issue alone and place their faith in the Constitution, the natural rights of all would—one day—be vindicated. In the meantime, Lincoln's goal was to put the public mind at rest by convincing his audience that faith in the Constitution was the appropriate course of action.

Before concluding this section, I must consider an objection to the arguments I have presented. A critic might ask, what are we to make of Lincoln's response to the Kansas-Nebraska Act of 1854 and the *Dred Scott* decision of 1857?[64] Lincoln seemed to think that neither was entitled to the sort of respect and reverence usually merited by the law. How does such skepticism fit with my emphasis on legalism in his antebellum thought?

Of the two cases, the Kansas-Nebraska Act is doubtless the most challenging to my thesis. Consider Lincoln's condemnation of the act in an 1855 letter to his friend Joshua Speed: "In your assumption that there may be a *fair* decision of the slavery question in Kansas, I plainly see you and I would differ about the Nebraska law. I look upon that enactment not as a *law*, but as *violence* from the beginning. It was conceived in violence, passed in violence, is maintained in violence, and is being executed in violence."[65] Here, Lincoln's language is much closer to that of the abolitionists; he refused to characterize the "enactment" as valid law. Instead of looking upon the act as law, Lincoln told his friend, we ought to look upon it as violence. It was "*con-

ceived in violence," he argued, because it brought about the "destruction of the Missouri compromise." It was "*passed* in violence," he contended, "because it could not have passed at all but for the votes of many members in violence of the known will of their constituents." And it was "*maintained* in violence," he insisted, "because the elections since, clearly demand its repeal, and this demand is openly disregarded."[66]

Lincoln's public statements about the Kansas-Nebraska Act were, of course, very critical, but his public language was not quite as stark as that in his private correspondence with Speed. When discussing the act in public, Lincoln often said essentially the same things he stated in the letter—that the legislation was an act of "destruction" because it discarded the Missouri Compromise, that it was more the product of political machinations than of popular will, and that it was thoroughly repudiated by the midterm election results in 1854—but he did not question whether the act qualified as a legitimate law.

What are we to make of the fact that Lincoln refused (at least in private correspondence) to "look upon" the Nebraska "enactment" as a law? Lincoln's letter to Speed seems to indicate that the reverence owed to various laws was conditional, not absolute. In this case, Lincoln objected to treating this law with the same reverence owed to laws generally because it deviated from the will of the people and was a radical departure from the legal order established by the founding generation and perpetuated by the Missouri Compromise. From Lincoln's perspective, the Kansas-Nebraska Act did violence to democratic principles because it had been "passed" against the "known will" of the people and "maintained" despite its thorough repudiation in the 1854 midterm elections. Lincoln's other reason for looking upon the Kansas-Nebraska Act as an act of violence rather than an act of law—that it was "conceived" in order to destroy the Missouri Compromise—is more deeply rooted in his natural rights philosophy. The Missouri Compromise, Lincoln believed, represented the continuation of the legal order established by the founding generation that was, at its core, meant to maintain the peace and "place slavery in the course of ultimate extinction." In other words, the legal regime supported by the Missouri Compromise was the one that Lincoln thought would keep the "public mind" at rest on the slavery question and, eventually, vindicate natural rights by allowing slavery to die a natural death. The Kansas-Nebraska Act, he argued, was more an act of violence than an act of law because it was an attempt to replace a legal regime that was committed to peace and the eventual vindication of natural rights with one that was likely to produce agitation and was at best indifferent, and at worst hostile, to the fate of natural rights.

What does all this tell us about Lincoln's legalism? First, it is worth noting the difference between his private and public tone with regard to the Kansas-Nebraska Act. As a matter of principle, I believe the letter to Speed is very revealing. In it, we find evidence that Lincoln's legalism was conditional, not absolute. As a public figure, though, Lincoln's toned-down language about the act is also revealing. Recall that Shklar's conception of legalism is both a "cast of mind" and a "social ethos." It is clear that the Kansas-Nebraska Act was, in Lincoln's mind, of dubious legitimacy. To speak of it "not as law, but as violence" in public could have undermined the legalist "social ethos" Lincoln promoted throughout his life as a statesman to keep the public mind at rest. In addition, the letter to Speed indicates that Lincoln was not a legalist for the sake of legalism. In other words, his legalism—as I stated earlier—was instrumental; he believed it was the best means to vindicate natural rights in the long run.

Lincoln's views of *Dred Scott* are also worth considering. In his famous address at Springfield in 1857, Lincoln explained his position in some detail:

> We believe, as much as Judge Douglas, (perhaps more) in obedience to, and respect for the judicial department of government. We think its decisions on Constitutional questions, *when fully settled*, should control, not only the particular cases decided, but the general policy of the country, subject to be disturbed only by amendments of the Constitution as provided in that instrument itself. More than this would be revolution. But we think the Dred Scott decision is erroneous. We know the court that made it, has often overruled its own decisions, and we shall do what we can to have it over rule this. We offer no *resistance* to it.[67]

Lincoln went on to explain that the "authority" of judicial decisions (and the extent to which they ought to be considered "fully settled") can be determined by attention to several "circumstances." Was the decision unanimous? Was the decision made without partisan bias? Was the decision consistent with "legal public expectation"? Was the decision consistent with "historical facts"? If the answer to any of these questions is no, there is reason, Lincoln thought, to cast some doubt on whether the decision ought to be regarded with the same reverence as settled law. In other words, Lincoln's skepticism of *Dred Scott* seems to be less an exception to his legalism than a reaffirmation of it. The majority in *Dred Scott*, he argued, made a decision that was at odds with settled law, exhibited partisan bias, deviated from public expectations, and was based on dubious history. For these reasons, he concluded, we ought to refuse to "obey it as a political rule."[68] This refusal, though, must not take the form of "resistance" or "revolution." This would be an affront to the entire legal order and, as such, would be deeply at odds with Lincoln's legalism. Instead, citizens and statesmen should refuse to treat *Dred Scott*'s revolutionary doctrines as settled law and utilize peaceful political means to overturn it.

THE LINCOLN PARADOX: LEGALISM AND THE PROMISES OF LIBERALISM

In an 1845 letter to Liberty Party activist Williamson Durley, Lincoln declared that our "paramount duty . . . to liberty itself (paradox though it may seem)" is to leave slavery alone where it exists.[69] My aim in this essay has been to explain how Lincoln attempted to resolve this paradox. In an 1860 "fragment" on "The Constitution and the Union," Lincoln attempted to articulate his resolution. He began by declaring that "the *Constitution*" and "the *Union*" are important causes of our "great prosperity" in the United States, but they are not the "primary cause." That place, he continued, belongs to "the principle of 'Liberty to all'" that finds its "expression" in "our Declaration of Independence." In the next few lines, Lincoln explored the relationship among the Constitution, the union, and the promise of universal liberty made in the Declaration:

> The assertion of that principle, at that time, was the word, "fitly spoken" which has proved an "apple of gold" to us. The Union, the Constitution, are the picture of silver, subsequently framed around it. The picture was made, not to conceal, or destroy the apple; but to adorn, and preserve it. The picture was made for the apple—not the apple for the picture. So let us act, that neither the picture, or apple, shall ever be blurred, or broken. That we may so act, we must study, and understand the points of danger.[70]

This passage is one of Lincoln's most eloquent defenses of the idea that the natural rights described in the Declaration were supposed to be preserved by the Constitution (and those laws authorized by it). His moral prescription—"let us act, that neither the picture, or apple, shall ever be blurred, or broken"—reflects his hope that legalism and natural rights might be reconciled.

In this essay, I have made the case that we need not conclude that Lincoln's antebellum political thought was disingenuous. Contra the racial contract thesis, he *did* believe that African Americans were the bearers of natural rights, and contra the political expediency thesis, he was *not* simply a closeted abolitionist who lied about his true beliefs to get elected. Instead, Lincoln genuinely believed that he could be simultaneously committed to natural rights for all people and opposed to the idea that there was an obligation to abolish slavery. To justify this set of beliefs, Lincoln blended legalist ideas with natural rights doctrine. Rather than imposing a duty to do whatever was necessary to bring about the immediate fulfillment of the promise of natural rights for all people (as the abolitionists would have it), Lincoln's legalist natural rights philosophy posited a duty to act in such a way that was most likely to bring about the *eventual* protection of the natural rights of all people. For Lincoln, a social ethos that placed respect and reverence for the law at the center of the moral universe was the best way to keep the public mind at rest while the public heart evolved toward justice.

In the end, leaders in the South did not believe that Honest Abe was telling the truth, and after his election to the presidency, the country descended into civil war. While it is clear that the Confederates were unconvinced by Lincoln's attempt to reconcile natural rights doctrine and legalism, how should we judge it? At a certain level of abstraction, there is something appealing about Lincoln's argument. If he was right that there was no morally acceptable and politically viable way to end slavery immediately, then perhaps the best way to advance natural rights was to maintain a legal order that protected the liberty of some and, arguably, promised to recognize the liberty of others in the future. Legalism provided Lincoln with a means to redefine moral relationships in a way that allowed him—and, he hoped, the public—to accept the idea that devotion to the rule of law would, in the long run, vindicate natural rights. Viewed through the lens of justice, though, Lincoln's antebellum resistance to abolition reveals the problem with his attempt to reconcile natural rights with legalism. He was confronted with a question that continues to trouble us to this day: what are we to do when the rule of law—an indispensable institution, to be sure—functions as an obstacle to the achievement of justice? When confronted with this problem prior to the Civil War, Lincoln time and again placed his faith in the law, hoping it would one day deliver justice. The sad truth is that, all too often, such a response is more a product of faith than of reason, and it is often deaf to the pleas of those oppressed by the status quo. As we continue to pursue other forms of emancipation in the present, we ought to remember that legalism can be both a friend and a foe of liberation.

NOTES

1. Harold Holzer, ed., *The Lincoln-Douglas Debates* (New York: HarperCollins, 1994), 63; hereafter cited as *Debates*.

2. Ibid., 189.

3. My focus in this essay is on Lincoln's antebellum political thought. Once the Civil War began, Lincoln's views evolved—at least in part—due to political and military necessity.

4. I hold that hostility to abolition is fundamentally illiberal because a commitment to the freedom of all individuals is essential to liberalism. The moral obligation to abolish slavery is especially strong according to the liberalism of natural rights. I discuss this matter in greater detail later in this essay.

5. Judith Shklar, "The Liberalism of Fear," in *Political Thought and Political Thinkers* (Chicago: University of Chicago Press, 1998), 8.

6. Roy P. Basler, ed., *Abraham Lincoln: His Speeches and Writings* (Cambridge, MA: Da Capo Press, 2001), 291; hereafter cited as *Speeches and Writings*.

7. I am not the first to describe Lincoln as a "legalist." John Burt, for example, argues that Lincoln's legalism "never . . . allowed his primary moral hostility to slavery to license him to ignore the Constitution's limitations upon his power to act directly against slavery." John Burt, *Lincoln's Tragic Pragmatism* (Cambridge, MA: Belknap Press of Harvard University Press, 2013), 315.

8. Judith Shklar, *Legalism* (Cambridge, MA: Harvard University Press, 1964), 1.

9. Ibid., 9. I should note that some aspects of Shklar's definition do not fit Lincoln well. Legalism, Shklar argues, is a "political ideology," and its adherents, "in their determination to preserve law from politics, fail to recognize that they too have made a choice among political values." Legalists are guilty, Shklar contends, of succumbing to the "tendency to think of law as 'there' as a discrete entity, discernibly different from morals and politics" (ibid.). I think Lincoln appreciated the political nature of law and the ideological choice expressed by elevating it to sacred status. Nor was Lincoln a legalist in the sense described by Eric Posner, who observed that legalism "loses sight of the function of law and sees it as an end in itself." Eric A. Posner, *The Perils of Global Legalism* (Chicago: University of Chicago Press, 2009), xii. Lincoln did not see law as an end in itself; he believed a legalistic attitude ought to be adopted to achieve ends, as I discuss later.

10. The doctrine of natural rights has been identified by many scholars as a central component of Lincoln's political thought. See, for example, James Oakes, "Natural Rights, Citizenship Rights, States' Rights, and Black Rights," in *Our Lincoln*, ed. Eric Foner (New York: W. W. Norton, 2008), 112: "Lincoln said it so often, so clearly, and so eloquently that there is no room for doubt: Slavery was wrong because is deprived men and women of the natural rights to which every human being was equally entitled."

11. *Speeches and Writings*, 305–306.

12. Ibid.
13. Ibid., 577.
14. Ibid., 360.
15. Ibid., 361.
16. *Debates*, 63.
17. Ibid., 290.
18. Ibid., 116.
19. See, for example, Richard Striner, *Lincoln and Race* (Carbondale: Southern Illinois University Press, 2012), 22–30.
20. Richard Striner, *Father Abraham* (New York: Oxford University Press, 2006), 10, 11, 49.
21. Shklar, "Liberalism of Fear," 8.
22. A utilitarian conception of liberalism that deviates too far from respect for individual rights would, of course, cease to qualify as liberalism. It is worth noting, though, that there is a significant difference in moral vocabularies and points of emphasis between natural rights and utilitarian liberals. Consider, for example, the status of rights in the philosophy of someone like Robert Nozick, on the one hand, and Friedrich Hayek, on the other.
23. This statement assumes that the natural rights thinker in question believes slaves to be bearers of natural rights—a position Lincoln accepted as true.
24. Charles Mills, *The Racial Contract* (Ithaca, NY: Cornell University Press, 1997).
25. Ibid., 57.
26. The most radical application of the racial contract thesis to Lincoln's thought is offered by Lerone Bennett Jr., *Forced into Glory: Abraham Lincoln's White Dream* (Chicago: Johnson Publishing, 1999). Bennett argues that Lincoln "was a man who defined himself and chose himself as a racist committed to the subordination of nonwhites." According to Bennett, Lincoln viewed the Constitution as "the white man's charter of freedom" (66), and his primary goals were always to advance the interests of white people and to undermine the interests of nonwhites.
27. *Speeches and Writings*, 363.
28. Ibid., 423.
29. *Debates*, 189.
30. Ibid., 355–356.
31. I say "sole explanation" because I do not think the racial contract can be rejected completely. As I explain later, I do not think we can rule out the idea that Lincoln's antebellum rejection of racial egalitarianism played at least some role in his illiberal view of abolitionism.
32. *Debates*, 189.
33. Ibid., 285.
34. Rogers Smith, *Civic Ideals* (New Haven, CT: Yale University Press, 1999), 6.
35. For an informative discussion of the political culture in which Lincoln found

himself, see George Frederickson, *Big Enough to Be Inconsistent: Abraham Lincoln Confronts Slavery and Race* (Cambridge, MA: Harvard University Press, 2008), 35–40.

36. Shklar, *Legalism*, 1.

37. W. E. B. DuBois, "Abraham Lincoln," *Crisis*, July 1922.

38. Michael Zuckert, "Human Dignity and the Basis of Justice," *Hedgehog Review* 9, 3 (2007): 40.

39. Shklar, *Legalism*, 9.

40. Posner, *Perils of Global Legalism*, xii.

41. *Debates*, 350.

42. For an extensive and illuminating discussion of this speech, see John Burt's essay in this volume.

43. *Speeches and Writings*, 76–77.

44. Ibid., 81.

45. Shklar, *Legalism*, 109.

46. *Speeches and Writings*, 81.

47. I suppose an abolitionist version of the speech might have been entitled "What Would Make Our Political Institutions Worth Perpetuating?"

48. To draw attention to the differences between Lincoln's views and the views of this imaginary abolitionist, I italicized the altered language.

49. Junius P. Rodriguez, *Slavery in the United States: A Social, Political, and Historical Encyclopedia* (Santa Barbara, CA: ABC-CLIO, 2007), 302.

50. *Debates*, 171–172.

51. George Fletcher argues that "legalism" fits best with the "Confederate" mind-set, and Lincoln is best understood as a "higher law" thinker. See George Fletcher, *Our Secret Constitution* (New York: Oxford University Press, 2003), 6.

52. Striner, *Father Abraham*, 50.

53. *Speeches and Writings*, 491–492.

54. Ibid., 492.

55. *Debates*, 63.

56. See, for example, Frederick Douglass, "Is Civil Government Right?" [1851], in *The Life and Writings of Frederick Douglass*, ed. Philip Foner (New York: International Publishers, 1950–1975), 5:208–214.

57. Douglass came to believe that the Constitution was best read as a "glorious liberty document" that provided a legal basis for the overthrow of slavery.

58. As I explain shortly, this is a necessary but not sufficient condition for Lincoln.

59. *Speeches and Writings*, 479.

60. *Debates*, 290.

61. *Speeches and Writings*, 395–396.

62. *Debates*, 348.

63. Ibid., 350.

64. Thanks to Julia Shaw, Chana Cox, and Chief Justice Tom Balmer for suggesting I consider this aspect of Lincoln's thought.

65. *Speeches and Writings*, 333.
66. Ibid., 335.
67. Ibid., 355.
68. Ibid., 396.
69. Ibid., 170.
70. Ibid., 513.

PART THREE

Lincoln and Equality

CHAPTER FIVE

"The Vital Element of the Republican Party": Antislavery, Nativism, and Lincoln

Bruce Levine

Abraham Lincoln's election to the presidency urgently posed a series of questions about both the man and his young party. Just who was Abraham Lincoln politically? Precisely what did he and his allies truly stand for? What could be expected from the new administration? And, since elections not only decide the identity of the future government but also take the electorate's political temperature, what did Lincoln's election reveal about the values and priorities of that majority of northern voters who had just given him their support? These were and are simple, straightforward questions, but the answers to some of them have long been hotly contested.

To many, what spawned and sustained Lincoln's party seemed obvious: a preoccupation with slavery and its future. Lincoln had forcefully said as much on innumerable occasions, as in his high-profile 1858 debates with Stephen A. Douglas. "The sentiment that contemplates the institution of slavery in this country as a wrong is the sentiment of the Republican party," Lincoln emphasized in Alton, Illinois. And it was that sentiment, he added, "around which all their actions, all their arguments, circle, from which all

---

This essay was originally published in *Journal of the Civil War Era* 1, 4 (2011): 481–505. For their kind assistance and criticisms during the preparation of this essay, I would like to thank John Ashworth, James Barrett, Richard Carwardine, James Cornelius, Eric Foner, Ruth Hoffman, James McPherson, Matthew Pinsker, David Roediger, and Scott Ware. They bear no responsibility, of course, for the uses to which I put their advice.

their propositions radiate. They look upon it as being a moral, social, and political wrong."[1]

Abolitionist Frederick Douglass, who could be very critical of Lincoln's party, nonetheless agreed with Lincoln about both the focus of that party's argument with the Democrats and how rank-and-file Republicans viewed that clash. "Slavery," Douglass observed in August 1860, "is the real issue— the single bone of contention between all parties and sections," and "the anti-slavery sentiment in the Northern States is the vital element of the Republican party."[2]

Many observers more hostile to the Republicans bitterly agreed. "The great point upon which the political parties of the country are at variance, is that of slavery," declared the Democratic *Illinois State Register*.[3] The *New York Herald* denounced the Republicans in 1860 exactly because they "were founded on and animated by the antislavery idea."[4] The *Charleston Mercury* had warned a few months earlier that in the North now "a party predominates whose vital principle is hostility to African slavery in the South."[5] One secession advocate after another made the same point in 1860–1861.[6] Over the years, many scholars have seen things similarly, and today this constitutes a broadly based consensus among historians of the subject.

At the time, however, some steadfastly denied that the desire to contain and ultimately destroy bondage was the essence of the Republican creed or appeal. During the mid-1850s, Stephen Douglas asserted that the Republicans were a party of ethnic hatred and cultural tyranny. Much of the Republicans' support came, according to Douglas and many of his party colleagues in the North, from anti-immigrant bigots. In making that case, such opponents depicted the Republican Party as the virtual clone of another organization that emerged during that decade—the anti-immigrant, anti-Catholic American Party, better known as the Know-Nothings, which notoriously aimed to exclude the foreign born from political life in the United States. "Abolitionism, Know Nothingism, and all other isms are akin to each other and are in alliance," declared Douglas. The Republicans, such critics charged, have "no objection to Know-Nothingism and its distinctive and proscriptive doctrines."[7] Both those parties "combine against the political rights and religious freedom" of those "who were born on European soil." The growth of Republicanism, these northern Democrats concluded, thus reflected "the powerful influence" of sheer "bigotry" in much of the northern electorate.[8]

During the past few decades, some scholars have revived the notion that Republicans secured much of their support by endorsing nativist sentiments and measures. In 1856, they point out, Know-Nothing presidential candidate Millard Fillmore received 22 percent of the popular vote, in the process depriving the Republicans of the crucial electoral votes of Illinois, Indiana, Pennsylvania, and New Jersey—and thereby of the White House. Four years later, however, Lincoln obtained nearly all the electoral votes of those same states, in no small part by winning the support of a great many former Fillmore supporters.[9]

The Republicans accomplished this feat, according to Joel Silbey, William E. Gienapp, and others, by adapting to the prejudices of the Know-Nothings. Their "blatant solicitation of nativist support" involved adding a big admixture of nativism, especially anti-Catholicism, to their message and program, thereby "making themselves attractive to the Know Nothings on the latter's terms." By the time this makeover was completed, they hold, "Know Nothings had . . . every reason to be satisfied" with the result.[10]

And what worked for the Republican Party as a whole, in this view, also worked for Abraham Lincoln the individual. Although Lincoln was unhappy with Know-Nothingism, William Gienapp asserts, the Illinoisan gained the Republican nomination and became a successful candidate partly because he deliberately refrained from publicly expressing his views on the subject.[11] Other historians, most notably Eric Foner and Tyler Anbinder, have sharply challenged these interpretations. But both Gienapp and David Herbert Donald subsequently reasserted the claim about Lincoln's public silence and its importance to his presidential nomination and election in well-received Lincoln biographies.[12]

To be sure, some historians advancing such claims have stressed them more than others in accounting for the rise and triumph of Lincoln and the Republicans. But in all these cases, the effect has been to minimize and divert attention from the most important political dynamic of the antebellum decades—the escalating polarization of public opinion nationally concerning chattel slavery. The present essay reexamines nativism's role in the rise of the Republican Party and of Abraham Lincoln as its leader in 1860. In the process, it aims to restore the transformation of northern views about slavery to its proper place in the history of that era.

Just a year before being elected president, Abraham Lincoln famously stated that he had "always [been] a Whig in politics."[13] What Lincoln left unsaid, however, was that for most of its life, the Whig Party's politics were the subject of vigorous internal dispute.

Uniting Whigs generally was a devotion to economic development and the government support that such development seemed to require. Other issues, however, tended to divide their party. At the two poles of that debate stood conservatives and liberal democrats. Differentiating these two camps were their contrasting reactions to the development of political democracy and calls to expand the scope of democratic rights and increase the number of those who enjoyed them. These differences, in turn, revealed themselves in disputes about two major questions of the day—what to do about chattel slavery, and how to cope with the era's massive immigration from Europe.

Whig conservatives, like Federalists before them, considered republics to be fragile structures. A broad franchise and open political conflict seemed to threaten social order and private wealth. An electorate that included men with little or no property, formal education, or cultural refinement, they were sure, was susceptible to dangerous manipulation by demagogues and therefore quite incapable of assuring the social peace and calm so essential to national prosperity.

In many urban centers, these fears and suspicions of mass-based political democracy expressed themselves most openly and forcefully in hostility toward an expanding and enfranchised immigrant population, an especially large proportion of which owned little or no property. Irish- and German-born working people proved to conservative Whig observers that they were poor citizen material. They proved that in part by rallying to Democratic politicians who professed sympathy for the plight of the man of small means who was oppressed by the power of "concentrated capital."[14]

Such northern Whig conservatives therefore gravitated toward nativist politicians and policies, especially the attempt to deny immigrants the right to vote, either permanently or at least for some extended period following federal naturalization. Nativism, wrote Philadelphia Whig attorney Sidney George Fisher in his diary in 1844, "is decidedly conservative, because by excluding foreigners so much democracy is excluded, so much of the rabble, so much ignorance & brutality from political power." Nativism therefore "harmonizes with the instincts & secret wishes & opinions of the Whigs."[15]

Conservative northern Whigs also brought their distinctive fusion of enthusiasm for economic development and distrust of democratic politics into the escalating controversy over slavery's future. Although critical of slavery, they generally strove to muffle controversies about that institution for fear of polarizing political life, endangering transregional political parties, and dissolving national cohesion.

Whig liberals kept their distance from more conservative party colleagues with regard to both immigration and slavery. They were more devoted to the principles of civic equality and political democracy. They believed, with New York's William H. Seward, that history was moving away from legal inequality and physical coercion, that "the democratic principle is leading the way to universal liberty."[16] Although few of them stood for full racial equality, Whig liberals were more convinced than Whig conservatives that slavery was not only economically stunting but also morally repugnant and politically toxic. The perfect embodiment of aristocratic, antidemocratic principles, it endangered the republic as a whole.[17]

Liberal democratic Whigs also differed with conservatives concerning the proper political status of immigrants. To be sure, they were not modern multiculturalists. They shared with conservatives an Anglo-American cultural tradition that associated Catholicism with moral laxity, economic stagnation, and antirepublican politics. And here again, social realities—the large contingent of immigrants who were poor, working-class, Catholic, and pro-Democratic—reinforced those associations and inflamed those longstanding prejudices. Many politicians and journalists with liberal Whig antecedents continued to express suspicion of and hostility to such immigrants through the 1860s and beyond.

But those sentiments led few Whig liberals to favor aggressive anti-immigrant policies. Charles Sumner, George Julian, and Joshua Giddings were especially vocal in their repudiation of nativism on principle.[18] So was William H. Seward, in whose opinion northern economic development and a welcoming attitude toward immigrants went hand in hand. The South had for a couple of centuries found the labor force it needed in the form of black slaves; the North was now easing its own labor shortage through the large-scale immigration of free laborers. To attract these new arrivals, Seward believed, "an asylum should be offered to the immigrant and exile of every creed and nation."[19] Such an enticing asylum must offer newcomers the same rights it granted to the native born.

In the late 1840s and early 1850s, both sources of internal Whig dissension—immigration and the sectional conflict over slavery—grew dramatically in political salience. The bonds that had previously held together the Whig Party's two warring factions in the North, long fraying, finally snapped. The Wilmot Proviso, Zachary Taylor's insufficiently proslavery conduct during the crisis of 1849–1850, and widespread northern resistance to the Fugitive Slave Act alienated a great many of the Whigs' supporters in the South and weakened the party's cohesion in the North. Meanwhile, a spike in immigration engendered widespread resentment among the native born.

That popular anti-immigrant animosity proved a godsend for Whiggish conservatives, giving them much of the traction they needed to break with the by-now virtually paralyzed Whig organization and launch a new party defined by their own principles. And so the Americans (or Know-Nothings) came into existence, pledged both to restrict the rights of immigrants and to muffle and defuse the explosive slavery issue.[20]

In the event, however, the slavery issue refused to be defused. On the contrary: it reemerged with a vengeance within the Know-Nothing Party itself, eventually unmaking it. And as that party disintegrated, it cast adrift a growing number of Whiggish northern voters and politicians, some of whom gravitated, either sooner or later, toward that other party born of the national Whig organization's demise—that is, the Republicans—a party in which liberal democratic Whigs featured prominently.[21]

The future political allegiance of the rest of those ex–Know-Nothing voters was a matter of great interest to Republicans generally during the second half of the 1850s. If those voters could be won over, the Republicans might well look forward to victory in the next presidential election. But opinions varied about how that task was to be accomplished.

Some Republicans did try to reshape their party's program to accommodate the politics of Whiggish conservatism between 1856 and 1860. Those who did so included some ex–Know-Nothings who had already joined the Republican Party and had decided that, with the nativist party's decline, "the only reasonable course" left to them was "to Americanize" the Republican organization.[22] Working with them were other Republicans (such as Horace Greeley) who, while not themselves nativists or "soft" on slavery, were quite willing to woo voters who were by bending in their direction, attempting to soften the Republican Party's adamant opposition to slavery's expansion or to infuse nativist themes into its platform and rhetoric.

This concerted effort to pull the Republican program in a conservative direction yielded some results. The most important adoption of nativist policy within the Republican Party occurred in Massachusetts, where in 1857 and 1858 a Republican-controlled state legislature voted to sustain a Know-Nothing–initiated policy of barring immigrants from the vote for a term of years beyond that required for federal naturalization.[23]

But this campaign to temper the Republican opposition to slavery's expansion and to court nativist-minded voters aroused strong resistance within the Republican Party. The result was a major, protracted struggle over Republicanism's basic tenets and public stance. In that struggle, Republican conservatives ultimately failed to impose their will.[24]

A variety of forces and factors strengthened the resistance to them. One of these was the adhesion to the Republican Party of some groups that were both militantly antislavery and antinativist and had initially kept their distance, notably, German American liberals and radicals.[25] But perhaps even more important to the Republican conservatives' ultimate failure was the national political dynamic that had so badly damaged the Democrats in 1854 and then precipitated the decline of the Know-Nothing Party—the deepening intransigence (indeed, aggressiveness) of proslavery forces that was, reciprocally, convincing more and more northerners that all attempts to conciliate the "slave power" were hopeless and that only firmness could meet the southern challenge.

Resistance to the conservative campaign within the national Republican Party helped induce the Massachusetts legislature to sharply reduce the waiting period imposed in that state on naturalized voters from the twenty-one years originally stipulated by the Know-Nothings to two years—a reduction carried out over the protests of the Know-Nothings themselves.[26] Just as telling, the ratification in 1859 of a "Two-Year Amendment" to the state constitution brought down upon the Massachusetts party a barrage of criticism by Republicans elsewhere. And no other Republican-controlled state legislature in the country approved a measure like the one passed in the Bay State.

This intraparty struggle between conservatives and liberal democrats over the Republicans' program came to a head in May 1860 at the National Convention in Chicago. Republican notables of Know-Nothing antecedents (along with others seeking to appease nativist voters) tried to bestow the Republican presidential nomination upon a man with nativist credentials. They also tried to weaken both the Republican Party's condemnation of slavery and its determination to block slavery's expansion through federal action.

A succession of historians has claimed that these sundry conservatives, nativists, and opportunists were successful in that attempt. Reinhard Luthin declared more than six decades ago that the 1860 Republican platform addressed the immigration question "in language that would not alienate the Know-Nothings" and that its stand on slavery was "comparatively conservative."[27] A decade later, Charles Granville Hamilton authored a booklet that flatly asserted that Know-Nothings had voted for Lincoln's party because "there was no word of anti-nativism in the Republican platform of 1860, which also soft-pedaled the anti-slavery attitudes of 1856."[28]

More than thirty years after Hamilton wrote, William Gienapp argued that the Republicans' determined attempt to attract the 1856 Fillmore voters had led them to adopt a platform in 1860 that was "both in its tone and program . . . more moderate than its predecessor." Even in the plank on immigrant rights, he added, "the language was designed not to offend the Know-Nothings."[29]

All these claims were well wide of the mark, however. If some of the 1856 platform's most fiery denunciations of slavery were absent from the 1860 version, both in substance and in tone the latter nevertheless rebuffed leaders of the party's more conservative wing. First, the Chicago platform reaffirmed the defining Republican doctrine on slavery, which held that bondage was inherently unconstitutional in any and all federal territories and that federal power should be used to prevent its establishment there. Second, the platform took solid antinativist ground. At the behest of German-born members of the platform committee, the convention explicitly repudiated any federal or state laws "by which the rights of citizens hitherto accorded to immigrants from foreign lands shall be abridged or impaired."[30]

Nativists recognized in these words a slap at themselves and their pet measures. Republican conservatives objected to the plank precisely for that reason. It "is a bad thing for our cause here," fretted one Bostonian, "and in Pennsylvania and New Jersey."[31] For that matter, grieved a Connecticut party leader, New Englanders generally "have been, and are now, strong in Americanism, and believe in just what that 'sec' [section] condemns."[32]

Republican conservatives and conciliators fared no better in their attempt to dictate the Republican Party's choice of presidential candidate. They were able to block William H. Seward's nomination, but their own favorite, Edward Bates of Missouri, made a far weaker showing than did the New Yorker. On the first convention ballot, Seward received 173 votes, Illinois's Abraham Lincoln received 102, while Bates got only 48. Bates's total never rose higher, and Lincoln received the Republican nomination on the third ballot.[33]

Which brings us back to the question of Lincoln's political identity generally and his stand on immigration and immigrant rights in particular.

Lincoln did not begin his career in the Whig Party as a member of its liberal wing. In those early years, he had instead taken the rather conservative Henry Clay as his model. As late as 1858, indeed, Lincoln was still referring to Clay as "my beau ideal of a statesman."[34] But in truth, he had by then come to champion a brand of Whiggery different in crucial ways from that of his supposed "beau ideal." The difference is especially apparent in the case of nativism and slavery.

Lincoln had since boyhood felt a strong revulsion toward slavery. He believed it was an institution grounded in "injustice." He believed, as he would later put it, that if slavery was not wrong, nothing was.[35] In 1845 he declared it northerners' duty to "never knowingly lend ourselves directly or indirectly, to prevent that slavery from dying a natural death," never to help "find new places for it to live in, when it can no longer exist in the old."³⁶ And when, a few years later, supporters of the Wilmot Proviso attempted to bar slavery from the lands taken from Mexico, Lincoln stood with them.

In 1850 fears for the union led Lincoln and many other like-minded Whigs to backtrack and applaud Clay's 1850 Compromise, which not only failed to exclude slavery by federal law from the Utah and New Mexico territories but also included a new and stronger fugitive slave law. But in 1854 the Kansas-Nebraska Act convinced Lincoln that slaveholders and their allies were determined to reinforce slavery and extend its domain as widely as possible. Lincoln concluded that the systems of free and slave labor could not indefinitely and peacefully coexist within the borders of the United States. One of them would have to subdue the other, and it would do so through the deliberate, organized efforts of its champions. Antislavery citizens in the North would have to take control of the federal government to block the further extension of bondage and thereby "put it in the course of ultimate extinction."³⁷ That conclusion led Lincoln into the leadership of the Illinois Republican Party.

To strengthen his new party, Lincoln wanted very much to attract ex–Know-Nothing voters to it. He wished (as he later put it) to fuse with as many people as possible. But he insisted on doing so without departing from Republican principles.³⁸ So he warned Republicans against "the temptation to lower the Republican Standard in order to gather recruits" from various quarters.³⁹ He was "against letting down the [R]epublican standard [of 1856] a hair's breadth."⁴⁰ He was adamantly opposed to any concession that would "surrender the o[b]ject of the Republican organization—of preventing the spread and nationalization of Slavery."⁴¹

This was the same Lincoln who rejected the antidemocratic impulse at nativism's core and refused to compromise his party's defense of immigrant rights. Of Know-Nothings and their ideas, he explained to Owen Lovejoy in 1855, "I think little better than I do of the slavery extensionists."⁴²

Lincoln's hostility to nativism sprang from a commitment to democratic principles that had grown over the years (and continued to grow).⁴³ Lincoln identified antiforeign and anti-Catholic measures as fundamentally alien and opposed to his deepening commitment to the democratic tenets represented by the Declaration of Independence. "Our progress in degeneracy seems to me pretty rapid," Lincoln complained to his old friend Joshua Speed in 1855. "As a nation," he recalled, "we began by declaring that 'all men are created equal.' We now practically read it 'all men are created equal except negroes.' When the Know-Nothings get control, it will read 'all men are created equal, except negroes, and foreigners, and catholics.'"⁴⁴ He made the same point four years later in a letter to German-born journalist Theodore Canisius, explicitly linking his opposition to nativism to his liberal democratic worldview. "Understanding the spirit of our institutions to aim at the elevation of men," he wrote, "I am opposed to whatever tends to degrade them." He added, "I have some little notoriety for commiserating [with] the oppressed condition of the negro; and I should be strangely inconsistent if I could favor any project for curtailing the existing rights of white men, even though born in different lands, and speaking different languages from myself."⁴⁵

Historians who detect an attempt by the Republican Party in 1860 to waffle on the issue of immigrants' rights have often depicted Lincoln's nomination as part of such a stratagem. "Abraham Lincoln kept very silent in public about his disapproval of Know-Nothingism," wrote David Potter.⁴⁶ "Cognizant of the Know Nothings' power in Illinois," wrote William Gienapp, Lincoln "had never publicly criticized the Know Nothings" but had instead carefully "confined his criticism to private exchanges." And it was precisely this calculated public silence on that subject, according to Gienapp, that in 1860 rendered Lincoln "acceptable to nativists."⁴⁷ David Donald's biography of Lincoln advanced the same claim.⁴⁸ Lincoln's alleged refusal to speak publicly on this subject, according to this argument, also explains why so many northerners who had cast their lot four years earlier not with the Republicans but with the Know-Nothings could vote for Lincoln and his party in 1860.

It is quite true, of course, that Lincoln's antinativist letters to Speed and Lovejoy were private communications. But by the time he wrote them, Lincoln had repeatedly placed the same views on the public record.

Nativism had emerged as a serious force during the 1840s. In 1844, when nativists rioted in Philadelphia, Illinois Whigs gathered in their state's capital to dissociate themselves from that bloody outburst. This meeting saw Abraham Lincoln do more than protest wanton violence generally. He explicitly rejected the nativist program. He called on those assembled to affirm publicly that naturalization laws "should be so framed, as to render admission to citizenship under them, as convenient, cheap, and expeditious as possible" and to pledge their party to "now, and at all times, oppose as best we may" all attempts to make naturalization more difficult "than it now is."⁴⁹

When the Know-Nothing Party arose in the early 1850s, Lincoln hoped it would soon break down under the weight of its own internal contradictions and without the need for vigorous external assistance. The Know-Nothings initially attracted some Whigs with whom he had previously worked, with whom he expected to work again (as in the ad hoc anti-Nebraska coalitions that had formed in Illinois and elsewhere in 1854), and whose sensibilities he therefore wished not to offend and whose enmity he hoped not to provoke.[50] For that reason, he sometimes avoided attacking nativist individuals or organizations by name.[51] But the political exigencies of the times nonetheless led Lincoln repeatedly to denounce nativist ideology and policies. And on several occasions, doing that involved repudiating the specific people and parties that espoused them.

During the summer of 1854, as Lincoln prepared to run for a seat in the state legislature as an anti-Nebraska Whig, a committee of self-styled "Native Americans" interviewed Lincoln to determine whether he merited their endorsement. A member of that committee subsequently recalled that during that interview, Lincoln reminded his interrogators of the fate suffered by the original Native Americans, the indigenous population of the continent. "We pushed them from their homes," Lincoln noted pointedly, "and now [we] turn upon others not fortunate enough to come over as early as we or our forefathers."[52] Lincoln told the nativists that they certainly "might vote for him if they wanted to," but "he was not in sentiment with this new party" because it "is wrong in principle."[53]

Illinois Democrats nonetheless sought to hang the nativist albatross around Lincoln's neck that fall. In the face of such attacks, Lincoln did not keep silent. Silence might have cost him the support of the many antislavery German voters in his state, voters whose support he considered essential but who were keenly sensitive to the nativist views espoused by some other members of anti-Nebraska coalitions of 1854. So Lincoln specifically and publicly reiterated his distaste for any "organization, secret or public," that "had for its object interference with the rights of foreigners."[54]

Early in 1856 Lincoln attended a meeting in Decatur called to launch what would become the Illinois branch of the national Republican Party. As those assembled strove to frame a provisional political platform, a German American newspaper editor, Chicago's George Schneider, proposed a plank that clearly opposed political discrimination on the grounds of either birthplace or religion. Lincoln promptly seconded the editor's proposal. After all, Lincoln explained, Schneider's resolution merely restated the ideas "already contained in the Declaration of Independence." It would be a serious mistake, Lincoln continued, to try to build the new party on a more exclusionary foundation than that—to try to base it on "proscriptive principles." The antinativist plank was adopted at Decatur and was subsequently incorporated into the platform of the Illinois Republican organization, which pledged to discriminate against no one "on account of religious opinions, or in consequence of place of birth."[55]

While campaigning for Republican candidates later that year, Lincoln reportedly strove to emphasize that "he [Lincoln] did not like the Know Nothings" and went out of his way to make the kind of friendly public overtures to foreign-born voters that were famously anathema to nativists—the same kind that had, for example, turned them with such fury upon Whig presidential candidate Winfield Scott in 1852.[56]

Lincoln once again sharply and publicly distanced himself from the Know-Nothing Party during his 1858 bid for a Senate seat.[57] And in the 1859 letter to Theodore Canisius referred to earlier, he condemned Massachusetts's "Two-Year Amendment" as both "foolish and unprincipled."[58] The letter promptly appeared in the *Illinois State Journal*, from which other newspapers then copied and reprinted it.[59] Nor was this public airing of Lincoln's antinativist views an accident. Lincoln plainly intended that the letter's contents be widely known. Canisius and other German Americans were at the time cross-examining politicians about their views concerning nativism. As Lincoln knew, both those queries and the replies thereto swiftly became public documents. That Lincoln was content to have Canisius secure publication of his letter is also apparent. Within two weeks, Lincoln had purchased a printing press and a set of German type and turned them over to Canisius so that the latter could begin publishing a German-language Republican newspaper in Springfield.[60] And the *Illinois State Journal*, which had reprinted the letter, was an enthusiastic Lincoln supporter. It would not have published the letter without Lincoln's approval—without, indeed, his active encouragement.[61] Lincoln was anxious to avoid unnecessarily antagonizing those with whom he was prepared to work in concert, but he was equally determined to make clear his rejection of nativism and nativist measures.

Finally, at the 1860 Republican National Convention in Chicago, well-known Lincoln supporters (such as German-born Gustave Koerner) played central roles in drafting the party platform's antinativist immigration plank. And during debates within various state delegations about the relative merits of the contenders for the party's presidential nomination, Lincoln's advocates repeatedly trumpeted his antinativist credentials. They did so, for example, while lobbying both the Pennsylvania and Indiana delegations, despite the fact that in both those state parties, nativists were known to be influential.[62]

In short, the Lincoln whom convention delegates picked to head their national ticket was a firm and publicly identified opponent of both slavery's expansion and nativism.

The national Republican Party's refusal, as the 1860 elections approached, to alter its stands on either immigrant rights or slavery in the territories angered many Whiggish conservatives, including those who had become Republicans in an attempt to "Americanize that party."[63] Missouri's Edward Bates gave vent to his frustration in his diary. Bates was proud to have been the favorite candidate at the Chicago convention of "the most moderate and prudent" Republicans, those who had sought to "secure the alliance of the remnants of the Whig and American parties." The failure of his candidacy and the convention's rejection of the political program for which it stood were all too evident to him. The platform adopted in Chicago, thought Bates, was too "exclusive and defiant," calculated "only to gratify a handful of extreme abolitionists." Excessively radical on the slavery issue, it was also far too generous toward immigrants. "To please the Germans unreasonably," Bates complained, "it galls (not to say insults) the Americans [Know-Nothings] and all the Republicans who came in through the American party." The Missourian was no more enthusiastic about the party's selection of its national standard-bearer—Abraham Lincoln—a man who, Bates wrote, "is as fully committed as Mr. Seward is, to the extremist doctrines of the Republican party."[64]

Illinois's own Orville H. Browning saw things in the same light. Bates counted Browning as a political friend, and Browning had favored Bates for the presidential nomination precisely "to give some check to the ultra tendencies of the Republican party" and "to bring to our support the old Whigs in the free states, who have not yet fraternized with us." In passing over Bates and nominating Lincoln, Browning therefore fretted, the party had made "a mistake."[65]

Sentiments like these were, of course, a far cry from the expressions of satisfaction with the outcome of the Republican convention that some modern writers have attributed to the nativists of 1860. It was the foreign-born and more militantly antislavery members of the Republican Party, rather than those anxious to accommodate nativism or sectional conciliators, who had reason to cheer Lincoln's nomination. One German-language newspaper in New York, although originally aligned with Seward, happily observed after the convention, "The struggle [against] a corrupt clique ... which had smuggled a narrow-minded Know-Nothingism into the very bosom of free and honest Republican principles" has now been successfully "fought out upon the field of the Republican nomination."[66]

But in the convention's aftermath, some Republican notables called on the party and its candidate to change course and "repudiate" the Chicago platform's antinativist plank.[67] Others urged that when Lincoln publicly accepted the party's nomination he at least take care to "say nothing about the platform."⁶⁸

That was not the course Lincoln chose. His letter of acceptance made a point, in fact, not only of endorsing the Chicago platform but also of specifically and pointedly pledging "not to violate, or disregard it, in any part."⁶⁹ And during the campaign proper, both that platform and Lincoln's position on immigrant rights were laid squarely before the electorate. An important and widely distributed piece of Republican campaign literature was Horace Greeley's *Political Text-Book for 1860*, an anthology of documents (including, of course, the Chicago platform) offered as essential reading for the informed voter. By the time of the fall election, that volume had gone through fourteen editions and had circulated throughout the free states.⁷⁰ Lincoln's antinativist letter to Theodore Canisius occupied a place of honor in that widely read book, one of only six samples of the candidate's writings included therein. Another of those six samples was Lincoln's aforementioned public acceptance of the presidential nomination and his emphatic endorsement of the party platform.⁷¹

How was it, then, that in the 1860 election so many northerners who four years earlier had voted for Millard Fillmore now cast ballots for Abraham Lincoln? No doubt some who did so believed that even a Lincoln administration would prove more sympathetic to nativism than one led by a Democrat. And some Republican officials and journalists were happy to encourage such hopes.

But attentive nativists and proponents of a weakened stand against slavery could hardly mistake Lincoln for one of their own. Most of the conservative Whigs and former Know-Nothings who voted for Lincoln did so not because he or his national party had made major concessions to their views about either of those subjects. They threw in with the Republicans as the sharpening terms of the sectional conflict demonstrated to them the urgency of stopping the "slave power," thereby undermining the appeal and prospects of the parties of the political center. Lincoln, in short, had not moved toward those voters; it was they who had moved toward him.

A case in point was conservative New York Whig George Templeton Strong, a patrician attorney whose diary had earlier overflowed with denunciations of both antislavery militants and foreign-born voters. But Strong's resentment of slaveholder bullying was driving him toward the Republicans even in 1856. In 1860, because "the crack of the plantation whip" had again grown "too audible" to tolerate in national politics, he once more concluded that "the North must assert its rights, now, and take the consequences."⁷²

Philadelphia's Sidney George Fisher, another rather conservative Whig (whose approval of nativism was noted above), followed a political trajectory similar to Strong's during the 1850s. By 1858, "disgust and indignation produced by the outrageous conduct of the South and of the [Buchanan] administration, which is a mere tool of the South," had left Fisher pleased with the growing strength of Republicanism in his state. "The overwhelming and exciting subject now before the country is slavery," he understood in 1860, and "by its side all other issues are insignificant." Still worried that the Republicans were too extreme and in danger of "going too far," Fisher hung back from casting a ballot for them; he decided instead not to vote at all. But he was nonetheless made "glad" by the news that Lincoln's party "is to triumph."⁷³

The general line of Strong's and Fisher's reasoning echoed that of others. From Connecticut, a Republican leader reported around the same time that although the Know-Nothings "feel humiliated by a section of that [the Republican] platform, because it strikes directly at them," they had "reluctantly swallowed the pill."⁷⁴ The picture was much the same in the Old Northwest. An acute Ohio observer informed Lincoln that many nativist-inclined voters had decided "to support you, notwithstanding the German plank in our platform," and even though "they know too that Lincoln and Hamlin are exclusively republicans"—that is, pure and unadulterated Republicans, rather than Know-Nothing–Republican hybrids.⁷⁵

A long-standing tradition traces the outcome of the 1860 election to a variety of factors other than the slavery issue and northern voters' response to it—tariffs; internal improvements; cultural antisouthernism; the peculiarities of the political system; politicians' irresponsibility, unbridled careerism, and hyperbolic rhetoric; and voter ignorance, gullibility, volatility, and prejudices of all sorts. Often inspiring that argument is the presumption (implicit or explicit) that since the slavery controversy had already existed for so many decades, people's opinions and the intensity of their feelings about it could not have altered enough over time to precipitate a seismic rearrangement in the political landscape—much less a sudden transition from peaceful to violent forms of struggle.⁷⁶

That presumption overlooks one of the most important hallmarks of historical turning points like the Civil War era: the rapidity with which popular views changed under the pressure of a dramatically transforming reality. It misses the basic fact to which George Templeton Strong referred in explaining his own political odyssey during the 1850s: "One's opinions change fast in revolutionary times."[77]

Northerners gravitated toward the Republicans during the 1850s because of the political education they received from the turbulent events of that era. As Indiana's George Julian recorded, the increasing aggressiveness of proslavery forces acted "to strengthen the growing hostility to slavery" among residents of the free states. And that process served as "a first-rate training school for Republicanism."[78] For many years, Frederick Douglass later noted, "the people of the North had been accustomed to ask, 'What have we to do with slavery?'" But the lessons taught them by the protracted struggle over Kansas, the Senate-floor beating of Charles Sumner, and the *Dred Scott* decision "settled this question" in the public mind.[79]

Once again, Sidney George Fisher offered pertinent testimony here. Fisher had long been personally inclined to preserve, if possible, both slavery and the union—and he was put off by "a blind, reckless & enthusiastic hatred of slavery" that foolishly ignored "the character of the Negro race" and "the consequences of abolition." But Fisher also recognized in 1860 that "northern opinion is averse to slavery, is becoming more hostile to it every day, & this hostility is constantly increased by the outrages of the South."[80]

Increasingly convinced that slavery and the political agenda of the slaveholders threatened their interests, many northerners who had previously regarded Republicans as dangerous sectional extremists or who had been repelled by the Republicans' friendly attitude toward immigrants now reconsidered those antipathies. And those who were less hesitant than Fisher decided that, in choosing which men to place in political office, the primary desideratum was the need to block the further expansion of the slave-labor system.[81] Over the previous decade and a half, the same basic process had increased the portion of the northern electorate voting for antislavery presidential candidates from 3 percent in 1844 (for the Liberty Party's James G. Birney) to 14 percent in 1848 (for the Free-Soil Party's Martin Van Buren) to 45 percent in 1856 (for Republican John C. Frémont).

Abraham Lincoln, one of the shrewdest politicians of his age, recognized and came to count on this potent political dynamic during the late 1850s. The irrepressible conflict between free and slave labor had an intrinsic logic, one able to mold events as well as minds. The continuing escalation of that conflict, Lincoln concluded, would weaken the hold over the electorate that intermediate, pro-compromise forces momentarily enjoyed while it strengthened the hands of both slavery's more consistent champions and its more determined opponents. "Every incident," he wrote, "every little shifting of scenes or of actors—only clears away the intervening trash, compacts and consolidates the opposing hosts, and brings them more and more distinctly face to face."[82] It was this appraisal of the political situation that had earlier led him to anticipate accurately that the Know-Nothing Party would soon come to grief. A similar fate, Lincoln expected, also awaited others who tried to evade the issue of slavery and its future.

He said as much in reflecting on his loss of the 1858 Illinois senatorial contest. Stephen Douglas had prevailed that year, Lincoln told a colleague, by presenting his own candidacy before different kinds of audiences as at once "the best means to break down, and to uphold the slave power." But, Lincoln continued, the short-term, merely personal success of that subterfuge had left the underlying national conflict still "not half settled." The further maturation of that conflict would clarify in the public's mind where all parties and public figures actually stood and what their political programs meant and were worth. In consequence, Lincoln predicted, "new splits and divisions will soon be upon our adversaries," and "step by step the object of the[ir] leaders will become too plain for the people to stand them."[83] If the Republican Party stood by and propagated its original principles, it would benefit from this political sorting-out process and then, having drawn the voters toward it, be able to act upon those principles from a position of strength.

That, once again, is just what happened, as southern leaders pointed out on the morrow of the election. Lincoln's victory, many of them recognized, signaled that the northern electorate had now come to embrace views incompatible with slavery's safety in the union. "The rights of the South, and the institution of Slavery," observed Georgia's governor Joseph Brown, were "not endangered by the triumph of Mr. Lincoln, as a man." The election's outcome was important because it showed "the direction in which the wind blows," which was toward "a great triumphant political party, the principles of which are deadly hostile to the institution of Slavery."[84]

That perceptive assessment identified a decisive element of the new political situation, one that remained central to political developments during the critical postelection period. Within weeks of his victory at the polls, Lincoln came under enormous pressure from many quarters to preserve the union by reneging on the Republican platform and accepting John J. Crittenden's proposed constitutional amendments. Those amendments would have given ironclad protection to the expansion of slavery into all federal territories "now held, or hereafter acquired" south of the old Missouri Compromise line.

Lincoln, as we know, rejected the Crittenden measures. "Entertain no proposition for a compromise in regard to the *extension* of slavery," he instructed his congressional allies. "On that point hold firm, as with a chain of steel."[85] The national Republican Party's refusal during the 1860 campaign to dilute its principles, and its success in winning a northern majority to those principles, gave Lincoln the solid base of popular support he needed to take that firm, momentous stand.[86]

NOTES

1. Seventh and Last Debate with Stephen A. Douglas at Alton, Illinois, October 15, 1858, in *The Collected Works of Abraham Lincoln*, 9 vols., ed. Roy P. Basler (New Brunswick, NJ: Rutgers University Press, 1953), 3:312; hereafter cited as *Collected Works*. See also, for example, Lincoln's speech at Edwardsville, Illinois, that season, in the same volume (92).

2. Philip S. Foner, ed., *The Life and Writings of Frederick Douglass*, 5 vols. (New York: International Publishers, 1950–1955), 2:510–511, 490.

3. *Springfield Daily Illinois State Register*, September 28, 1860, in *Northern Editorials on Secession*, 2 vols., ed. Howard Cecil Perkins (Gloucester, MA: Peter Smith, 1964), 1:42.

4. *New York Herald*, September 19, 1860, in Perkins, *Northern Editorials on Secession*, 1:36.

5. Dwight L. Dumond, ed., *Southern Editorials on Secession* (New York: Peter Smith, 1964), 152.

6. Charles B. Dew, *Apostles of Disunion: Southern Secession Commissioners and the Causes of the Civil War* (Charlottesville: University Press of Virginia, 2001), 11.

7. Stephen Douglas to Howell Cobb, October 6, 1855, in *The Letters of Stephen A. Douglas*, ed. Robert W. Johannsen (Urbana: University of Illinois Press, 1961), 342; Joel H. Silbey, *The Partisan Imperative: The Dynamics of American Politics before the Civil War* (New York: Oxford University Press, 1985), 129–130.

8. Silbey, *Partisan Imperative*, 184, 180.

9. William E. Gienapp, "Who Voted for Lincoln?" in *Abraham Lincoln and the American Political Tradition*, ed. John L. Thomas (Amherst: University of Massachusetts Press, 1986), 65; William E. Gienapp, "Nativism and the Creation of a Republican Majority in the North before the Civil War," *Journal of American History* 12 (December 1985): 555. In the latter essay, Gienapp estimates that the proportion of 1856 Fillmore voters that cast ballots for Lincoln in 1860 was 74 percent in Illinois, 40 percent in Indiana, and 83 percent in Pennsylvania.

10. Gienapp, "Nativism and Creation of a Republican Majority," 558–559; Silbey, *Partisan Imperative*, 128–129, 131–132, 150, 164.

11. Gienapp, "Nativism and Creation of a Republican Majority," 554–555.

12. See David Herbert Donald, *Lincoln* (New York: Simon & Schuster, 1995),

170, 255; William E. Gienapp, *Abraham Lincoln and Civil War America: A Biography* (New York: Oxford University Press, 2002). According to Gienapp: "Lincoln's unwillingness to speak out against the Know Nothings at this time, despite his strong feelings, would be a crucial factor in his successful bid for the Republican nomination in 1860," since it made him, at the Chicago convention, "the one possible nominee who was acceptable to all factions of the party," including "former Know Nothings" (55, 69).

13. Lincoln to George M. Parsons and others, December 19, 1859, in *Collected Works*, 3:512; Gabor S. Boritt, *Lincoln and the Economics of the American Dream* (Memphis, TN: Memphis State University Press, 1978); Olivier Fraysee, *Lincoln, Land, and Labor, 1809–1860* (Urbana: University of Illinois Press, 1994).

14. John Ashworth, *"Agrarians" and "Aristocrats": Party Political Ideology in the United States, 1837–1846* (Cambridge: Cambridge University Press, 1987).

15. Nicholas B. Wainwright, ed., *A Philadelphia Perspective: The Diary of Sidney George Fisher Covering the Years 1834–1871* (Philadelphia: Historical Society of Pennsylvania, 1967), 177. On Fisher's background, social position, and general views, see William H. Riker, "Sidney George Fisher and the Separation of Powers during the Civil War," *Journal of the History of Ideas* 15 (June 1954): 401.

16. "Annual Message to the Legislature," January 1, 1839, in *The Works of William H. Seward*, 5 vols., ed. George E. Baker (New York: Redfield, 1853–1884), 2:197.

17. Eric Foner, *Free Soil, Free Labor, Free Men: The Ideology of the Republican Party before the Civil War* (1970; reprint, New York: Oxford University Press, 1995), 250–253.

18. David Herbert Donald, *Charles Sumner and the Coming of the Civil War* (Chicago: University of Chicago Press, 1981), 275; George Julian, *Political Recollections, 1840 to 1872* (1884; reprint, New York: Negro Universities Press, 1970), 141; Tyler Anbinder, *Nativism and Slavery: The Northern Know-Nothings and the Politics of the 1850s* (New York: Oxford University Press, 1992), 166.

19. William H. Seward, *The Autobiography of William H. Seward from 1801 to 1834, with a Memoir of His Life*, ed. William H. Seward and Frederick W. Seward (New York: D. Appleton, 1877), 54.

20. For a fuller presentation of this interpretation, see Bruce Levine, "Conservatism, Nativism, and Slavery: Thomas R. Whitney and the Origins of the Know Nothing Party," *Journal of American History* 88 (September 2001): 455–488.

21. Gregg Cantrell, *Kenneth and John B. Rayner and the Limits of Southern Dissent* (Urbana: University of Illinois Press, 1993), 100–107; Anbinder, *Nativism and Slavery*, 167, 207; [Henry Winter Davis], *The Origin, Principles, and Purposes of the American Party* (n.p.: [1855]), 38–39.

22. L. Ellis to Daniel Ullmann, July 2, 1860, Daniel Ullmann Papers, New-York Historical Society.

23. Gienapp, "Nativism and Creation of a Republican Majority," 529–559; Foner, *Free Soil, Free Labor, Free Men*, 250–253; Dale Baum, *The Civil War Party System: The Case of Massachusetts, 1848–1876* (Chapel Hill: University of North Carolina Press, 1984), 44–45.

24. Kenneth M. Stampp, *America in 1857: A Nation on the Brink* (New York: Oxford University Press, 1990), 131, 135–143.

25. On this subject, see Bruce Levine, *The Spirit of 1848: German Immigrants, Labor Conflict, and the Coming of the Civil War* (Urbana: University of Illinois Press, 1992).

26. Anbinder, *Nativism and Slavery*, 248–252.

27. Reinhard Luthin, *The First Lincoln Campaign* (1944; reprint, Gloucester, MA: Peter Smith, 1964), 225.

28. Charles Granville Hamilton, *Lincoln and the Know-Nothing Movement* (Washington, DC: Public Affairs Press, 1954), 12.

29. Gienapp, "Who Voted for Lincoln?" 53–56. Here, Gienapp suggests that to court more conservative northern voters, Republicans in 1860 weakened their antislavery stance. In his essay "Nativism and Creation of a Republican Majority," which appeared almost simultaneously, Gienapp seems to advance a different argument—that such voters came over to the Republican Party because (and only when) it opted to run on the same mix of strongly nativist and strongly antislavery themes that the Know-Nothings had earlier embraced. In the North, he writes, the Know-Nothings' initial supporters "were antislavery extension as well as nativist in sentiment, and they voted for the American party because it represented both principles" (Gienapp, "Nativism and Creation of a Republican Majority," 532–533). Later, however, "thousands of members deserted it for the Republicans precisely because the Republican appeal emphasized both sectionalism and nativism" (ibid., 558–559). Neither argument, I believe, properly represents the relationship between Know-Nothings and Republicans on the slavery issue. Whereas the first underestimates the antislavery thrust of the Republicans' 1860 campaign, the second exaggerates the antislavery militancy of the American Party. The Republican organization was, from its birth through 1860, significantly more radical and militant in its antislavery stance than either the national Know-Nothing Party or its northern leaders in general, including most of those who broke with that party over its equivocation about Kansas-Nebraska in 1855–1856. See Henry Wilson, *History of the Rise and Fall of the Slave Power in America*, 2 vols. (Boston: J. R. Osgood, 1872–1877), 2:427; Levine, "Conservatism, Nativism, and Slavery."

30. Platform of the Republican Party in 1860, in Kirk H. Porter and Donald Bruce Johnson, eds., *National Party Platforms, 1840–1960* (Urbana: University of Illinois Press, 1961), 32–33; F. I. Herriott, "The Conference in the Deutsches Haus, Chicago, May 14–15, 1860," *Illinois State Historical Society Transactions* 35 (1928): 101–191; James M. Bergquist, "The Forty-Eighters and the Republican Convention of 1860," in *The German Forty-Eighters in the United States*, ed. Charlotte L. Brancaforte (New York: Peter Lang, 1989), 141–156. On the 1860 platform, see especially Don E. Fehrenbacher, *Prelude to Greatness: Lincoln in the 1850s* (Stanford, CA: Stanford University Press, 1962), 156n; Foner, *Free Soil, Free Labor, Free Men*, 132–133, 211–213, 271, 277; and Richard H. Sewell, *Ballots for Freedom: Antislavery Politics in the United States, 1837–1860* (New York: Oxford University Press, 1976), 343–365.

31. L. K. Pangborn (of the *Boston Daily Atlas and Bee*) to Josiah M. Lucas, May 22, 1860, Abraham Lincoln Collection, Library of Congress.

32. Nehemiah D. Sperry to Abraham Lincoln, May 27, 1860, Lincoln Collection. Sperry was chairman of Connecticut's Republican State Committee. On the convention's treatment of nativism and the nativists' response, see also Anbinder, *Nativism and Slavery*, 267–270.

33. M[urat]. Halstead, *Caucuses of 1860: A History of the National Political Conventions of the Current Presidential Campaign* (Columbus, OH: Follett, Foster, 1860), 146–149.

34. Lincoln, "Debate with Stephen A. Douglas at Ottawa, Illinois on August, 21, 1858," in *Collected Works*, 3:29.

35. He went on record with that view almost a quarter of a century before he entered the White House. Lincoln, "Protest in Illinois Legislature on Slavery," March 3, 1837, in *Collected Works*, 1:75.

36. Lincoln to Williamson Durley, October 3, 1845, ibid., 347–348.

37. Speech at Edwardsville, Illinois, May 18, 1858, in ibid., 2:453.

38. "In respect to fusion, I am in favor of it whenever it can be effected on Republican principles, but upon no other condition. A fusion upon any other platform would be as insane as unprincipled." Lincoln to Theodore Canisius, May 17, 1859, in ibid., 3:380.

39. Lincoln to Mark W. Delahay, May 14, 1859, in ibid., 3:379.

40. Lincoln to Canisius, May 17, 1859, ibid., 380–381. In fact, as Gustave Koerner accurately noted, by 1860, Lincoln was taking a considerably firmer stand on the issue than was the supposedly more radical William H. Seward. Gustave Philipp Koerner, *Memoirs of Gustave Koerner, 1809–1896, Life-Sketches Written at the Suggestion of His Children*, 2 vols., ed. Thomas J. McCormack (Cedar Rapids, IA: Torch Press, 1909), 2:92.

41. Lincoln to Mark W. Delahay, May 14, 1859, in *Collected Works*, 3:379. Lincoln repeated and further elaborated this line of thinking in a letter to Nathan Sargent, June 23, 1859, ibid., 387–388.

42. Lincoln to Owen Lovejoy, August 11, 1855, in ibid., 2:316.

43. As a young man in the mid-1830s, Lincoln had apparently echoed the early Whig opposition to universal white male suffrage and the Illinois party's insistence that only those who paid taxes (or at least bore arms on the country's behalf) should be granted the franchise. But over the next several years Lincoln moved away from that vestigial elitism. In predominantly Democratic rural and small-town Illinois, he fashioned a viable political career by linking his lifelong enthusiasm for economic development to a popular-democratic rhetoric, style, and program. By the end of the 1840s, Lincoln was declining to assist his law partner William Herndon in a case that required endorsing a restrictive franchise. Lincoln now told Herndon that he was "opposed to the limitation." Far from wishing to curtail the right to vote, Lincoln explained, he was "in favor of its Extension—Enlargement." See Donald, *Lin-*

coln, 59; To the Editor of the *Sangamo Journal*, June 13, 1836, in *Collected Works*, 1:48; Ida M. Tarbell, *In the Footsteps of the Lincolns* (New York: Harper & Brothers, 1924), 240–242, 266–269; David Herbert Donald, *Lincoln's Herndon: A Biography* (New York: Da Capo, 1989), 20–21; and Douglas L. Wilson and Rodney O. Davis, eds., *Herndon's Informants: Letters, Interviews, and Statements about Abraham Lincoln* (Urbana: University of Illinois Press, 1998), 705.

44. Lincoln to Joshua Speed, August 24, 1855, in *Collected Works*, 2:323. See also Lincoln to Delahay, May 4, 1859, ibid., 3:378–379; Lincoln to Sargent, June 23, 1859, ibid., 387–388; Lincoln to Schuyler Colfax, July 6, 1859, ibid., 390–391; Notes for Speeches at Columbus and Cincinnati, Ohio, September 16, 17, 1859, ibid., 432–433, 435.

45. Lincoln to Canisius, May 17, 1859, ibid., 380. These words anticipated his later, more famous description of the Union cause in the Civil War: "On the side of the Union, it is a struggle for maintaining in the world, that form, and substance of government, whose leading object is, to elevate the condition of men—to lift artificial weights from all shoulders—to clear the paths of laudable pursuit for all—to afford all, an unfettered start, and a fair chance, in the race of life. Yielding to partial, and temporary departures, from necessity, this is the leading object of the government for whose existence we contend" (ibid., 4:438).

46. David M. Potter, *The Impending Crisis: 1848–1861* (New York: Harper & Row, 1977), 253. In support of this claim, Potter cites only Charles Granville Hamilton's pamphlet.

47. Gienapp, "Nativism and Creation of a Republican Majority," 554.

48. Donald, *Lincoln*, 170, 247.

49. Speech and Resolution Concerning Philadelphia Riots, June 12, 1844, in *Collected Works*, 1:337–338.

50. Lincoln to Lovejoy, August 11, 1855, ibid., 2:316.

51. See Lincoln to Abraham Jonas, July 21, 1860, in ibid., 4:85–86.

52. David Donald views Lincoln's words as an attempt to feign ignorance of the meaning of the committee's "native Americanism" and thereby to evade the thorny issue as a whole. But surely it was Donald who missed the meaning of Lincoln's typically tongue-in-cheek but politically transparent declaration. See Donald, *Lincoln*, 170.

53. Noah Levering, "Recollections of Abraham Lincoln," *Iowa Historical Record* 12 (July 1896): 496. Thanks to Matthew Pinsker for pointing me toward Levering's memoir.

54. Speech at Bloomington, Illinois, September 26, 1854, in *Collected Works*, 2:234. For Lincoln's concern with holding German support, see his letter to James Berdan, July 10, 1856, ibid., 347.

55. The Decatur meeting denounced "all attacks upon our Common School System, or upon any of our institutions of an educational character, or of civil polity by the adherents of any religious body whatever." These words represented a rejection of the Catholic Church's attempts to use public money to support parochial schools.

But the meeting also resolved, "We are in favor of the widest tolerance upon all matters of religious faith," that "in regard to [political] office we hold merit, not birth place, to be the test," and that "we shall maintain the naturalization laws AS THEY ARE, believing as we do, that we should welcome the exiles and emigrants of the Old World, to homes of enterprise and of freedom in the New." Remarkably, David Donald calls this passage "so vague that it did not alienate the Know Nothings." Since the Know-Nothings insisted that immigrants' political rights be curtailed or eliminated precisely on the basis of their places of birth, it is hard to see how the nativists could find this platform plank unexceptionable. George Schneider, "Lincoln and the Anti-Know-Nothing Resolutions," *McLean County Historical Society Transactions* 3 (1900): 88–90; *Illinois State Journal*, February 25, 27, 1856; *Illinois State Register*, February 25, 1856; A. T. Andreas, *History of Chicago from the Earliest Period to the Present Time*, 3 vols. (Chicago: A. T. Andreas, 1884–1886), 1:390; Paul Selby, "The Editorial Convention of 1856," *Illinois State Historical Society Journal* 5 (July 1912): 343–349; William E. Gienapp, *The Origins of the Republican Party, 1852–1856* (New York: Oxford University Press, 1988), 289–290; Arthur Charles Cole, *The Era of the Civil War, 1848–1870* (Urbana: University of Illinois Press, 1987), 143–144; Donald, *Lincoln*, 191.

56. Speech at Jacksonville, Illinois, September 6, 1856, in ibid., 2:373. See also Lincoln's speech at Belleville, Illinois, ibid., 379–380.

57. He did so, according to yet another Democratic newspaper, in a "severe, personal manner." Speech at Meredosa, Illinois, October 18, 1858, in ibid., 3:328–329. See also Lincoln's letter to Edward Lusk, October 30, 1858, ibid., 333.

58. Lincoln to Canisius, May 17, 1859, ibid., 380–381; F. I. Herriott, "The Premises and Significance of Abraham Lincoln's Letter to Theodore Canisius," *Deutsch-Amerikanische Geschichtsblaetter von Illinois* 15 (1915): 181–254; James Manning Bergquist, "The Political Attitudes of the German Immigrant in Illinois, 1848–1860" (Ph.D. diss., Northwestern University, 1966), 273–290, 306.

59. Lincoln to Canisius, May 17, 1859, in *Collected Works*, 3:380; *Illinois State Journal*, May 18, 1859.

60. Contract with Theodore Canisius, May [30?], 1859, in *Collected Works*, 3:383–384.

61. Bergquist, "Political Attitudes of the German Immigrant," 273–290, 306; Donald, *Lincoln*, 170.

62. Koerner, *Memoirs*, 2:86–89.

63. L. Ellis to Daniel Ullmann, July 2, 1860, Ullmann Papers. Daniel Ullmann, a leader of the New York Know-Nothings, moved closer and closer to the Republicans during the latter half of the 1850s and was therefore "severely criticized by many old friends" for trying to persuade his American Party colleagues to fuse with the Republican organization. *New York Times*, July 17, 1860; Ralph Basso, "Nationalism, Nativism, and the Black Soldier: Daniel Ullmann, a Biography of a Man Living in a Period of Transition, 1810–1892" (Ph.D. diss., St. John's University, 1986), 223–227. One leading New York nativist refused to even open unity negotiations until the Re-

publicans became "less sectional in their platforms and their political action." A second thought it "evident that we can never unite with the vast body of the Republican Party, nor is that desirable, if possible," because major units of the Republicans were "almost completely Abolitionized and Foreignized" and because that party was committed to an absolute congressional ban on slavery in the territories (rather than the much more flexible Kansas-Nebraska formula of "popular sovereignty"). A third denounced the Republicans' "anti-national and treasonable" stance on slavery and its "persistent disposition . . . to truckle to the wishes of the German Catholics." A fourth despised the Republicans' determination to stir up "hatred on the part of the North to the South." J. W. Reynolds to Daniel Ullmann, May 28, 1859; L. L. Pratt to Ullmann, May 31, 1859; M. H. Goodwin to Ullmann, James Barker, and others, May 28, 1859; and J. M. Hefford to Ullmann, May 31, 1859, all in Ullmann Papers.

64. Howard K. Beale, ed., *The Diary of Edward Bates, 1859–1866*, in *Annual Report of the American Historical Association* 4 (1930): 128–129. See also Foner, *Free Soil, Free Labor, Free Men*, 257–258.

65. Theodore Calvin Pease and James G. Randall, eds., *The Diary of Orville Hickman Browning*, 2 vols. (Springfield: Illinois State Historical Library, 1925), 1:407–410.

66. Editorial in the *New Yorker Demokrat*, translated and reprinted in the *Cincinnati Daily Commercial*, May 24, 1860.

67. L. K. Pangborn to Josiah M. Lucas, May 22, 1860, Lincoln Collection.

68. Elihu Washburne to Lincoln, May 20, 1860; James E. Harvey to Lincoln, May 21, 1860, both in Lincoln Collection. Washburne was an Illinois Whig; Harvey was a Whig journalist.

69. Lincoln to George Ashmun, May 23, 1860, in *Collected Works*, 4:52. Ashmun presided over the 1860 Republican National Convention in Chicago.

70. Allan Nevins, *The Emergence of Lincoln*, 2 vols. (New York: Charles Scribner's Sons, 1950), 2:277, 299, 302. Lincoln also arranged for the publication (as a campaign booklet) of the text of his 1858 debates with Stephen Douglas, in which Lincoln had openly identified the goal of restricting slavery's spread as the "ultimate extinction" of slavery per se.

71. Horace Greeley and John F. Cleveland, eds., *Political Text-Book for 1860* (1860; reprint, New York: Negro Universities Press, 1969), 206–207.

72. Allan Nevins and Milton Halsey Thomas, eds., *The Diary of George Templeton Strong, 1835–1875*, 3 vols. (New York: Macmillan, 1952), 1:94; 2:174, 274, 281–282, 287–288, 305, 475–476; 3:42, 52, 54, 56–57, 59.

73. Wainwright, *Philadelphia Perspective*, 308, 367.

74. James F. Babcock to Mark Howard, August 4, 1860, Mark Howard Papers, Connecticut Historical Society, Hartford.

75. Richard M. Corwine to Lincoln, May 28, 1860, Lincoln Collection.

76. For two explicit assertions of this assumption, see Michael F. Holt, *The Political Crisis of the 1850s* (New York: Wiley, 1977), 2–3, and Marc Egnal, *Clash of Extremes: The Economic Origins of the Civil War* (New York: Hill & Wang, 2010), 5.

77. Nevins and Thomas, *Diary of Strong*, 3:95.

78. Julian, *Political Recollections*, 169–171.

79. Frederick Douglass, *Life and Times of Frederick Douglass* (1892; reprint, London: Collier Books, 1962), 293.

80. Wainwright, *Philadelphia Perspective*, 367, 373.

81. Here I agree with David Potter's observation that the northern electorate's support for the Republicans in 1860 signified "the triumph of a new attitude" toward the slavery question, "a vast transformation" that represented "nothing less than a revolution" in public opinion. Potter, *Impending Crisis*, 445–446.

82. Lincoln, fragment of a speech, ca. December 28, 1857, in *Collected Works*, 2:452–453.

83. Lincoln to Eleazar A. Paine, November 19, 1858; Lincoln to Alexander Sympson, December 12, 1858, both in ibid., 3:340, 346.

84. Joseph Brown's open letter for secession, December 7, 1860, reprinted in *Secession Debated: Georgia's Showdown in 1860*, ed. William W. Freehling and Craig M. Simpson (Baton Rouge: Louisiana State University Press, 1992), 147–148.

85. Lincoln to William Kellogg, December 11, 1860, and Lincoln to Elihu Washburne, December 13, 1860, both in ibid., 4:150–151, emphasis in original.

86. The best account of this aspect of the secession era remains Kenneth Stampp, *And the War Came: The North and the Secession Crisis, 1860–61* (1950; reprint, Baton Rouge: Louisiana State University Press, 1970).

CHAPTER SIX

Lincoln's Competing Political Loyalties: Antislavery, Union, and the Constitution

Manisha Sinha

Shortly before the Civil War, Abraham Lincoln wrote, "I have always hated slavery, I think, as much as any abolitionist." Lincoln, of course, was no abolitionist. Indeed, among Lincoln's many virtues lauded by historians are his moderation, pragmatism, political acumen, and philosophical temperament, a "blend of political cunning and bedrock idealism" that allowed him to slowly but surely navigate the road to emancipation during the Civil War.[1] Abolitionists, in contrast, have been caricatured in mainstream historical narratives and popular culture as radical fanatics, anti-intellectual activists who had little to do with the coming of emancipation and whose extremism in the cause of black freedom threatened to sabotage the very cause they championed.[2] Such a dichotomy is based not just on a lack of appreciation of the rich political and intellectual history of abolition but also on discussions of Lincoln's moderation and intellect that set him apart from the antislavery and abolition movements of his time.[3]

There is no reason to doubt Lincoln's claim during the war that he had always been "naturally antislavery," even though he balanced antislavery principles with competing loyalties to the union and the Constitution.[4] Lincoln's commitment to the American experiment in republican government simultaneously reinforced and moderated his antislavery views, preventing him from adopting any position that might threaten the union with slaveholders or the constitutional compromises on slavery. The most remarkable aspect of Lincoln's views on slavery and race is their continuous evolution from antislavery sentiment to a growing acceptance of the abolitionist ideal of black citizenship at the end of his life. Lincoln achieved greatness not by redeeming the founding fathers' republican experiment in white liberty and black slavery but in initiating the transformation of the slaveholding republic into an interracial democracy.[5] In doing so, he inhabited abolitionist ground.

It is important to comprehend how Lincoln's competing political loyalties to the union and the Constitution moderated his antislavery beliefs through much of his political career. The union and the Constitution or the American state became the vehicles for antislavery and emancipation only during the Civil War. Long ago, David Potter, in his masterly synthesis *The Impending Crisis*, made a cogent argument about the competing values of most antislavery northerners: "The problem for Americans who, in the age of Lincoln, wanted slaves to be free was not simply that southerners wanted the opposite, but that they themselves cherished a conflicting value: they wanted the Constitution, which protected slavery, to be honored, and the Union, which was a fellowship with slaveholders, to be preserved. Thus they were committed to values that could not be logically reconciled." This, I argue, was essentially Lincoln's dilemma. It was not just a matter of a "ranking of values" but of competing, dissonant political loyalties. Recently, Dorothy Ross has given us a sophisticated reformulation of Potter's argument in which Lincoln reconciled liberty and nationalism through the discourse of American exceptionalism. But she argues further that, for Lincoln, even at the moment of emancipation, preserving the nation always trumped ending slavery. Lincoln's antislavery conviction in this reading is instrumental rather than genuine, a lesser rather than a competing value.[6] My purpose in this essay is to show that Lincoln struggled to reconcile these conflicting political loyalties, rather than to claim a precedence of one over the other. Lincoln's commitment to the union and the Constitution balanced his antislavery inclinations through much of his political career.

From the start, while Lincoln shared abolitionists' moral abhorrence of slavery, he distanced himself from their tactics and their program for the immediate abolition of slavery and the achievement of racial equality. Lincoln's earliest public statements on slavery reveal what historian Mark Neely calls a "consistent antislavery record." In 1837, when Lincoln was an Illinois state representative, he refused to vote for proslavery resolutions condemning the abolition movement and defending slaveholders' "right to property in slaves." A protest signed only by Lincoln and a fellow Whig representative from Sangamon County who had been appointed to a judgeship clarified that "slavery is founded on both injustice and bad policy," but abolition tended to "increase rather than abate its evils." It also vindicated the constitutional power of Congress to abolish slavery in the District of Columbia, an early demand of most abolitionist petitions, with the admonition that it should do so with the consent of the residents. A year later Lincoln gave his Lyceum speech in which he condemned the vigilante actions of proslavery mobs during the Mississippi slave insurrection scare; the lynching of a black man, Floyd McIntosh, in Missouri, which led abolitionist Elijah Lovejoy to relocate his newspaper to Alton, Illinois; and the subsequent murder of Lovejoy and the destruction of his press, calling such acts the biggest threats to the rule of law.[7] Lincoln did not join the abolitionists, but like many antislavery politicians, including the far more radical Thaddeus Stevens of Pennsylvania, he condemned the wave of antiabolitionist violence that engulfed the country in the 1830s.

As a Whig lawyer-politician, however, Lincoln's devotion to the Constitution, the law, and the union moderated his antislavery beliefs. Unlike other Republicans, such as the radical Salmon Chase of Ohio, known as the "attorney general of fugitive slaves" for his long record of representing them, or his more moderate Illinois colleague Lyman Trumbull, Lincoln fought on both sides of the issue, representing slaves as well as slaveholders. Unlike abolitionists and radicals in his own party, such as Charles Sumner (who always referred to the Fugitive Slave Act of 1850 as a "bill" because he refused to recognize its constitutionality), Lincoln did not challenge the fugitive slave clause of the Constitution and the federal laws that implemented it. As a one-term Whig congressman in 1849, he proposed a plan for gradual, compensated emancipation in the District of Columbia to which he attached a fugitive slave clause, leading abolitionist orator Wendell Phillips to call him the "Slave-hound of Illinois" in 1860.[8] Lincoln's position anticipated his opposition to the extension of slavery in the 1850s, a constitutionally permissible position and the lowest common denominator of antislavery politics, rather than favoring the abolition of slavery.

Lincoln's growth in antislavery politics can be traced from his support of the fugitive slave law to his passionate condemnation of the 1857 *Dred Scott* decision, both based on the premise that African Americans were noncitizens. His evolution coincided with his move from the Whig to the Republican Party. As a northern Whig, Lincoln had opposed the Mexican War as a land grab for slavery, and he had voted several times for the Wilmot Proviso, which prohibited the introduction of slavery into territories acquired from Mexico. But unlike many antislavery Whigs, including Sumner and Joshua R. Giddings (with whom he boarded in Washington), he did not join the Free-Soil Party. Lincoln's "beau ideal" of a statesman (as he said in his famous debates with Stephen A. Douglas) was the "Great Pacificator" Henry Clay, author of nearly all the major antebellum compromises on slavery from the Missouri Compromise of 1820 to the Compromise of 1850. Lincoln supported the compromise and the draconian new fugitive slave law, even though he believed provisions to protect free blacks from illegal enslavement should be added to it. Lincoln balanced his competing loyalties to the union, the Constitution, and the antislavery cause until the emergence of the Republican Party, which not only revived his moribund political career but also allowed him to articulate and develop his antislavery views.

In his first explicitly antislavery speech, delivered in Peoria in 1854 in the aftermath of the passage of the Kansas-Nebraska Act, rescinding the Missouri Compromise line, Lincoln began his long-running political battle on the meaning of American democracy with Douglas, the Democratic senator from Illinois and author of the act. Lincoln condemned American slavery for making a mockery of American republicanism: "In our greedy chase to make profit of the negro, let us beware, lest we 'cancel and tear to pieces' even the white man's charter of freedom." Declaring slavery a "monstrous injustice," Lincoln pointed to the dilemma it posed for the American republic, allowing its "enemies . . . with plausibility, to taunt us as hypocrites" and its "friends" to "doubt our sincerity." He argued that slavery violated the principles of the Declaration of Independence: "If the negro is a man, why then my ancient faith teaches me that 'all men are created equal'; and that there can be no moral right in connection with one man's making a slave of another." And he dwelled on the American paradox of "self-government" for whites and "despotism" for blacks. The North, he said, suffered under the Constitution, which created a government that gave slaveholders the advantage and asked the free states to perform the "dirty, disagreeable job" of apprehending fugitive slaves. This, Lincoln argued, was "manifestly unfair," but he was still prepared to stand by the Constitution "fairly, fully, and firmly."[9] Lincoln tried to resolve the self-evidently antislavery founding principles of American republicanism with the political edifice erected by the founders, the constitutional compromises over slavery that made possible a union with slaveholders. The free-soil platform of the Republican Party offered one solution to his quandary. Unlike abolition, the nonextension of slavery, the Republicans argued, was a politically legitimate program that allowed the federal government to exercise its constitutional powers to regulate the territories, even though southern extremists threatened secession at the very idea of any restriction on slavery.

Throughout the 1850s Lincoln perfected his antislavery politics, combining the stirring "language of abolitionism" with a constitutionally unassailable antislavery program: nonextension. By 1857, Lincoln condemned the *Dred Scott* decision not only for declaring the free-soil platform of the Republican Party unconstitutional but also for debasing African Americans. It was in response to *Dred Scott* that Lincoln issued his most memorable condemnation of the enslavement of blacks in the United States:

> All the powers of earth seem rapidly combining against him. Mammon is after him; ambition follows, and philosophy follows, and the Theology of the day is fast joining the cry. They have him in his prison house; they have searched his person, and left no prying instrument with him. One after another they have closed the heavy iron doors upon him, and now they have him, as it were, bolted in with a lock of a hundred keys, which can never be unlocked without the concurrence of every key; the keys in the hands of a hundred different men, and they scattered to a hundred different and distant places; and they stand musing as to what invention, in all the dominions of mind and matter, can be produced to make the impossibility of his escape more complete than it is.[10]

This was no paean to the American republic but a remarkable understanding of the entrenched nature of both slavery and racism in the "white man's democracy."

It is perhaps more useful to explore why relatively conscientious nineteenth-century American citizens such as Lincoln, who theoretically abhorred the existence of slavery, did not join the abolitionists. One conventional answer is racism. Lincoln's preferred solution to the problems of slavery and race in the American republic was the colonization of black Americans in Africa. But if Lincoln was not a racial egalitarian, neither was he a hardened racist. Lincoln's unequivocal condemnation of slavery resembled abolitionist logic, but he limited his antislavery position to nonextension. Likewise, his ideas on race were far in advance of those of most of his countrymen, yet he advocated the colonization of African Americans rather than black citizenship. Lincoln shared Clay's distaste of slavery as well as his ardent views on unionism and colonization. Like Thomas Jefferson, Clay, also a slaveholder, had hoped for the gradual abolition of slavery and the expatriation of all freed blacks to Africa. As the longtime president of the American Colonization Society (ACS), founded in 1816, Clay had touted this program, a forgotten part of his plan for economic modernization—the "American System" of banks, tariffs, and internal improvements to encourage manufacturing. Colonization was widely rejected by most African Americans and abolitionists such as William Lloyd Garrison; instead, the abolition movement demanded racial equality and black citizenship in the United States. Lincoln, however, recommended colonization, claiming that it required only political "will" based on a better appreciation of "self-interest" and that it made "moral sense" to "transfer the African to his native clime"—an odd characterization, as African Americans had lived in the country for generations. Lincoln also tried to portray colonization as compatible with the antislavery cause, likening it to the exodus of the children of Israel from Egyptian bondage. During the Civil War, he borrowed the words of Reverend Leonard Bacon, an antislavery colonizationist from Connecticut: if "slavery is not wrong, nothing is wrong."

Unlike Jefferson, Clay, and most other colonizationists, Lincoln did not subscribe to crude racist ideas. Apparently, the closest he came to expressing racism was in homespun jokes, but he never flirted with the pseudoscience of race, whose flowering in the 1850s lent a powerful impetus to the proslavery argument. Lincoln's public statements on race were always hedged with qualifications. In Peoria, Lincoln argued that his preference was for gradual emancipation and the colonization of African Americans to Liberia, the ACS colony in West Africa. He admitted, however, that it was an impractical plan, and he would not presume to dictate to southerners how to end slavery. To free black people and "make them politically and socially our equals," as abolitionists demanded, his "own feelings will not admit of this; and if mine would, we know the great mass of white people will not." Conceding that racism may not accord with "justice and sound judgment," he argued that a "universal feeling, whether well or ill-founded, can not be safely disregarded." When it came to race, Lincoln's argument was based on political expediency and self-interest, grounds he had rejected when it came to slavery. But even on race, Lincoln was far ahead of hardened racists, who wanted to write black people out of humanity. Privately, he belittled racist ideas. In a brilliant reductio-ad-absurdum refutation of the racial logic of slavery worthy of an abolitionist, Lincoln wrote:

> You say A is white and B is black. It is colour, then; the lighter have the right to enslave the darker? Take care. By this rule you are to be slave to the first man you meet with a fairer skin than your own.
>
> You do not mean colour exactly? You mean the whites are intellectually the superiors of blacks, and therefore have the right to enslave them? Take care again. By this rule you are the slave of the first man you meet with an intellect superior than your own.[11]

Lincoln surely knew that advocating black equality would be the kiss of death for his career and for the Republican Party. Even so, Lincoln's strong criticisms of slavery worried his friends, who thought he had lost the 1858 senatorial election to Douglas because of them. One Democratic newspaper in Illinois argued, "His niggerism has as dark a hue as that of Garrison or Fred Douglass." Despite Democratic attempts to class Republicans with abolitionists as "nigger worshippers," Lincoln highlighted partisan differences on race. Republicans argued that "the negro is a man; that his bondage is cruelly wrong, and that the field of his oppression should not be enlarged. The Democrats deny his manhood; deny, or dwarf to insignificance, the wrong of his bondage; so far as possible, crush all sympathy for him, and cultivate and excite hatred and disgust against him." Lincoln met head-on Democratic accusations that Republicans promoted racial "amalgamation" or intermixture. There was nothing in the Republican platform on racial intermarriage, he noted. Like the abolitionists, Lincoln pointed out that it was slaveholders who pressured enslaved women into "forced concubinage." At one point, he joked that he had no objections if a white man wanted to marry a black woman if the black woman could "stand it," even though he personally would not do it. Lincoln deliberately used the example of a black woman to make a free-labor argument on natural equality for blacks:

> I protest against the counterfeit logic which concludes that just because I do not want a black woman for a slave, I must necessarily want her for a wife. I need not have her for either. I can just leave her alone. In some respects she is certainly not my equal; but in her natural right to eat the bread she earns from her own hands, without asking leave of anyone else, she is my equal, and the equal of all others.[12]

Natural equality clearly did not mean political and civil rights or citizenship for the black woman, who was doubly disfranchised by race and gender in the antebellum American republic.

During their 1858 debates, Lincoln was constantly race-baited by Douglas; he was always on the defensive on the issue of racial equality and explicitly disavowed the abolitionist goal of promoting black citizenship. Illinois, with its large southern-born population and "black laws" that systematically discriminated against free blacks, was not fertile ground when it came to advocating black equality, especially not for a politician trying to win votes. Lincoln clearly displayed his displeasure with having to deal with "all this quibbling about this man and the other man, this race and that race and the other race being inferior, and therefore must be placed in an inferior position." He asked his audience to "discard all these things" and unite on the "standard" that all men are created equal. In Ottawa, Lincoln read aloud the relevant portion of his Peoria speech and clarified that he had never advocated racial equality but stuck to the natural rights and free-labor arguments against the enslavement of blacks:

> There is a physical difference between the two, which, in my judgment, will probably forever forbid their living together upon the footing of perfect equality, and inasmuch as it becomes a necessity that there must be a difference, I, as well as Judge Douglas, am in favor of the race to which I belong having the superior position. I have never said anything to the contrary, but I hold that, notwithstanding all this, there is no reason in the world why the negro is not entitled to all the natural rights enumerated in the Declaration of Independence, the right to life, liberty, and the pursuit of happiness. I hold that he is as much entitled to these as the white man. I agree with Judge Douglas he is not my equal in many respects—certainly not in color, perhaps not in moral or intellectual endowment. But in the right to eat the bread, without the leave of anybody else, which his own hand earns, he is my equal and the equal of Judge Douglas, and the equal of every living man.

At Charleston in southern Illinois, Lincoln elaborated that he was "not in favor of negro citizenship," but he qualified that declaration by stating that, in his opinion, "different States have the power to make a negro a citizen under the Constitution of the United States, if they choose . . . if the State of Illinois had that power, I should be opposed to the exercise of it."[13] With this argument, Lincoln repudiated the proslavery logic of the *Dred Scott* decision, which denied that blacks could ever be citizens of the United States (most of the New England states had already given black men the right to vote), without adopting the abolitionist demand for black citizenship. In fact, he and Trumbull, a Democrat who had joined the Republican Party, refused to sign a petition to rescind Illinois's black laws presented by H. Ford Douglas, a black abolitionist and former slave from Virginia. This was Lincoln's public position on black rights on the eve of the Civil War, one that put him behind most abolitionists and radical Republicans. He deplored slavery and racism but refused to endorse abolition and black citizenship.

Clearly, racism is not an adequate explanation for Lincoln's antislavery moderation, even though it may explain why some northern whites found it easier to be free-soilers rather than abolitionists. Lincoln's antislavery position was grounded in his staunch belief in the Enlightenment ideals of universal individual natural rights enshrined in the Declaration of Independence and in the American experiment in representative government. He thus parsed natural versus political and civil rights for blacks, calling for the colonization of African Americans. Indeed, Lincoln's support for colonization could have arisen from his pessimism about the entrenched nature of racism in the United States. Whereas Garrisonian abolitionists developed a radical critique of the slaveholding republic, Lincoln's antislavery sentiment, like that of some political abolitionists and free-soilers, was grounded in redeeming the republic's founding revolutionary creed. It led Lincoln to reject nativism, which, like slavery and racism, he considered a species of despotism or tyranny. Lincoln complemented his theoretical commitment to natural equality with humanitarianism, protesting attempts to write blacks out of humanity or to consider them only as chattel, a sensibility he shared with abolitionists. Just as Lincoln was antislavery but not an abolitionist, he was an antiracist but not an advocate of black citizenship. His views on slavery and race were not opposed but complementary. It is not inconsequential or anachronistic to reconstruct Lincoln's views on race from the historical record, just as we have done with slavery, if for no other reason than to debunk the argument that Lincoln's alleged racism or a belief in racial inequality lay at the heart of his antislavery moderation.[14]

In the run-up to the 1860 presidential election, most Republicans went out of their way to portray themselves as members of the "white man's party" in an effort to appeal to the more conservative lower northern states. This made them suspect in the eyes of abolitionists. In his 1860 Cooper Union speech, "the speech that made Abraham Lincoln President," Lincoln distinguished the antislavery (nonextension) platform of the Republican Party, with its nebulous hope for slavery's "ultimate extinction," from abolitionist immediatism, especially John Brown's raid on Harpers Ferry. In this speech (which was not as conservative as is generally thought) Lincoln assured his audience that free-soilism was the antislavery program of the founders, involving the constitutional exercise of the powers of the federal government. Free-soilism was not abolition, but it could lead to the "extinction" of slavery by establishing a cordon sanitaire of freedom around it and slowly but surely choking it to death. While assuring slaveholders that he and the Republicans were not abolitionists, Lincoln made it clear that most northerners could not "be disinfected from all taint of opposition to slavery." Denying that the Republican Party was "sectional," he nonetheless addressed southerners as "you" and referred to the northern position with the pronouns "us" and "we." The Constitution, *pace* John C. Calhoun, Lincoln claimed, building on the arguments of political abolitionists and antislavery politicians, did not recognize property in slaves. It was southern slaveholders who defied the constitutional compact and the union between free and slave states by wanting to "overrun" the "National Territories" and the North. In an 1854 editorial against the Kansas-Nebraska Act, Lincoln had made the same argument in a more homely fashion: the land had been divided between John and Abraham. After running his side dry, Calhoun had taken down the fence and wanted his "herd of cattle" to have free run of Lincoln's meadow.[15]

Lincoln's Cooper Union speech highlighted the basic sectional divide pointed out in earlier, more radical speeches, including his own "House Divided" speech and William H. Seward's "The Irrepressible Conflict," delivered in 1858 in the abolitionist stronghold of Rochester, New York. Quoting the Gospels, as the Quaker abolitionist Thomas Genin had done thirty years earlier, Lincoln had announced, "A house divided against itself cannot stand. I believe this government cannot endure, permanently half *slave* and half *free*." Seward also underscored that the "two radically different political systems," one resting on slave labor and the other on free labor, were "incongruous" and "incompatible." Seward—who, like Lincoln, had made the journey from Whiggery to Republicanism—was known for his famous "Higher Law" speech against the Compromise of 1850. As governor of New York, Seward had supported black suffrage and opposed fugitive slave rendition.[16]

While Seward and Chase were seen as too radical for the Republican presidential nomination, Lincoln was acceptable to all factions of the party.[17] He shared the radicals' antislavery views, the moderates' reverence for the union and the Constitution, and the conservatives' pet project of colonization. But no matter how much Lincoln and other Republicans invoked the founders—especially Jefferson, the primary author of the Declaration of Independence and the 1787 Northwest Ordinance restricting the spread of slavery north of the Ohio River, and whose party's name they adopted—their antislavery position was an implicit repudiation of the founders' political project: the union of free and slave states. Even before the war, Lincoln expected that the union would be remade, either all slave or all free. Appropriating the mantle of the revolutionary generation, Lincoln and the Republican Party pointed the way to the destruction of slavery and the remaking of the American republic. In the end, Lincoln's attempt to reconcile antislavery with the union and the Constitution failed. Most southern slaveholders did not appreciate the constitutional nature of the

Republicans' nonextension platform, nor did most abolitionists, radical Republicans, and African Americans believe that racial separation or colonization was the ideal solution to the race problem. During the Civil War and Reconstruction the union and the Constitution would be remade along antislavery lines, with abolition, equal protection of the law regardless of race or previous condition of servitude, and black voting inscribed into the Constitution with the Thirteenth, Fourteenth, and Fifteenth Amendments. This was not the union and the Constitution of the founders but an abolitionist conception of them. Neither Lincoln nor most of his contemporaries could have foreseen that result, as only the "fanatical" abolitionists had asked all along that the union and the Constitution be remade along antislavery lines.

The origins of this constitutional transformation lay in the sectional debate over the nature of the Constitution and its relationship to slavery. Most slaveholders insisted on a literal interpretation of the Constitution, a secular parallel to their fundamentalist reading of the Bible, in order to defend slavery and render it immune to political or moral criticism. Proslavery constitutionalism was based on a rigid defense of states' rights and on a strict construction of the Constitution developed by planter-politicians, most preeminently by Calhoun since South Carolina's nullification of the federal tariff laws. Even slaveholders' and their northern allies' use of the repressive powers of the state to realize the goals of proslavery imperialism— whether for waging war in the Mexican and Seminole Wars, planning to acquire Cuba and Central America, or implementing the federal fugitive slave law (on whose enforcement mechanisms, ironically, Trumbull modeled the 1866 Civil Rights Act)—did not shake this parochial, antistatist, conservative political tradition. Conversely, abolitionists and antislavery politicians, even when resorting to the southern gospel of states' rights to oppose the federal fugitive slave law, strove to interpret the Constitution for antislavery purposes and evoked the power of the state to dislodge the entrenched position of slaveholders in the federal government and union—the "slave power."[18]

Abolitionists evoked the spirit of both the Bible and the Constitution as essentially antislavery. In the 1830s abolitionist Theodore Dwight Weld authored two books on the antislavery nature of the Bible and the constitutionality of abolition. In *The Power of Congress over the District of Columbia* (1838) Weld did not simply assert the constitutional power of the federal government to abolish slavery in areas where it had jurisdiction; he also made a broader argument for abolition by law. Marshaling the opinions of the founders and the political history of the young republic, Weld argued that slavery could be abolished by legislative authority, as it had been in the northern states, or by Congress, as in the case of the Northwest Ordinance and the abolition of the African slave trade. Weld contended that slavery had been brought into existence by "*statute law*," not common law, which, with its proclivity for freedom, was "the grand element of the Constitution." Since slavery was a legal system, a "creature of legislation," it could be abolished by it. In rejecting the idea that legislative abolition was barred by the constitutional sanction against the confiscation of property without due process, Weld was upholding not the bourgeois sanctity of property but the abolitionist notion that there could be no property in human beings. With perfect abolitionist logic, and presciently anticipating the Civil War, he argued that the federal government could constitutionally abolish slavery and that it owed slaves protection from their masters in return for their allegiance. Weld also researched the "rights of colored citizens under the US Constitution," insisting, like most abolitionists, that the Constitution's privileges and immunities clause applied to free African Americans, who were, after all, citizens of the northern states. From the narrow question of DC abolition, Weld made a case for black rights based on the abolitionist premise that African Americans were citizens.[19]

This was much further than Lincoln was willing to go before the Civil War. Weld's argument was far broader and more radical than antislavery constitutionalism, whose abolitionist roots extended beyond Weld's treatise. Abolitionist constitutionalism justified emancipation by the state and argued for the civil and political rights that were denied to most African Americans. It was reinforced by northern free blacks' demands and struggles for citizenship rights. Abolitionists also developed their constitutional ideas in fugitive slave court cases and by lobbying for northern state laws to ensure due process for free blacks and suspected fugitives. The abolitionist project was never just a matter of getting rid of slavery; it was always intended to establish black citizenship. Whatever their personal beliefs and interactions, most abolitionists of all factions—political, evangelical, and Garrisonian—subscribed to this programmatic commitment to racial equality.[20]

Unlike Lincoln, then, abolitionists insisted that African Americans were entitled to not just the universal natural rights of the Declaration but also the civil liberties enumerated in the Bill of Rights. Political abolitionist Alvan Stewart, for instance, argued that the Constitution's guarantees of citizenship, which were violated by slavery, allowed the federal government to abolish slavery in the southern states. Stewart pronounced slavery unconstitutional on the basis of the Fifth Amendment, which stipulated that no person could be deprived of life, liberty, and property without the due process of law. A lawyer and one of the founders of the Liberty Party, Stewart urged in "A Constitutional Argument on the Subject of Slavery" that the federal government ought to abolish slavery to fulfill the constitutional guarantee of republican government in the southern states and in accordance with the general welfare. Stewart died in 1849, and although free-soilers rejected his constitutional views, he influenced radical political abolitionists such as Gerrit Smith, William Goodell, and, after his break with the Garrisonians, Frederick Douglass. Similarly, Massachusetts lawyer and political abolitionist G. W. F. Mellen's 400-page book, published in 1841, detailed the history of the republic and debates in the constitutional and state conventions and argued for the unconstitutionality of slavery. Anticipating the 1857 *Dred Scott* decision, Mellen wrote that if the country's "courts decide that the descendants of Africa are to be thrown out of all government protection," then it would be better for "these United States to be broken up at once ... we saw no object in their Union."[21]

Mellen's conclusion merited praise from Garrison, whose followers argued that the Constitution's clauses protecting slavery made it unsalvageable. In 1839–1840 the abolition movement was torn by a schism between political and evangelical abolitionists and the Garrisonians. The emergence of political abolitionism forced Garrison and his allies to develop their own stance on politics, often mischaracterized as an outdated adherence to moral suasion or as apolitical. Rejecting electoral politics, Garrisonians developed a politics of agitation and a transnational commitment to radical reform that questioned the very foundations of the slaveholding republic. The fugitive slave controversy played a crucial role in Garrison's rejection of a proslavery union and Constitution. In 1842 the US Supreme Court declared in *Prigg v. Pennsylvania* that the northern personal liberty laws that gave free blacks and suspected fugitives certain legal protections were unconstitutional. That year, Garrison announced his doctrine of disunion in the *Liberator*, stating, "a repeal of the Union between northern liberty and southern slavery is essential to the abolition of one, and preservation of the other." For Garrisonians, disunionism was a concerted attack on slaveholders' political power and not a retreat into inaction. By 1844, the official policy of the Garrison-led American Anti-Slavery Society (AASS) became "no union with slaveholders." The union Garrison referred to in his "Address to the Friends of Freedom and Emancipation in the United States" had been bought "*at the expense of the colored population of the country*." Garrison had expected opposition to such a "bold" and "revolutionary" step, but he argued that in advocating disunion, the AASS had taken "the highest possible ground" against slavery. In 1846, unknown to most historians, Garrison used the words of black abolitionist clergyman James W. C. Pennington—ironically, a man associated with the political and evangelical wing of the abolition movement—to denounce the Constitution in biblical terms as "a covenant with death" and "an agreement with hell."[22]

Wendell Phillips, a lawyer by education, presented the full-blown Garrisonian case in *The Constitution, a Pro-Slavery Compact* (1844). Mining James Madison's notes on the Constitutional Convention debates (which had been published in 1840) to prove the founding fathers' intent to protect slavery, Phillips concluded that the Constitution was an "infamous" bargain that proved "the melancholy fact" that "our fathers bartered honesty for gain, and became partners with tyrants, that they might profit from their tyranny"—a radical abolitionist indictment of the sacrosanct liberty-loving reputation of the founders. A year later, in "Can Abolitionists Vote or Take Office under the United States Constitution?" Phillips argued that the AASS's opposition to a proslavery government and laws should not be mistaken as endorsing a "no government" or nonresistant position. It had simply judged all institutions, no matter how "venerable," by the "touchstone of anti-slavery principle" and found them wanting.[23] This was precisely the kind of exercise that Lincoln and other men of antislavery sentiment were not willing to undertake; instead, they submerged their qualms—or, as Lincoln put it, "crucified their feelings"—to preserve the slaveholding republic at the expense of black freedom and rights.

The political abolitionist platform—especially that of the radical minority, which insisted that the federal government had the power to abolish slavery in the southern states—proved to be just as unacceptable to Lincoln and to antislavery politicians like him. William Goodell's *Views of American Constitutional Law, in Its Bearing upon American Slavery* (1844) and Massachusetts lawyer Lysander Spooner's *The Unconstitutionality of Slavery* (1845) were the lengthiest expositions of that position. Goodell's book began with the deceptively simple premise that the American government and Constitution cannot be viewed as "neutral" or even only "partial" on the subject of slavery; they must be either completely for or against liberty, as even a slight toleration of slavery would endanger all liberty. If they were proslavery, then abolitionists would have the option of the "right to revolution" or submission. Employing slaveholders' cherished method of strict construction, Goodell argued that the Constitution did not recognize slavery, since slavery reduced human beings to chattel, property, things, and the Constitution alluded only to "persons." Moreover, the democratic "spirit" of the Constitution was antislavery, with its positive exhortations on liberty and rights, like the spirit of English common law, the Declaration, and the New Testament, although it did not include specific abolitionist injunctions. According to Goodell, all antislavery men need not be republicans, but all republicans must be antislavery. In a public letter to John G. Whittier, Gerrit Smith called the Constitution "a noble and beautiful temple of liberty" based on the defense of human rights that had simply been perverted to proslavery ends. Even the three-fifths clause, he predicted, calling for political action, could not prevent a northern majority from electing an antislavery government.[24]

Similarly, according to Spooner, all law, especially fundamental constitutional law, must be based on principles of natural rights and justice. The fact that the African slave trade and slavery were "tolerated" in the American colonies was no argument for their legality. Making a historical argument, Spooner wrote that slavery was not recognized in either the state constitutions or the Articles of Confederation, and if slavery did not have a "constitutional existence" earlier, it certainly did not under the Constitution, which recognized all people, including blacks, as "citizens." Like Goodell, Spooner argued that the Constitution recognized only persons and not chattel; persons held to service were referred to as servants, not slaves. Furthermore, the preamble applied to all the people of the United States, not just whites or free people, as citizens of the country. Despite the "arrogant" and "bombastic" claims of slaveholders, the only guarantee in the Constitution concerned not slavery but a republican form of government, which slavery contravened. Despite the "practice" of the US government, the Constitution was based on the principles of the "rights of man" and republicanism, and it did not sanction slavery. Spooner concluded that the antislavery nature of the Constitution guaranteed that all the children of slaves were born free and ought to be freed immediately by federal judges. In his 1847 review of Spooner's book, Phillips proceeded to dismantle each one of his historical and constitutional arguments but ended with genuine admiration for their "ingenuity."[25] Political abolitionists' liberal interpretation of the Constitution influenced northern antislavery politicians, even though the latter rejected calls for the immediate abolition of slavery by the federal government.

Antislavery constitutional theory emerged from the abolitionist debate on the relationship of slavery to the Constitution. It built on the abolitionist idea that slavery was the creature of positive state law and in contravention to English common law, natural law, and the Constitution. Most antislavery constitutionalists evoked the Somerset principle from 1772, which did not recognize slavery if it was not instituted by local laws. The person who best developed the concept of "constitutional antislavery" was Ohio lawyer-politician Salmon P. Chase, who joined the Liberty Party in 1841 and became an advocate of broadening its appeal in the North. Chase worked to convince northerners of the constitutionality of the antislavery political project. For the average northern citizen who, like Lincoln, revered the union and the Constitution, the Garrisonian position was anathema. However, unlike radical political abolitionists, and conceding a lot of ground to the Garrisonians, Chase argued that although the Constitution protected slavery in the southern states, the founders had been antislavery because they visualized an end to slavery. He contended that the founding principles of the country and the Constitution made it the duty of the federal government to act against slavery in areas under its exclusive control, including the District of Columbia and the federal territories, as well as to intervene in the interstate slave trade and even in the rendition of fugitive slaves. His notion of the "divorce" of the federal government from slavery was incorporated into the Liberty Party platform of 1844, and his slogan espousing the "Denationalization of Slavery" or Sumner's "Freedom National" became the rallying cry of the Free-Soil Party four years later. On the eve of the Civil War, when the Republican Party swept into power, Chase could point out that a majority of northerners believed that "the general government has the power to prohibit slavery everywhere outside of the slave States."[26] It was perhaps appropriate that this intrepid promoter of antislavery politics and constitutional theory ended his career as chief justice of the Supreme Court, appointed by Lincoln to replace Roger Taney, author of the *Dred Scott* decision and the personification of proslavery constitutionalism.

Chase advocated the broadening—some would argue the diluting—of the abolitionist platform as a formula for political success in the North. With the rise of the sectional controversy over the expansion of slavery after the Mexican War and the Kansas wars, his acolytes would win the day in the Republican Party. The so-called federal consensus that the federal government could abolish slavery in areas under its jurisdiction and prevent its expansion, but that it lacked the constitutional power to abolish slavery in the southern states, owed its existence to Chase. This position sought to counter an increasingly aggressive proslavery constitutional theory that challenged the ability of the federal government to legislate on any matter concerning slavery directly or indirectly. The Calhounian states' rights position was an unprecedented demand for state sovereignty that made a mockery of federalism, strict construction, and states' rights when it came to implementing proslavery demands. In the 1850s, when Lower South planter-politicians started flirting with secession, a federal slave code, the reopening of the Atlantic slave trade, and extralegal military expeditions to Central America and Cuba and considered challenging the enumerated powers of the federal government and the principles of democratic governance, antislavery politicians such as Chase, Sumner, Lincoln, and even Seward (of "higher law" fame) could claim to have the Constitution and the rule of law on their side.[27]

Unlike abolition, restricting the extension of slavery proved to be a winning political formula because it was viewed as the constitutionally legitimate position, established by the precedents of the Northwest Ordinance of 1787 and the constitutionally permissible prohibition of the African slave trade in 1808. It was precisely the kind of antislavery program that moderates and northern Whigs like Lincoln could subscribe to without jeopardizing their loyalty to the union and the Constitution. The Free-Soil and Republican Parties also jettisoned the abolitionist commitment to equal rights for African Americans in their platforms. Leading radicals with roots in the abolition movement, however, defended suspected fugitives and sought to remove all political and civil obstacles to black citizenship. Chase represented so many fugitive slaves that he earned a silver pitcher from Cincinnati's black community. Sumner's close ties with Boston's free black community and local abolitionist struggles such as the desegregation of the public school system set him on the path to becoming the preeminent congressional champion of black political and civil rights during Reconstruction. When Seward alluded to a "higher law" during debates over the Compromise of 1850, he evoked the abolitionist demand to judge all man-made laws according to an antislavery standard based on divine and natural law and alarmed northern conservatives and moderates. For radicals, antislavery was always the ruling element of their politics, whereas for Lincoln and other moderates, it was simply one among several competing and sometimes conflicting values. Sumner, for instance, refused to recognize the constitutionality of the Fugitive Slave Act of 1850. In his maiden antislavery speech on the law, "Freedom National, Slavery Sectional," he claimed it violated the rights of African American citizens. For Sumner, the antislavery cause took precedence over reverence for the Constitution and compromises with slaveholders to preserve the union; for Lincoln, it did not.[28]

In the decade before the Civil War, despite the growing popularity of free-soil politics, abolitionist constitutionalism did not disappear. It lived on in the ideas of the radical Republicans as well as in the continuing debate between Garrisonians and political abolitionists on the nature of the Constitution. Garrison famously burned copies of the Constitution, the fugitive slave law, and the decision of the federal commissioner ordering the rendition of the runaway slave Anthony Burns in 1854, shocking moderate antislavery men. Abolitionists and their radical allies united to oppose the implementation of the fugitive slave law in northern streets, legislatures, and courts as a gross violation of black citizenship rights and the due process of law. Lincoln and moderate antislavery men, in contrast, stressed the federal restriction on the expansion of slavery as the constitutionally permissible way to provide for the "ultimate extinction of slavery" in the American republic.

The most innovative constitutional theorist of this era, however, was not Lincoln or any of the other politically prominent Republicans. It was former slave and great black abolitionist Frederick Douglass. By 1851, Douglass disavowed his Garrisonian belief that the Constitution protected slavery and, like his new mentor Gerrit Smith, argued that it was antislavery in spirit. Like most political abolitionists, Douglass combined a literal reading of the nation's founding legal document, which mentioned neither slavery nor slaves, with the abolitionist insistence that constitutional guarantees of citizenship rights included African Americans. But he went further. Douglass held that the original intent of its framers, many of whom were slaveholders, was irrelevant. This claim was bold and sacrilegious in the context of nineteenth-century American constitutionalism, when both slaveholding southern politicians and antislavery northern politicians regularly sought to enlist the founders on their side of the sectional conflict. Instead, Douglass, anticipating modern constitutional theorists, argued that the Constitution was a living document whose democratic promise must be extended by subsequent generations. As Douglass put it in a speech that was later published as a pamphlet titled *The Constitution of the United States: Is It Pro-Slavery or Anti-Slavery?* slaveholders had given the Constitution a "proslavery interpretation," but the Constitution "will afford slavery no protection when it shall cease to be administered by slaveholders." The real purpose of abolitionist constitutionalism was not simply to stay true to the Constitution or the intent of its framers, he believed, but to use it for antislavery purposes. Douglass invoked the founding generation and its ideals, but in the matter of constitutional interpretation, he asked his and future generations to imagine both abolition and black citizenship.[29] By refusing to be held hostage to the intent of the Constitution's framers, Douglass went well beyond contemporary constitutional debates over slavery and anticipated its remaking. In short, he imagined an interracial democracy in the United States and the overthrow of the lily-white slaveholding republic. In this sense, both the Garrisonians and the radical political abolitionists such as Douglass shared common goals, although they squabbled over the means of achieving them. In the end, both were proved right. Slavery was abolished through state action, but in the midst of the enormous bloodletting of the Civil War, a covenant with death indeed.

During the revolutionary crisis generated by secession and war, Lincoln's competing political loyalties to antislavery, the union, and the Constitution became compatible. The slaveholders' rebellion solved the problem for him. Lincoln adhered to antislavery moderation with great tenacity upon his election to the presidency and after the secession of the Lower South states, refusing to compromise on nonextension but disavowing any intention to "interfere" with or abolish slavery in the South. It is worth noting that when Lincoln refused to compromise on nonextension, he privileged his antislavery convictions above the union. In his annual message to Congress on December 3, 1861, Lincoln said he hoped the Civil War "shall not degenerate into a violent and remorseless revolutionary struggle against slavery." He also recommended colonizing blacks to "some place, or places, in a climate congenial to them." During the first year of the war, Lincoln proposed gradual, compensated emancipation to the border states and continued to recommend colonization. Abolitionists criticized Lincoln's slowness to act on emancipation and his support for colonization. Congress stole a march on the president by passing two confiscation acts that allowed for the confiscation of all slaves used for military purposes by the Confederacy and all slaves of rebel slaveholders. It also passed a militia act that addressed the recruitment of black men in the Union army. Hundreds of slaves defected to Union army lines, seeing the president and the army as their liberators before they saw themselves in that role.[30]

Within little more than a year, the war became a revolutionary war against slavery—the "Second American Revolution." In 1863 the president issued the Emancipation Proclamation, which immediately abolished slavery in the areas under the Confederacy, and the Union army marched to the tune of "John Brown's Body." Lincoln's proclamation urged all freed slaves to "labor faithfully for reasonable wages" and "to abstain from violence, unless in necessary self-defense." While the first admonition was central to Lincoln's ideas about free labor, the second was the same rationale abolitionists and fugitive slaves had employed in resisting the rendition of runaways under the federal law. Lincoln did not move from union to abolition, as is commonly argued, even though he explicitly called for preservation of the union at the start of the war; he moved from antislavery to abolition. In 1862, after Lincoln had already made the decision to issue the Emancipation Proclamation, his famous reply to Horace Greeley's demand for abolition explained his long-standing antislavery moderation. By his Second Inaugural address, however, Lincoln gave words to the abolitionist conception of the war as divine chastisement for the nation's crime of slavery. Remembered chiefly for the platitude "with malice toward none, with charity for all," in that address he stated more eloquently: "Fondly do we hope—fervently do we hope—that this mighty scourge of war may speedily pass away. Yet if God wills that it continue, until all the wealth piled by the bondsman's two hundred and fifty years of unrequited toil shall be sunk, and until every drop of blood drawn by the lash, shall be paid by another drawn by the sword, as was said three thousand years ago, so still it must be said 'the judgments of the Lord are true and righteous altogether.'"[31] According to Douglass, who had met Lincoln, it was a "sacred effort."[32]

The war allowed Lincoln to finally align his commitment to the union and the Constitution with abolition. Emancipation, Lincoln stated, was "the central act of my administration, and the great event of the nineteenth century." For Lincoln, antislavery, union, and Constitution went from being competing to complementary values, thanks to the slaveholders' rebellion. The manner in which Lincoln issued the proclamation, as a military necessity and evoking his war powers, ensured that its constitutional bona fides would not be challenged. He also revoked the emancipation orders issued by Generals Frémont and Hunter, who had overstepped their constitutional authority in initiating emancipation, since only Lincoln, as commander in chief of the Union army, had the authority to do that. This did not prevent Democratic copperheads, northern conservatives, and racists, not to mention southern slaveholders and Confederates, from accusing Lincoln of treason to the Constitution and the union. It nearly cost him the presidency in 1864. It was not clear at that moment whether emancipation would further divide the nation rather than save and unite it. Lincoln's battle to secure passage of the Thirteenth Amendment was a testimony to his determination to embed abolition in the Constitution and make it irreversible.[33]

The key to understanding Lincoln's cautious move toward emancipation lies in his attempt to balance his antislavery views with his sworn duty, as president of the United States, to uphold the union and the Constitution. Lincoln's constitutionalism was the source of both his antislavery moderation before the war and the manner in which he promulgated emancipation during it. It shaped his various proposals for compensated, gradual emancipation; the form and content of the final Emancipation Proclamation; his advocacy of the Thirteenth Amendment; and, finally, his support for limited black citizenship. Every step the president took toward emancipation and black rights, however, made antislavery the dominant principle of his politics and brought him ever closer to abolitionist ground. Emancipation gave the Civil War greater meaning and purpose than a war for simply the union.[34] For Lincoln, abolition and union became complementary values, but he understood that this "new birth of freedom" necessitated a transformation of the Constitution and the union.

Although radical Republicans composed the antislavery vanguard of their party, it would be a mistake to view Republicanism as abolitionism writ large. It was Lincoln rather than the radicals who represented the large group of moderates who defined the mainstream Republican position on slavery and the Constitution on the eve of the Civil War. Only the wartime emergency and the actions of the enslaved themselves convinced the president as well as the nation to redefine the union and the Constitution on antislavery terms. It helped, of course, that in the winter and spring of 1860–1861 a majority of the slave states had destroyed the union and challenged the Constitution. At the start of the war, Lincoln's proposal for gradual, compensated emancipation to the border states was characteristic of his attempt to balance his antislavery views with his support for the union and the Constitution. By uncoupling slavery from the union and the Constitution—a political reality the border states fiercely and obdurately sought to deny—the war allowed Lincoln and the Republican Party to act on antislavery principle. It allowed them to become emancipationists if not abolitionists.

During the debates over emancipation, abolitionists and radicals such as Sumner evoked John Quincy Adams and urged Lincoln to use his war powers for emancipation. Adams, who had led the long fight against the gagging of abolitionist petitions, had pointed out that during a military emergency, the president could employ his war powers to constitutionally abolish slavery. Lincoln had revoked Frémont's and Hunter's wartime emancipation orders not because he thought military emancipation was unconstitutional but because he thought the two generals lacked the constitutional authority to enact emancipation. Only he, as president and commander in chief, could take that step. The Union's contraband policy, invented by that consummate lawyer-politician General Benjamin F. Butler, and the confiscation acts justified confiscating the property of enemy combatants under the laws of warfare, an idea that Alexander Hamilton had first defended during the Revolutionary War. Ironically, in the aftermath of the War of 1812, Adams had fought for the restoration of or compensation for slaves as private property from the British. During the Civil War, antislavery lawyer William Whiting popularized the notion that the president could use his war powers to promulgate emancipation as an act of war. As solicitor in the War Department, Whiting would also argue that black soldiers were entitled to the rights of citizenship. German political thinker and professor Francis Lieber codified the freeing and arming of former slaves in his code of war written for the Union army. Lieber encoded an axiom of abolitionist constitutionalism, missing from the laws of war until then, that slavery had no existence in "the law of nature and nations" and that it existed only in "municipal law." Moreover, the slaves of enemy belligerents were defined as free persons, and to return them would be tantamount to enslaving free men. Lincoln had called on armed black men to put down the slaveholders' rebellion, and Lieber's code reiterated that "the law of nations knows no distinction of color." The military nature of emancipation—immediate, uncompensated, and based on a recognition of the rights of the enslaved—was the fruit of abolitionist constitutionalism. "Lincoln's code," as it related to emancipation and black Union soldiers, was abolitionist even though Lieber was not an abolitionist. In his retaliatory order responding to the Confederacy's enslavement of black prisoners of war, Lincoln's words were reminiscent of Sumner's 1860 abolitionist speech, "The Barbarism of Slavery." He called that policy a "relapse into barbarism."[35]

The wartime demand for black military service was led by the radical governor of Massachusetts, John Andrew, and others who took the initiative and formed black regiments. Lincoln's proclamation allowed for the arming of black men and their recruitment into the Union army. This provision, more than anything else, helped convert the Civil War into a revolutionary war that paved the way for black citizenship. The enlistment of black men, supported and led by abolitionists, raised the question of racial equality as black soldiers and their abolitionist and radical allies successfully fought for equal pay and access to the officer ranks. Even though black soldiers fought in segregated units, the value that Lincoln attached to their military service helped him move toward the idea of black citizenship. In 1863 he wrote that black Union soldiers could aspire to the ideal of American citizenship better than white secessionists and copperheads. When peace arrives, "there will be some black men who can remember that, with silent tongues, and clenched teeth, and steady eye, and well-poised bayonet, they have helped mankind onto this great consummation; while, I fear, there will be some white ones, unable to forget that, with malignant heart, and deceitful speech, they have strove to hinder it."[36]

Not surprisingly, the issue of black rights and citizenship, long held in abeyance, now made a comeback. Criticized by abolitionists and radicals for his wartime Reconstruction plans that did not include black political or civil rights, and having received delegations of southern blacks demanding the right to vote, Lincoln made his last pronouncements on the subject of black citizenship just before his death. In a letter to Louisiana's military governor, Michael Hahn, he suggested that "the very intelligent, and especially those who have fought gallantly in our ranks" be given the franchise. It would help, "in some trying time to come, to keep the jewel of liberty within the family of freedom." In a speech on Reconstruction in Louisiana, Lincoln argued that he would "prefer" it if suffrage were conferred on the "very intelligent" and "those who serve our cause as soldiers." He stated the same preference informally from the balcony of the White House to a crowd gathered below. In the audience was John Wilkes Booth, the Confederate sympathizer and actor who had pledged to kill the president for his championship of "nigger citizenship." He claimed this was the last speech Lincoln would ever make.

Lincoln's antislavery views at the end of his life encompassed black rights and citizenship, issues he had shied away from or explicitly repudiated before the war. With the failure of his many wartime colonization schemes, and no doubt in response to the goading and criticisms of abolitionists and radicals in his own party, Lincoln moved toward an acceptance of black citizenship. As late as 1862, Lincoln had touted colonization during his meeting with Washington's black leaders, whom he had summoned to the White House, and in his annual message to Congress. Black abolitionist orator and writer Frances Ellen Watkins Harper wrote trenchantly, "while we admit the right of every man to choose his home, . . . we neither see the wisdom nor expediency of our self-exportation from a land which has in great measure [been] enriched by our toil for generations, til we have a birthright on the soil, and the strongest claim on the nation for that justice and equity which has been withheld from us for ages." Not just black protest and coolness to his propositions but also the military service of black soldiers in the Union army finally convinced Lincoln to give up on colonization and endorse black citizenship. As H. Ford Douglas put it, "This war will educate Mr. Lincoln out of his idea of the deportation of the Negro."[37]

Every step the president took toward emancipation and black rights, however, made antislavery the dominant principle of his politics and brought him closer to abolitionist ground. As he came to accept partial black voting, Lincoln moved toward the abolitionist standard of racial equality. It is highly likely that he would have continued on that antislavery trajectory had he lived, rather than reversed that momentum, as his successor Andrew Johnson attempted. The agenda of radical Reconstruction—black citizenship—fueled by the refusal of former slaveholders to accept the results of emancipation, had long roots in abolitionist constitutionalism. After the fall of Reconstruction in 1877, reunion and a narrow reading of the Constitution would once again eclipse antislavery principles. It is safe to conclude that although Abraham Lincoln had finally resolved his competing loyalties to the union, the Constitution, and antislavery, the American nation had yet to do so.

NOTES

1. Roy P. Basler, ed., *The Collected Works of Abraham Lincoln*, 9 vols. (New Brunswick, NJ: Rutgers University Press, 1953–1955), 5:492 (hereafter cited as *Collected Works*); Sean Wilentz, *The Rise of American Democracy: Jefferson to Lincoln* (New York: W. W. Norton, 2005), 783. For some of the best iterations of this theme, see John Burt, *Lincoln's Tragic Pragmatism: Lincoln, Douglas, and Moral Conflict* (Cambridge, MA: Harvard University Press, 2013); William Lee Miller, *Lincoln's Virtues: An Ethical Biography* (New York: Vintage, 2002); William Lee Miller, *President Lincoln: The Duty of a Statesman* (New York: Knopf, 2008); Richard Striner, *Father Abraham: Lincoln's Relentless Struggle to End Slavery* (New York: Oxford University Press, 2006); Doris Kearns Goodwin, *Team of Rivals: The Political Genius of Abraham Lincoln* (New York: Simon & Schuster, 2005); Richard J. Carwardine, *Lincoln: Profiles in Power* (London: Longman, 2003); Allen C. Guelzo, *Abraham Lincoln, Redeemer President* (Grand Rapids, MI: Wm. B. Eerdmans, 1999); and Allen C. Guelzo, *Abraham Lincoln: A Man of Ideas* (Carbondale: Northern Illinois University Press, 2009).

2. Allen C. Guelzo, *Lincoln's Emancipation Proclamation: The End of Slavery in America* (New York: Simon & Schuster, 2004), 17–28. See the debate in Andrew Delbanco, with commentary by John Stauffer, Manisha Sinha, Darryl Pinckney, and Wilfred M. McClay, *The Abolitionist Imagination* (Cambridge, MA: Harvard University Press, 2012).

3. For Lincoln in the context of antislavery and abolition, see James Oakes, *The Radical and the Republican: Frederick Douglass, Abraham Lincoln and the Triumph of Antislavery Politics* (New York: W. W. Norton, 2007); Paul Kendrick and Stephen Kendrick, *Douglass and Lincoln: How a Revolutionary Black Leader and a Reluctant Liberator Struggled to End Slavery and Save the Union* (New York: Walker, 2007); John Stauffer, *Giants: The Parallel Lives of Frederick Douglass and Abraham Lincoln* (New York: Twelve, 2008); Eric Foner, *The Fiery Trial: Abraham Lincoln and American Slavery* (New York: W. W. Norton, 2010); Manisha Sinha, "Allies for Emancipation: Lincoln and Black Abolitionists," in *Our Lincoln: New Perspectives on Lincoln and His World*, ed. Eric Foner (New York: W. W. Norton, 2008), 166–196.

4. *Collected Works*, 7:281. Compare Michael Lind, *What Lincoln Believed: The Values and Convictions of America's Greatest President* (New York: Anchor, 2004).

5. See, for example, Richard Brookhiser, *Founder's Son: A Life of Abraham Lincoln* (New York: Basic Books, 2014).

6. David M. Potter, *The Impending Crisis, 1848–1861*, ed. Don E. Fehrenbacher (New York: Harper Perennial, 1976), 44–45; Dorothy Ross, "Lincoln and the Ethics of Emancipation: Universalism, Nationalism, and Exceptionalism," *Journal of American History* 96 (September 2009): 379–399.

7. Mark E. Neely Jr., *The Last Best Hope of Earth: Abraham Lincoln and the Promise of America* (Cambridge, MA: Harvard University Press, 1993), 34; *Collected Works*, 1:74–76; Foner, *Fiery Trial*, 25–28.

8. Brian Dirck, *Lincoln the Lawyer* (Urbana: University of Illinois Press, 2007); Foner, *Fiery Trial*, 43–51; *Liberator*, June 22, 1860.

9. Don E. Fehrenbacher, *Prelude to Greatness: Lincoln in the 1850s* (Stanford, CA: Stanford University Press, 1962); *Collected Works*, 2:247–283, Lewis E. Lehrman, *Lincoln at Peoria: The Turning Point* (Mechanicsburg, PA: Stackpole, 2008).

10. *Collected Works*, 2:404. I am grateful to Mike Thelwell for alerting me to this quotation a long time ago. See also Foner, *Fiery Trial*, 66.

11. *Collected Works*, 2:255–256, 323, 409, 7:281; Eric Foner, "Lincoln and Colonization," in Foner, *Our Lincoln*, 138–150; Lerone Bennett Jr., *Forced into Glory: Abraham Lincoln's White Dream* (Chicago: Johnson Publishing, 2000); George M. Fredrickson, *Big Enough to Be Inconsistent: Abraham Lincoln Confronts Slavery and Race* (Cambridge, MA: Harvard University Press, 2008); Henry Louis Gates Jr., ed., introduction to *Lincoln on Race and Slavery* (Princeton, NJ: Princeton University Press, 2009); Brian R. Dirck, ed., *Lincoln Emancipated: The President and the Politics of Race* (De Kalb: Northern Illinois University Press, 2007).

12. *Collected Works*, 2:405, 409; Don E. Fehrenbacher and Virginia Fehrenbacher, eds., *Recollected Words of Abraham Lincoln, 1832–1865* (Stanford, CA: Stanford University Press, 1996), 198, 303.

13. *Collected Works*, 2:501, 3:16, 179; James Oakes, "Natural Rights, Citizenship Rights, States' Rights, and Black Rights: Another Look at Lincoln and Race," in Foner, *Our Lincoln*, 109–134.

14. *Collected Works*, 2:409. For the argument that Lincoln supported black citizenship even before the war, see Burt, *Lincoln's Tragic Pragmatism*; for the opposing extreme, see Lind, *What Lincoln Believed*. Also see Brian R. Dirck, *Abraham Lincoln and White America* (Lawrence: University Press of Kansas, 2012).

15. *Collected Works*, 3:522–550, 2:230; Harold Holzer, *Lincoln at Cooper Union: The Speech that Made Abraham Lincoln President* (New York: Simon & Schuster, 2004); James Oakes, *The Scorpion's Sting: Antislavery and the Coming of the Civil War* (New York: W. W. Norton, 2014).

16. *An Oration Delivered before the Semi-Annual Meeting of the Union Humane Society . . . by Thos. H. Genin, Esq.* (Mount Pleasant, OH, 1818); *Collected Works*, 2:461; *The Irrepressible Conflict, a Speech by William H. Seward Delivered at Rochester, Monday, Oct 25, 1858* (New York, n.d.), 1–2.

17. Douglas R. Egerton, *Year of Meteors: Stephen Douglas, Abraham Lincoln and the Election that Brought on the Civil War* (New York: Bloomsbury, 2010), chap. 1.

18. On slaveholders' constitutionalism, see Manisha Sinha, *The Counterrevolution of Slavery: Politics and Ideology in Antebellum South Carolina* (Chapel Hill: University of North Carolina Press, 2000). Compare David Ericson, *Slavery in the American Republic: Developing the Federal Government, 1791–1861* (Lawrence: University Press of Kansas, 2011).

19. Theodore Weld, *The Power of Congress over the District of Columbia* (New York, 1838), 3, 15–16, 39–47; Gilbert H. Barnes and Dwight L. Dumond, eds., *Letters of Theodore Weld and Angelina Grimke Weld and Sarah Grimke, 1822–1844*, vol. 2 (Gloucester, MA: Peter Smith, 1965), 923, 954–955, 958. On Weld, see Robert Abzug, *Passionate Liberator: Theodore Dwight Weld and the Dilemma of Reform* (New York: Oxford University Press, 1980).

20. For this argument, see Manisha Sinha, *The Slave's Cause: A History of Abolition* (New Haven, CT: Yale University Press, 2016). Also see William M. Wiecek, *The Sources of Antislavery Constitutionalism in America, 1760–1848* (Ithaca, NY: Cornell University Press, 1977); Robert M. Cover, *Justice Accused: Antislavery and the Judicial Process* (New Haven, CT: Yale University Press, 1975); Thomas D. Morris, *Free Men All: The Personal Liberty Laws of the North, 1780–1861* (Baltimore: Johns Hopkins University Press, 1974); Paul Finkelman, *An Imperfect Union: Slavery, Federalism, and Comity* (Chapel Hill: University of North Carolina Press, 1981); Steven Lubet, *Fugitive Justice: Runaways, Rescuers, and Slavery on Trial* (Cambridge, MA: Harvard University Press, 2010).

21. Alvan Stewart, "A Constitutional Argument on the Subject of Slavery," in Jacobus Ten Broek, *Equality under Law* (New York: Collier, 1965), 281–295; G. W. F. Mellen, *An Argument on the Unconstitutionality of Slavery: Embracing an Abstract on the Proceedings of the National and State Conventions on This Subject* (Boston: Saxton & Pierce, 1841), 4–6, 433; Frederick J. Blue, *No Taint of Compromise: Crusaders in Antislavery Politics* (Baton Rouge: Louisiana State University Press, 2005), 20–21, 30–36.

22. *Liberator*, February 25, 1842, 29; April 22, 1842, 63; April 29, 1842, 65; May 13, 1842, 75; September 2, 1842, 139; January 20, 1843, 10; May 17, 1844, 79; May 24, 1844, 81–82; May 31, 1844, 86–87; February 7, 1845, 21; April 4, 1845, 53; July 18, 1845, 114; *William Lloyd Garrison, 1805–1879 The Story of His Life Told by His Children*, vol. 3, *1841–1860* (Boston: Houghton, Mifflin, 1889), 88–90, 96–119; Henry Mayer, *All on Fire: William Lloyd Garrison and the Abolition of Slavery* (New York: W. W. Norton, 1998), 327–329, 365–371. Compare Elizabeth Varon, *Disunion! The Coming of the American Civil War, 1789–1859* (Chapel Hill: University of North Carolina Press, 2008), chap. 4; W. Caleb McDaniel, *The Problem of Democracy in the Age of Slavery: Garrisonian Abolitionists and Transatlantic Reform* (Baton Rouge: Louisiana State University Press, 2013); Manisha Sinha, "James W. C. Pennington and Transatlantic Abolitionism," in *Heidelberg Center for American Studies: Annual Report 2010–11* (Heidelberg, Germany, 2011), 168–169.

23. Wendell Phillips, *The Constitution, a Pro-Slavery Compact: or, Extracts from the Madison Papers, Etc.* (New York: American Anti-Slavery Society, 1844), 8; *TAE No. 13: Can Abolitionists Vote or Take Office under the United States Constitution?* (New York: American Anti-Slavery Society, 1845), 4; James Brewer Stewart, *Wendell Phillips: Liberty's Hero* (Baton Rouge: Louisiana State University Press, 1986), 123–125; Staughton Lynd, "The Abolitionist Critique of the United States Constitution," in *The Antislavery Vanguard: New Essays on the Abolitionists*, ed. Martin Duberman (Princeton, NJ: Princeton University Press, 1965), chap. 10.

24. William Goodell, *Views of American Constitutional Law, in Its Bearing upon American Slavery* (Utica, NY: Jackson & Chaplin, 1844), 10–11, 35–37, 63–65, 97–102, 149–151; *Gerrit Smith's Constitutional Argument* (Utica, NY: Jackson & Chaplin, 1844), 4–8.

25. Lysander Spooner, *The Unconstitutionality of Slavery* (Boston: Bela Marsh, 1845; Project Gutenberg e book, 2010); Wendell Phillips, *Review of Lysander Spooner's Essay on the Unconstitutionality of Slavery* (Boston: Andrew & Prentiss, 1847), 9–15, 93. For a modern and extended historical recapitulation of the constitutional position of political abolitionists, see Don E. Fehrenbacher with Ward M. McAfee, *The Slaveholding Republic: An Account of the United States Government's Relations to Slavery* (New York: Oxford Univeristy Press, 2001).

26. *Diary and Correspondence of Salmon P. Chase* (New York: American Historical Association, 1971), 115; J. W. Schuckers, *The Life and Public Services of Salmon Portland Chase* (New York: D. Appleton, 1874), 67–74; John Niven, ed., *The Salmon P. Chase Papers*, vol. 2, *Correspondence, 1823–1857* (Kent, OH: Kent State University Press, 1994), 84–87, 99–100, 119–120; Albert Bushnell Hart, *Salmon Portland Chase* (Boston: Chelsea House, 1899), chap. 4; Eric Foner, *Free Soil, Free Labor, Free Men: The Ideology of the Republican Party before the Civil War* (New York: Oxford University Press, 1970), chap. 3; Frederick J. Blue, *Salmon P. Chase: A Life in Politics* (Kent, OH: Kent State University Press, 1987), 41–52; Frederick J. Blue, *The Free Soilers: Third Party Politics, 1848–54* (Urbana: University of Illinois Press, 1973).

27. On the "federal consensus," see James Oakes, *Freedom National: The Destruction of Slavery in the United States, 1861–1865* (New York: W. W. Norton, 2013). On aggressive proslavery demands, see Sinha, *Counterrevolution of Slavery*, and Fehrenbacher, *Slaveholding Republic*; on their self-defeating nature in terms of evoking a greater antislavery response in the North, see Potter, *Impending Crisis*.

28. On the radicals, see Foner, *Free Soil, Free Labor, Free Men*, chap. 4. On Sumner's constitutional critique of the fugitive slave law, see Charles Sumner, *The Works of Charles Sumner*, 15 vols. (Boston: Norwood Press, 1870–1883), 3:49–67, 73–75, 95–196, 355–414, 426–432, 529–547; Edward L. Pierce, ed., *Memoir and Letters of Charles Sumner*, 4 vols. (Boston: Roberts Brothers, 1877–1893), 3:293–299. Also see Frederick J. Blue, *Charles Sumner and the Conscience of the North* (Arlington Heights, IL: Harlan Davidson, 1994); David Donald, *Charles Sumner and the Rights of Man* (New York: Da Capo Press, 1970).

29. Philip S. Foner, ed., *The Life and Writings of Frederick Douglass*, 4 vols. (New

York: International Publishers, 1950), 2:467–480. Also see Hoang Gia Phan, *Bonds of Citizenship: Law and the Labors of Emancipation* (New York: New York University Press, 2013); Nicholas Buccola, *The Political Thought of Frederick Douglass: In Pursuit of American Liberty* (New York: New York University Press, 2012); Nick Bromell, *The Time Is Always Now: Black Thought and the Transformation of US Democracy* (New York: Oxford University Press, 2013).

30. *Collected Works*, 5:48–49; Sinha, "Allies for Emancipation," 167–196; Oakes, *Freedom National.*

31. Abraham Lincoln, "Second Inaugural Address," in *Abraham Lincoln: Speeches and Writings*, 2 vols., ed. Don E. Fehrenbacher (New York: Library of America, 1989), 2:687.

32. Frederick Douglass, *The Life and Times of Frederick Douglass* (New York: Library of America, 1994), 804.

33. James McPherson, *Abraham Lincoln and the Second American Revolution* (New York: Oxford University Press, 1990); *Collected Works*, 6:28–30, 8:333; Guelzo, *Lincoln's Emancipation Proclamation*, 186; "Historian's Forum: The Emancipation Proclamation," *Civil War History* 59 (March 2013): 7–31. On Lincoln's constitutionalism, see Mark E. Neely Jr., *Lincoln and the Triumph of the Nation: Constitutional Conflict in the Civil War* (Chapel Hill: University of North Carolina, 2011); Brian R. Dirck, *Lincoln and the Constitution* (Carbondale: Southern Illinois University Press, 2012). On the reaction to the Emancipation Proclamation, see Michael Burlingame, *Abraham Lincoln: A Life*, vol. 2 (Baltimore: Johns Hopkins University Press, 2008), chap. 29. Also see Harold Holzer, *Emancipating Lincoln: The Proclamation in Text, Context and Memory* (Cambridge, MA: Harvard University Press, 2012).

34. Gary W. Gallagher, *The Union War* (Cambridge, MA: Harvard University Press, 2011).

35. Oakes, *Freedom National*, esp. 34–41; William Whiting, *The War Powers of the President and the Legislative Powers of Congress in Relation to Rebellion, Treason, and Slavery* (Boston: John L. Shorey, 1862); John Fabian Witt, *Lincoln's Code: The Laws of War in American History* (New York: Free Press, 2012), 71–79, 240–249.

36. Sinha, "Allies for Emancipation," 188–192; *Collected Works*, 6:410.

37. *Collected Works*, 7:53–56, 8:403; LaWanda Cox, *Lincoln and Black Freedom: A Study in Presidential Leadership* (Columbia: University of South Carolina Press, 1981); David Donald, *Lincoln* (New York: Simon & Schuster, 1995), 588; Sinha, "Allies for Emancipation," 184–185. For the argument that Lincoln never made the shift from colonization to black citizenship, see Philip W. Magness and Sebastian N. Page, *Colonization after Emancipation: Lincoln and the Movement for Black Settlement* (Columbia: University of Missouri Press, 2011).

PART FOUR

Lincoln as a Liberal Democratic Statesman

CHAPTER SEVEN

Four Roads to Emancipation: Lincoln, the Law, and the Proclamation

Allen Guelzo

To stand in the presence of Abraham Lincoln's Emancipation Proclamation is to be in the company of the single most sweeping presidential action in American history—greater in its impact on the lives of more people in one generation than any before it, and still alive with consequence for every generation after it. Lincoln's proclamation dwarfs in scope the Louisiana Purchase, the New Deal, the Panama Canal, and the Great Society; it achieved the reversal of the single greatest oversight of the Constitutional Convention—the failure to deal directly with slavery. It was the Emancipation Proclamation that lopped off its head and made it possible, two years and one month later, to drive a stake, in the form of the Thirteenth Amendment, through its vampire heart.

All honor, then, to Abraham Lincoln, as the proclamation's author. "He was happy in his life, for he was the restorer of the republic," said the premier American historian in 1865, George Bancroft. "He was happy in his death, for his martyrdom will plead forever for the Union of the States and the freedom of man."[1] William Cullen Bryant, a poet and editor, added this laurel:

> Thy task is done—the bond are free;
> We bear thee to an honored grave,
> Whose noblest monument shall be
> The broken fetters of the slave.

In many ways, Lincoln almost made the task of emancipation look too easy, causing us to wonder, if a presidential proclamation was all that was needed to paralyze slavery, why did he wait twenty-two months into his presidency to issue it?

The most obvious reason is Lincoln's acute sense of what was politically possible. Eleven states of the American union *loved* slavery so much that they had seceded, formed a southern Confederacy to protect it, and plunged the nation into civil war. But the remaining twenty-four states of the union did not *hate* slavery so badly that they were willing to fight for its end; four of the most important—the "border states" of Kentucky, Maryland, Missouri, and Delaware—actually kept legalized slavery in their statute books. And they did not mind telling Lincoln that emancipation proclamations of any sort would be the signal for them to desert to the Confederate side. As Lincoln himself bluntly explained to Orville Hickman Browning, "the very arms we had furnished Kentucky would be turned against us."[2]

Nor was that the only objection. Entirely apart from the practical considerations of stampeding Missouri or Kentucky into the arms of the Confederacy, Kentuckian Joshua Speed, his oldest friend, reminded Lincoln that federal proclamations, whether from presidents or generals, on the subject of slavery were "directly against the spirit of the law." The laws of slavery in Kentucky, as elsewhere, were state laws, and the federal Constitution gave the national government no authority to override those statutes: "Our [state] Constitution & laws both prohibit the emancipation of slaves among us—even in small numbers," Speed stated, and he knew of no constitutional power that a proclamation from Lincoln or any other federal authority could interpose. Yet another Kentuckian, congressman Aaron Harding, was just as direct: "This war should have nothing to do with the institution of slavery any more than with any other state institution." He explained:

> The Constitution of the United States secures to each State the right to have or not to have the institution of slavery—just as essentially so as it does the right to regulate your own common school system. We have no more right to make war upon the institution of slavery than upon any other local institution. The Constitution secures to each State the right of regulating its own domestic institutions; and it must necessarily protect slavery, as certainly as it protects your own common school system.[3]

Speed and Harding were, unhappily, right, and no one knew that better than Lincoln. Lincoln recognized that, "in ordinary civil administration," there was no constitutional authority to "practically indulge my primary abstract judgment on the moral question of slavery," but there was also nothing in the history of the so-called laws of war that authorized the emancipation of slaves. "The modern usage" of war, wrote soldier-turned-lawyer Henry Wager Halleck in his 1861 textbook on international law, "is, not to touch private property on land." Slaves were chattel property; ergo, the title of slave owners to their slaves should not be rewritten. "Even where the conquest of a country is confirmed by the unconditional relinquishment of sovereignty by the former owner, there can be no general or partial transmutation of private property, in virtue of any rights of conquest."[4]

This was Halleck's position not because he was indifferent or inhumane. On the contrary, restraining war's reach over property was supposed to be an example of humane proceedings. For 300 years, European jurists writing on international law had struggled to defang war's potential for barbarity and destructiveness by limiting the right to go to war to sovereign states and by making the legitimacy of war dependent on the satisfaction of certain formal conditions between the combatants, without regard to considerations of religion, justice, truth, or purity (all of which, it was feared, tended to inflame what was already a potentially brutal affair). American jurists shared this worry and even prided themselves on keeping American warfare in the hands of professional soldiers so as to "soften the extreme severity of the operations of war by land." In the charged atmosphere of the Revolution, both the Continental Congress and the individual states had cheerfully confiscated Tory property and justified doing so on the grounds that "vicious citizens who side with tyranny and oppression, or who cloak themselves under the mask of neutrality, should at least hazard their property, and not enjoy the benefits procured by the labours and dangers of those whose destructions they wished." But in peace, calmer counsels prevailed. So in 1789, when it came to property in war, the new US Constitution specifically banned bills of attainder (Article I, section 3)—"bills of pains and penalties"—that alienated even the property of traitors. And no less a figure than John Marshall declared in 1814 that "the modem usage of nations is to abstain from confiscating the debts due to an enemy, or his property found within the territory at the breaking out of war."[5]

According to this concept, when the property of one belligerent falls directly into the hands of another belligerent, "the right to the debts and the property is only suspended during the war, and revives with the return of peace." Even property used directly in the making of war—"contraband of war"—can be seized only for use, not for ownership. "War gives the right to confiscate," Marshall added, "but does not itself confiscate the property of the enemy." This included *slave* property: from the time of Hugo Grotius (1583–1645), the most celebrated of all international jurists, it was understood that, in war, "a slave also, who has fallen into the hands of an enemy, upon his release from thence, returns to the service of his former master." And Americans confirmed this by securing the rendition of slaves who fled to the British armies in both the Revolution and the War of 1812. Article 7 of the Treaty of Paris explicitly stipulated that British forces leaving the United States were to do so with "all convenient speed, and without causing any Destruction, or carrying away any Negroes or other Property of the American inhabitants," and George Washington made it clear to the British commander in chief, Sir Guy Carleton, that no African Americans who had fled as fugitives to British-occupied areas should be allowed to leave with their quondam British friends.[6] (Twenty-three of Thomas Jefferson's slaves ran away during the Revolution; he secured the return of at least five of them, whom he promptly reenslaved.) The Treaty of Ghent, likewise, explicitly guaranteed the rendition of "Slaves or other private property" in 1814. In neither case were the British enthusiastic parties to such renditions. An American demand to the governor of Bermuda to surrender American slaves who had been taken there by the Royal Navy during the War of 1812 provoked that "worthy Englishman, nettled at a requisition so derogatory to the honor of his country," to snarl in reply that he "would rather Bermuda, with every man, woman and child in it, were sunk under the sea, than surrender one slave that had sought protection under the flag of England." Deliberations over rendition dragged on until 1826, when the British finally settled all claims for $1.2 million in cash.[7]

The twin cliffs of the Constitution and the conventional laws of war did not, therefore, present Lincoln with many options for pursuing an emancipation agenda. And, given the additional restraint imposed by northern whites' chilliness toward the practical consequences of emancipation, it is a wonder that Lincoln ever gave the subject a second thought. It is certainly imaginable that he might have taken the low road and never introduced the subject of slavery and emancipation into the Civil War at all, since there were so many short-term incentives for him to do just that. But his revulsion at chattel slavery sprang from sources that were deeply embedded. "I am naturally anti-slavery," he said. "If slavery is not wrong, nothing is wrong. I cannot remember when I did not so think, and feel." Slavery was "founded in the selfishness of man's nature," a "monstrous injustice" that "deprives our Republican example of its just influence in the world—enables the enemies of free institutions, with plausibility to taunt us as hypocrites"; it was indistinguishable from the tyranny of kings.[8] Only convictions of such depth could have overcome the manifest disincentives to pursue an emancipation policy.

Despite the disincentives, there were, as it turned out, four roads that might have been taken toward emancipation; the problem for Lincoln was that each of them entailed certain risks, and with no guarantee of success, the path ahead disappeared into a murk of legal uncertainty. The first of these roads was one that Lincoln himself had always favored: a gradual emancipation program, sweetened by the offer of compensation to slave owners and authorized by state legislative action—or, as he put it in a letter to Horace Greeley in the spring of 1862, a plan with "three main features—gradual—compensation—and [the] vote of the people." Plans for gradual, compensated emancipation had been both successful and peaceful in many of the northern states, including Pennsylvania, New York, and New Jersey, and they had the imprimatur of a number of leading Americans. "I have seen no proposition so expedient on the whole," wrote Thomas Jefferson in 1814, "as emancipation of those born after a given day, and of their education and expatriation after a given age." What was more, gradualism was supposed to minimize the social shock of emancipation in ways that generated no *noticeable* racial hostility from the surrounding white populations. (The emphasis here is on noticeable from a *national* point of view, because the freed slaves of the northern states experienced no shortage of hostile restrictions in employment, education, and everyday living.) "This," Jefferson believed, "would give time for a gradual extinction of that species of labour & substitution of another, and lessen the severity of the shock which an operation so fundamental cannot fail to produce." Lincoln agreed. "In my judgment," he explained, "gradual, and not sudden emancipation, is better for all." It would allow slave states to "adopt some practical system by which the two races could gradually live themselves out of their old relation to each other, and both come out better prepared for the new."[9]

This was, of course, small consolation to the slaves, since it held out a *promise* of freedom rather than freedom itself. And lingering in the shadow of gradual emancipation was the not so discreet hint that such plans also included the freed slaves' transportation and colonization somewhere outside the United States (there were already two sizable but not very attractive freedmen's colonies in Liberia and Sierra Leone, in West Africa). Lincoln himself had given a perfunctory endorsement of colonization in his 1852 eulogy for Henry Clay and in speeches in 1854, 1857, and 1858 in Peoria, Springfield, and Edwardsville:

> If as the friends of colonization hope, the present and coming generations of our countrymen shall by any means, succeed in freeing our land from the dangerous presence of slavery; and, at the same time, in restoring a captive people to their long lost father land, with bright prospects for the future; and this too, so gradually, that neither races nor individuals shall have suffered by the change, it will indeed be a glorious consummation.[10]

But this was predicated on several *ifs*. It has never been clear how serious Lincoln was about colonization; surely, if he had been as deeply racist or as enthusiastic about colonization as his critics suggest, it is peculiar that he put so little energy into making colonization happen. As James Oakes observes, Lincoln regarded colonization as an option "not because blacks were irredeemably inferior but because so many whites were irredeemably racist." Emancipation alone, objected J. H. B. Latrobe in 1851, "could give political, but not social position" to the freed slaves. "It could empower the emancipated slaves to hold property and to vote, which has been already done in some of the States; but it could not remove the prejudice which the white population entertain against their race." And prejudice, Latrobe warned, "is traditionary; and even after the white generations which have seen slavery have died out, the prejudices, originating from that condition, will be handed down from generation to generation." Hence, Latrobe coldly reasoned, "the colonization of the free negroes, and of such slaves as may be emancipated, from time to time, is . . . the only remedy."[11] As Lincoln himself explained while trying to persuade a delegation of African American clergy to take the lead in promoting colonization:

> Even when you cease to be slaves, you are yet far removed from being placed on an equality with the white race. You are cut off from many of the advantages which the other race enjoy. The aspiration of men is to enjoy equality with the best when free, but on this broad continent, not a single man of your race is made the equal of a single man of ours. Go where you are treated the best, and the ban is still upon you. I do not propose to discuss this, but to present it as a fact with which we have to deal. I cannot alter it if I would. It is a fact, about which we all think and feel alike, I and you.[12]

The one experiment in colonization Lincoln did sponsor during the war—the short-lived colony at Ile a Vache, off the south coast of Haiti—was voluntary rather than compulsory, and it was so badly managed that Lincoln recalled the entire enterprise after just a few months. According to John Hay, he "sloughed off that idea" once and for all as a "hideous & barbarous humbug."[13] Colonization, in that light, may have been no more than sugarcoating in Lincoln's mind, aimed at appeasing white anxieties over the larger scheme of emancipation. Colonization projects like Ile a Vache were, wrote Frederick Edge, "adopted to silence the weak-nerved, whose name is legion—and to enable any of the slaves who see fit to emigrate to more genial climes."[14]

Still, gradualism and compensation certainly remained worthwhile options in Lincoln's mind. This, as Lincoln said, "is a world of compensations"—of trade-offs, so to speak—rather than absolutes or either-ors, and if the trade-off for emancipation was gradualism and compensation, he would take it. By the fall of 1861, he had already devised a compensated emancipation plan for the border state of Delaware: slaves born in Delaware after adoption of the plan would automatically be free, as would any slaves older than thirty-five; all others would become free when they turned thirty-five. The Delaware legislature would be provided with $719,200 in 6 percent US bonds to buy out the slave owners' interests. Depending on the timetable adopted by the Delaware legislature, slavery would cease to exist in Delaware no later than 1872. With that example in place, the same plan could then be offered to the other three border states. This would take so much wind out of the Confederacy's sails that the rebellion itself would collapse, and the process of emancipation could begin throughout the South. "If Congress will pass a law authorizing the issuance of bonds for the payment of the emancipated Negroes in the border states," Lincoln explained, "Maryland, Kentucky, and Missouri will accept the terms," gradually bringing slavery "to an end." As each border state embraced emancipation, each compensated emancipation program would spawn another. The majority of slaveholders in any given border state would accept the buyout; the uncooperative minority who insisted on clinging to slave labor would have no choice but to take their slaves into a neighboring border state, where the increased supply of slaves would drive down their individual value—and induce market-anxious slaveholders to respond favorably when Lincoln presented the state legislature with a buyout plan. At the same time, each border state that signed up for emancipation would thrust the boundaries of freedom closer to the fugitive slaves in the upper South and destabilize slavery there as well. Self-interest alone would bring slaveholders in the border and the upper tier to heel. Given that Delaware had only 1,700 slaves and that half of Maryland's African American population was already free, this was not an unrealistic scenario. And, Lincoln might have added, the border states would do this as a purely civil procedure originating within the states, thus neatly sidestepping any accusations of federal overreach.[15]

Congress, however, had its own ideas about the road to emancipation, and most of them harked back to policies of confiscation and the status of wartime contraband goods. In late May 1861 three fugitive slaves showed up at the gates of Fortress Monroe, the last surviving toehold of Federal authority in Confederate Virginia. Their master was a Confederate officer, and they had been put to work constructing Confederate fortifications; now he "purposed taking them to Carolina to be employed in military operations there," and since two of them had wives and children in Virginia, they wanted refuge. The commandant at Fortress Monroe, Benjamin Butler, was a Massachusetts Democrat who had quixotically supported Jefferson Davis for the presidency in 1860, but when the slaves' owner demanded their return, Butler declared them to be "contraband of war" and refused. The notion that slaves could be considered *contraband* was a nice joke at the expense of their Confederate owner. (Hadn't slave owners insisted all along that slaves were property? Very well, Butler would treat them like any other war-making property and confiscate them as contraband.) "The venerable gentleman, who wears gold spectacles and reads a conservative daily . . . is reluctant to have slaves declared freemen," wrote Edward Pierce in the *Atlantic Monthly*, "but has no objection to their being declared contrabands."[16]

After the debacle suffered by Union forces at Bull Run in July, it was too tempting for Congress not to grab on to this idea and expand it into the First Confiscation Act, providing that if slave owners allowed their slave "property" to be used in "promoting . . . insurrection or resistance to the laws," that property would be the "lawful subject of prize and capture," and they would "forfeit all right to such service or labor." This was followed eleven months later by the Second Confiscation Act, which expanded the application of confiscation to include "every person who shall hereafter commit the crime of treason against the United States." Confiscated slaves, moreover, "shall be declared and made free."[17]

Nor was Butler the only soldier who was tempted to lay a hand on slavery. Among them was a former Republican candidate for the presidency, Major General John Charles Frémont. Placed in charge of the Department of Missouri, Frémont quickly showed an extraordinary lack of military competence but a finely honed sense of the political, and in August 1861 he imposed martial law first on St. Louis and then on the rest of the state. Violators of the decree would suffer the seizure of "property, real and personal," and "their slaves, if any they have, are hereby declared free men." Butler had merely *confiscated* the slaves who knocked at his door; Frémont, purely by the authority of martial law, cut out the middleman of congressional statute and declared slaves *free*. Others, lacking Frémont's boldness, just looked the other way when fugitives sought out their camps and then pretended they had seen nothing when angry slave owners demanded the return of their property. Finally, in April 1862, the new commandant of the occupied districts along the Carolina coast, Major General David Hunter, implemented his own version of martial law, not only declaring all slaves within his district free but also enlisting 500 of them as the First South Carolina Volunteers.[18]

Finally, it must be noted that, in addition to Lincoln's plan of gradual emancipation and Congress's and the generals' plans for confiscation, the slaves had their own plan for achieving freedom: they intended to use the distraction of the war and the diversion of the South's white male population into the Confederate armies to simply run away, usually into the arms of an increasingly compliant US Army. "Slaves seized their chances to escape," wrote Secretary of War Edwin Stanton, "discontent and distrust were engendered, the hopes of the slave and the fears of the master, stimulated by the success of the Federal arm, shook each day more and more the fabric built on human slavery." Everywhere across the South, but especially wherever the Union armies marched, "hundreds of colored people obtained passes and free transportation to Washington and the North, and made their Escape to the Free States. Day after day the slaves came into camp and everywhere that the 'Stars and Stripes,' waved they seemed to know freedom had dawned to the slave." Slave owners in the inaptly named Georgia county of Liberty complained to their local Confederate commandant that "from ascertained losses on certain parts of our Coast, we may set down as a low estimate, the number of Slaves absconded & enticed off from our Seaboard as 20,000 & their value as from $12 to 15 millions of Dollars, to which loss—may be added the insecurity of the property along our borders & the demoralization of the negroes that remain." Although the fugitives' transience makes it difficult to peg the number of runaways with any accuracy, it is likely that between 200,000 and 250,000 slaves bolted from slavery.[19]

After all this, a very interesting question becomes which of these roads ended up being the one that led most directly to emancipation. And the answer is, as in so many maddening historical situations, *all* of them—and *none*.

Herbert Aptheker was probably the first, in 1938, to suggest the outlines of what has become known as the "self-emancipation" thesis, although it was Vincent Harding in 1981 who gave the most recognizable shape to this thesis—that the slaves freed themselves by resistance and by flight.[20] This has become a popular thesis, and no wonder: it has a rattlingly revolutionary ring to it, derived in part from its long-term connections to Marx's declaration (in the *Critique of the Götha Program* in 1875) that "the emancipation of the working class will be the task of the working class itself," and it satisfies a need to see emancipation as an object African Americans seized, rather than a gift bestowed by white people who expected unending gratitude for their generosity. According to the self-emancipation thesis, these self-freed slaves, along with their white abolitionist allies, exerted such pressure on Lincoln that he was compelled to end his long hesitation and issue the Emancipation Proclamation on January 1, 1863.

Ironically, there is more than a little truth to the idea that the slaves exerted pressure for emancipation. I say *ironically* for two reasons. First, most of the pressure exerted by fugitives came in the decade before the Civil War, when the flight of fugitives from the Upper South helped radicalize pro-secession sentiment in the Gulf states, where they feared that the Upper South would someday abandon slavery entirely and become a new refuge for runaways, this time from the Deep South. Second, it was not the fugitive slaves who exerted pressure during the war itself but the still-enslaved black laborers in the Confederate armies. By performing the logistical and fatigue duties performed by white soldiers in the Union armies, Confederate slaves were making a direct contribution to the southern war effort, which even the most flint-hearted northern racists were willing to see undercut by emancipation.[21]

But there are two fundamental problems with imputing this "pressure" to the fugitives and contrabands. First, even *free* blacks in the northern states lacked access to the ballot box (and many other civil freedoms, for that matter), and without it, it is hard to imagine what pressure fugitives and contrabands were in a position to exert on Lincoln or anyone else. Second, while it is true that fugitive slaves could free themselves by running away, the freedom they achieved was only de facto freedom—the temporary freedom any fugitive from law or power enjoys—not de jure freedom—the freedom that enables one to stand up as a citizen in civil society without fear or trembling. And if, for any reason, the Union decided to come to the negotiating table with the Confederacy (which likely would have happened if Lincoln had lost the 1864 election to George B. McClellan), the past record of demanding the rendition of fugitives certainly would have set off an unholy pursuit of the contrabands by war-wearied northern whites, especially if rendition was a sine qua non of peace. (The British minister to the United States, Lord Lyons, actually took steps in advance of the election to guarantee the passage of fugitive slaves to the nearest British dominions, precisely because he was convinced that if McClellan was elected and a negotiated settlement with the Confederacy was reached, "fugitive slaves who escaped to freedom behind Union lines would . . . be sacrificed without scruple.") That sort of freedom would require something of much greater impact than mere flight, no matter how heroic.[22]

Freedom de jure would not come, however, from the generals' proclamations of martial law, if only because there was no effective jurisprudence on the nature of martial law in American legal history. "Martial law is a thing not mentioned by name, and scarcely as much as hinted at, in the Constitution and statutes of the United States," admitted Caleb Cushing, onetime attorney general, in 1856. "I say, we are without law on the subject."[23] The generals might have declared a suspension of the writ of habeas corpus (a key assumption in the imposition of martial law), but suspending the writ did not give them the power to alter title to property. In any case, there was already a substantial contest going on between Lincoln and Chief Justice Roger Taney about suspending the writ of habeas corpus, without odds and ends of generals muddying the waters. It did not improve Lincoln's peace of mind to be told that "the proclamation of Genl. Fremont is most inopportune for the Union party." Kentucky senator Garrett Davis warned, "The general principle of the martial law is . . . so far modified by the constitution as to have no effect for a longer time than the life of the rebel."[24] Lincoln revoked Frémont's proclamation and then relieved him of command in Missouri; he did likewise to Hunter the following spring.

Something of the same problem attached to Congress's confiscation acts. Both acts limited their reach to those areas where the federal courts were no longer operating; they could do nothing about slaves in the loyal border states, where any attempt at a government "taking" would be stopped by appeals for due process. And even in the Confederacy, explained the bills' architect, Lyman Trumbull, "so far from striking at all the property of each and every citizen in the seceded States, it would not probably reach the property of one in ten of the rebels. . . . It only applies to the property of such rebels as are beyond the reach of judicial process. Wherever the person of the rebel can be reached and made subject to the punishment his crimes deserve, the bill does not propose to touch his property." Trumbull was painfully aware that this flew in the face of international law. "According to the modern usage of nations, private property of alien enemies on land has not generally been forfeited," and he could only plead that a "right of forfeiture . . . may be exercised if necessary to secure the just ends of the war, or in retaliation for forfeitures by the enemy."[25]

Although Lincoln signed both acts, he did so with ill-concealed reluctance, and (in the case of the Second Confiscation Act) not until Congress had passed a resolution affirming that confiscation would not function as a bill of attainder. What would happen at the end of the war, when calls for rendition of confiscated property became the target of litigation in the federal courts, Trumbull did not care to predict. Congress could pass as many confiscation acts as it liked, but Lincoln had to keep in mind the likelihood that they would be challenged as unconstitutional. In that case, the challenge would be handled, in the end, by Roger Taney, who would have been only too happy to put a permanent obstacle in the path of emancipation, just as he had blocked the move to keep slavery out of the western territories in the *Dred Scott* decision in 1857.

But Lincoln's cherished plan of gradual emancipation fared no better. Inducing state legislatures to do the work of emancipation themselves in exchange for a federal buyout made perfect sense to a lawyer like Lincoln. But white slave owners in Delaware and elsewhere preferred racism to profit, and all the gradual emancipation schemes he proposed for the states were thrown back in his face. Only in the District of Columbia, where Congress had direct constitutional jurisdiction, was a compensated emancipation plan finally hatched, and successfully. Elsewhere, Lincoln was tartly informed to mind his own business. "Confine yourself to your constitutional authority," the border state congressmen told him on July 14, 1862, "confine your subordinates within the same limits; conduct this war solely for the purpose of restoring the constitution to its legitimate authority."[26]

There was one more road to emancipation, but it was one that only Lincoln himself could walk, and he would have to do so very carefully. Whatever else the Constitution prevented Lincoln from doing as president, it did empower him in at least one key respect: it designated him "Commander-in-Chief of the Army and Navy of the United States . . . when called into the actual Service of the United States." It had never been very clear what powers the title of commander in chief actually conferred on the president, but as early as the 1830s, John Quincy Adams had announced that they encompassed a set of wide-ranging "war powers" that included emancipating slaves if a war emergency required it. "All the powers incidental to war are, by necessary implication, conferred upon the government of the United

States," Adams averred. This "war power" is "tremendous: it is strictly constitutional, but it breaks down every barrier so anxiously erected for the protection of liberty, of property, and of life." And "in war there are many ways by which Congress not only have the authority but are bound to interfere with the institution of slavery in the states." For example, Adams argued: Suppose a slave insurrection broke out. Congress would be obliged to come to the aid of the states in any and every way it could devise. Might not emancipation be one of those devices? "Can it for an instant be pretended that congress, in such a contingency, would have no authority to interfere with the institution of slavery, in any way, in the states? Why, it would be equivalent to saying that congress have no constitutional authority to make peace." It was based on this notion of "war powers" that Charles Sumner, as soon as he heard of the firing on Fort Sumter, informed Lincoln that the war had delivered into his hands a full and plenary authority to smite the Confederacy hip and thigh. "I . . . told him," Sumner said, "that under the war power the right had come to him to emancipate the slaves." The war power, argued Sumner, "is above the constitution, because, when set in motion, it knows no other law." He stated, "The civil power, in mass and in detail, is superseded, and all rights are held subordinate to this military magistracy. All other agencies, small and great, executive, legislative, and even judicial, are absorbed in this transcendent triune power, which, for the time, declares its absolute will, while it holds alike the scales of justice and the sword of the executioner."[27] With every other tool breaking in his hand, one week after being told by the border state delegations that he had no business thinking about emancipation, Lincoln submitted to his cabinet the first draft of an emancipation proclamation, predicated on these "war powers" as commander in chief.

He knew he had no direct precedent for doing this. For one thing, Adams had spoken of the "war power" as a congressional, not an executive, power. For another, none of the great commentators on the Constitution agreed with Adams that such a war power even existed. James Kent's famous *Commentaries* made no mention of any "war powers" inhering in the presidency. It was not even clear what a commander in chief was supposed to be, or do. The *Federalist Papers* opined that the president's title of commander in chief "would amount to nothing more than the supreme command and direction of the military and naval forces, as the first general and admiral of the Confederacy." Even then, the venerable Joseph Story actually believed that Congress ought to pass a consent resolution before allowing a president to take up personal military command.[28]

What made this shinnying out on such a narrow constitutional limb all the more perilous was that, in addition to all the questions of justice, policy, and timing, Lincoln had a hostile federal judiciary to deal with, with the scarecrow Taney at its head. One false legal step would set Taney at the exposed proclamation in a fashion that might set emancipation back for another generation. Whether "war powers" proclamations "are binding or not will be a question for the courts," Lincoln admitted. "Mere vague assertions that the decisions of the Courts are fraudulent, with appeals to me to reverse them, can [not] be entertained," he warned. Any "question of property in slaves," like the "confiscation of property," would be something "he must of course leave to the courts to decide." And, as he told Alexander Stephens in February 1865, "How the courts would decide it, he did not know and could give no answer."

> His own opinion was that as the proclamation was a war measure and would have effect only from its being an exercise of the war power, as soon as the war ceased, it would be inoperative for the future. It would be held to apply only to such slaves as had come under its operation while it was in active exercise. This was his individual opinion, but the courts might decide the other way and hold that it effectually emancipated all the slaves in the states to which it applied at the time. So far as he was concerned, he should leave it to the courts to decide.

Nevertheless, he insisted, "I think [the proclamation] is valid in law," and in any case, he had no better options. "I cannot recall my proclamations," he replied to Duff Green. But the problem of "whether they are binding or not ... for the courts" was on his mind from the start. That is why, when he issued the preliminary Emancipation Proclamation on September 22, 1862, he characterized the rationale for it not in terms of abstract justice but "by virtue of the power in me vested as Commander-in-Chief ... and as a fit and necessary war measure." That is also why he added such a lengthy list of exceptions when he signed the final version on January 1, 1863. The areas he exempted—thirteen parishes in Louisiana and the city of New Orleans, seven counties and two cities in Virginia, and the whole of West Virginia—had been returned to the civil jurisdiction of the United States and were no longer subject to his "war powers."[29]

Above all, that is why the Emancipation Proclamation is written in such deadeningly legalistic terms. It is easy to jump to the conclusion that, coming from a president capable of such rhetorical gems as the Gettysburg Address and his two inaugural addresses, the woodenness of the proclamation reveals a man whose heart was only half in the project, if that much. But this was certainly not Lincoln's own estimate, much less the estimate of the Confederates. Jefferson Davis's response was apoplectic. He harangued the Confederate Congress on January 12, 1863, stating, the "proclamation dated on the first day of the present month signed by the President of the United States in which he orders and declares all slaves within ten States of the Confederacy to be free, except such as are found in certain districts now occupied in part by the armed forces of the enemy," is "a measure by which several millions of human beings of an inferior race, peaceful and contented laborers in their sphere, are doomed to extermination, while at the same time they are encouraged to a general assassination of their masters." It is "the most execrable measure recorded in the history of guilty man," and Davis could find no more appropriate response than to recommend that "all commissioned officers of the United States that may hereafter be captured by our forces in any of the States embraced in the proclamation ... be dealt with in accordance with the laws of those States providing for the punishment of criminals engaged in exciting servile insurrection."[30]

Lincoln was hardly less sanguine. Once the Emancipation Proclamation took effect, Lincoln remarked, "the character of the war will be changed. It will be one of subjugation and extermination." Emancipation "will be pushed after the 1st [of January 1863] with all the power left in the federal arm," and thereafter, he would shape "his policy" in a direction "more radical than ever." The character of slavery would also be changed, for the slaves who fell within the ambit of the proclamation "shall be then, thenceforward, and forever free." Not merely loose or at large or on the run but *free*—legally and forever.[31]

It takes nothing away from the struggles of the slaves to say that freedom came to them through the act of a white man. Moreover, Lincoln did not issue the proclamation *as* a white man handing out gifts to people who would thereafter be resented if they did not behave like humble children; he did so as the president of the United States and the commander in chief. The slaves themselves certainly had no problem linking their fortunes to Lincoln's. African American war correspondent Thomas Morris Chester wrote that the proclamation "ends the days of oppression, cruelty and outrage, founded on complexion, and introduces an era of emancipation, humanity and virtue, founded upon the principles of unerring justice." It "protects the sanctity of the marriage relationship ... justifies the natural right of the mother over the disposition of her daughters, and gives to the father the only claim which Almighty God intended should be exercised by man over his son." Frederick Douglass agreed. "The fourth of July was great, but the first of January, when we consider it in all its relations and bearings is incomparably greater. The one had respect to the mere political birth to a nation, the last concerns the national life and character, and is to determine whether that life and character shall be radiantly glorious with all high and noble virtues, or infamously blackened, forevermore, with all the hell-darkened crimes and horrors which attach to Slavery."[32] When freedmen were interviewed by a congressional committee on Reconstruction in 1866 and asked when they considered themselves free, the answers were unanimous: "When the proclamation was issued." "I have been a slave from my childhood up to the time I was set free by the emancipation proclamation." "Under the Proclamation of the President of the United States, I consider myself a Free Man."[33]

There was, in the end, nothing easy about the Emancipation Proclamation. It involved numerous false hopes and false starts, and the fourth and final road Lincoln followed to reach emancipation, through a "war powers" proclamation, was full of legal dangers, some of which remain with us. One thing emancipation certainly did *not* do was guarantee that the freed slaves would automatically attain equal citizenship with all other Americans. It gave them freedom but not autonomy, in the sense of conferring political participation and identity.[34] A movement toward genuine autonomy brought the larger cast of emancipation agents back into play, and by joining the US Army, free blacks and freed slaves made a powerful argument for receiving that status. Frederick Douglass had been waiting for this moment for a long time; he was convinced that once the US government began enlisting African Americans as soldiers, there would be no logical stopping point between enlistment and full civil equality. "Once let the black man get upon his person the brass letters *US*, let him get an eagle on his button, and a musket on his shoulder, and bullets in his pocket, and there is no power on earth or under the earth which can deny that he has earned the right of citizenship in the United States." "Men of Colour, To Arms!" he cried:

> The day dawns; the morning star is bright upon the horizon! The iron gate of our prison stands half open. One gallant rush from the North will fling it wide open, while four millions of our brothers and sisters shall march out into liberty. The chance is now given you to end in a day the bondage of centuries, and to rise in one bound from social degradation to the place of common equality with all other varieties of men.[35]

But African American military service could not, on its own, translate into citizenship. There was no necessary reward of citizenship after military service, if only because the *Dred Scott* decision was still the Supreme Court's last word on the subject, and *Dred Scott* adamantly barred blacks from citizenship. The "right of citizenship" would require another set of interventions by Congress before citizenship became de jure. The Civil Rights Act of 1866 and, eventually, the Fourteenth Amendment supplied a definition of citizenship that (curiously) the Constitution lacked.

In the longest sense, there were limits to what even the law could do. Thomas Morris Chester might believe that emancipation "end[ed] the days of oppression, cruelty and outrage," but it did not. Emancipation did not prevent Jim Crow, lynching, grandfather clauses, and other instruments of citizenship's denial. But emancipation did change the nature of that "oppression, cruelty and outrage," making them illegal acts that had to be committed behind masks and by mob violence. It would take an agonizingly long time for practice to catch up to the logic of emancipation, and African Americans would have to lie down before the steamroller of prejudice, sacrificing themselves to draw attention to the oft-ignored demands of the law, just as a century before they had taken up the button and the eagle to demonstrate their claim to citizenship. But it would come.

In the process, law itself would fall into a shadow of contempt, and the rebound from that has a great deal to do with the careless fashion in which Lincoln and the Emancipation Proclamation are regarded. Today, we are dismissive of a regard for legal danger; in an age that is awake to the demands of humanitarian justice, we are inclined to look cynically on law as merely the tool of the powerful. But while law is lasting, power is not, and Lincoln's anxiety to connect the proclamation with law, even at great risk, was a hallmark of statesmanship, not hesitancy. The passage of a century and a half may have reduced our perception of those risks, but they were real at the time. Yet, even in the face of those risks, Lincoln was adamant: "I think I shall not retract or repudiate it. Those who shall have tasted actual freedom I believe can never be slaves, or quasi-slaves again."[36] Or ever would be.

NOTES

1. *Hon. George Bancroft's Oration: Pronounced in New York, April 25, 1865, at the Obsequies of Abraham Lincoln* (New York: Schermerhorn, Bancroft, 1865), 13.

2. Lincoln to Orville Hickman Browning, September 22, 1861, in *The Collected Works of Abraham Lincoln*, 9 vols., ed. Roy P. Basler (New Brunswick, NJ: Rutgers University Press, 1953), 4:532; hereafter cited as *Collected Works*.

3. John Singleton Mosby, *The Memoirs of Colonel John S. Mosby*, ed. C. W. Russell (Boston: Little, Brown, 1917), 19; Joshua Speed to Lincoln, September 1, 1861, Abraham Lincoln Papers, Library of Congress; Aaron Harding, "Emancipation of Slaves in Rebel States," December 17, 1861, in *Congressional Globe*, 37th Cong., 2nd sess. (appendix), 29–30.

4. Abraham Lincoln, "Letter to Albert Hodges," in *Abraham Lincoln: Speeches and Writings*, vol. 2, *1859–1865* (New York: Library of America, 1989), 585; Henry Wager Halleck, *International Law: Or, Rules Regulating the Intercourse of States in Peace and War* (New York: D. Van Nostrand, 1861), 456.

5. Henry Wheaton, *Elements of International Law* (Boston: Little, Brown, 1857), 429; "Documents Bearing on the Treaty of 1783," in *Proceedings in the North Atlantic Coast Fisheries Arbitration before the Permanent Court of Arbitration at The Hague* (Washington, DC: Government Printing Office, 1912), 201; Daniel Hamilton, *The Limits of Sovereignty: Property Confiscation in the Union and the Confederacy during the Civil War* (Chicago: University of Chicago Press, 2007), 15–17.

6. Alan Gilbert, *Black Patriots and Loyalists: Fighting for Emancipation in the War for Independence* (Chicago: University of Chicago Press, 2012), 177–178.

7. John Fabian Witt, *Lincoln's Code: The Laws of War in American History* (New York: Free Press, 2012), 32, 77, 199; *Armitz Brown v. the United States* (1814), in *Condensed Reports of Cases in the Supreme Court of the United States* (Philadelphia: John Grigg, 1831), 3:60; Hugo Grotius, *The Rights of War and Peace: Including the Law of Nature and of War*, ed. A. C. Campbell (Pontefract, UK: B. Boothby, 1814), 3:262–263; William Jay, "A View of the Action by the Federal Government, on Behalf of Slavery," in *Miscellaneous Writings on Slavery* (Boston: John P. Jewett, 1853), 251.

8. Lincoln, "Speech at Peoria, Illinois," October 16, 1854, and Lincoln to Albert G. Hodges, April 4, 1864, in *Collected Works*, 2:271, 275, 7:281.

9. Jefferson to Edward Coles, August 25, 1814, in *Thomas Jefferson: Writings*, ed. Merrill D. Peterson (New York: Library of America, 1984), 1345; Lincoln, "Message to Congress," March 6, 1862, and Lincoln to Horace Greeley, March 24, 1862, in *Collected Works*, 5:144, 169.

10. Lincoln, "Eulogy on Henry Clay," July 6, 1852, in *Collected Works*, 2:132.

11. James Oakes, *The Scorpion's Sting: Antislavery and the Coming of the Civil War* (New York: W. W. Norton, 2013), 83; J. H. B. Latrobe, *Colonization: A Notice of Victor Hugo's Views of Slavery in the United States* (Baltimore: John D. Toy, 1851), 12, 22.

12. Lincoln, "Address on Colonization to a Deputation of Negroes," August 14, 1862, in *Collected Works*, 5:370.

13. Gabor Boritt, "Did He Dream of a Lily-White America? The Voyage to Linconia," in *The Lincoln Enigma: The Changing Faces of an American Icon* (New York: Oxford University Press, 2001), 8; Philip S. Paludan, *The Presidency of Abraham Lincoln* (Lawrence: University Press of Kansas, 1994), 132–133; John Hay, diary entry for July 1, 1864, in *Inside Lincoln's White House: The Complete Civil War Diary of John Hay*,

ed. Michael Burlingame and J. R. T. Ettlinger (Carbondale: Southern Illinois University Press, 1997), 217.

14. Frederick Edge, *Major General McClellan and the Campaign of the Yorktown Peninsula* (London: Trubner, 1865), 61.

15. H. Clay Reed, "Lincoln's Compensated Emancipation Plan and Its Relation to Delaware," *Delaware Notes* 7 (1931): 36–39; Lincoln to Henry L. Pierce, April 6, 1859, and "Drafts of a Bill for Compensated Emancipation in Delaware," in *Collected Works*, 5:29–30; Lincoln to David Davis and to Gilbert Greene, in *Recollected Words of Abraham Lincoln*, ed. D. Fehrenbacher and V. Fehrenbacher (Stanford, CA: Stanford University Press, 1996), 132, 182.

16. Edward Pierce, "The Contrabands at Fortress Monroe," *Atlantic Monthly* 8 (November 1861): 626–627; Adam Goodheart, *1861: The Civil War Awakening* (New York: Knopf, 2011), 295–340; Louis Masur, *Lincoln's Hundred Days: The Emancipation Proclamation and the War for the Union* (Cambridge, MA: Harvard University Press, 2012), 15–20; John V. Quarstein, *Hampton and Newport News in the Civil War: War Comes to the Peninsula* (Lynchburg, VA: H. E. Howard, 1998), 23–25.

17. "Confiscation," in *The Political History of the United States of America during the Great Rebellion*, ed. Edward McPherson (Washington, DC: Philp & Solomons, 1864), 195–196.

18. John C. Frémont, "Proclamation," August 30, 1861, in *The War of the Rebellion: A Compilation of the Official Records of the Union and Confederate Armies* (Washington, DC: Government Printing Office, 1899), series 1, 3:466–467 (hereafter cited as *OR*); Edward A. Miller, *Lincoln's Abolitionist General: The Biography of David Hunter* (Columbia: University of South Carolina Press, 1997), 94–100; "General Orders No. 11," in *OR*, series 1, 14:341.

19. George Congdon Gorham, *Life and Public Services of Edwin M. Stanton* (Boston: Houghton Mifflin, 1899), 2:221; John M. Washington, *A Slave No More: Two Men Who Escaped to Freedom, Including Their Own Narratives of Emancipation*, ed. David Blight (Orlando, FL: Houghton Mifflin, 2007), 198; Patricia C. Clink, *Time Full of Trial: The Roanoke Island Freedmen's Colony, 1862–1867* (Chapel Hill: University of North Carolina Press, 2001), 231; R. Q. Mallard and others to Hugh Mercer, August 1, 1862, in *Free at Last: A Documentary History of Slavery, Freedom, and the Civil War*, ed. Ira Berlin et al. (New York: New Press, 1992), 62.

20. Herbert Aptheker, "Negro Participation in the Civil War," *New Masses*, July 26, 1938; Vincent Harding, *There Is a River: The Black Freedom Struggle in America* (New York: Harcourt Brace, 1981).

21. W. Caleb McDaniel, "The Bonds and Boundaries of Antislavery," *Journal of the Civil War Era* 4 (March 2014): 91; Glenn David Brasher, *The Peninsula Campaign and the Necessity of Emancipation: African Americans and the Fight for Freedom* (Chapel Hill: University of North Carolina Press, 2012), 103–123.

22. Ira Berlin, "Who Freed the Slaves? Emancipation and Its Meaning," in *Union and Emancipation: Essays on Politics and Race in the Civil War Era*, ed. David Blight and

Brooks Simpson (Kent, OH: Kent State University Press, 1997), 108–110; Brian Jenkins, *Lord Lyons: A Diplomat in an Age of Nationalism and War* (Montreal: McGill-Queen's University Press, 2014), 229–230.

23. Caleb Cushing, "Martial Law," in *Official Opinions of the Attorneys General of the United States* (Washington, DC: W. H. & O. H. Morrison, 1872), 358.

24. Garrett Davis to Salmon Chase, September 3, 1861, in "Diary and Correspondence of Salmon P. Chase," in *Annual Report of the American Historical Association for the Year 1902* (Washington, DC: Government Printing Office, 1903), 2:502–503.

25. Lyman Trumbull, *The Constitutionality and Expediency of Confiscation Vindicated: Speech of Hon. Lyman Trumbull, of Illinois* (Washington, DC: Congressional Globe, 1862), 4; *Speech of Hon. Lyman Trumbull, of Illinois, on Introducing a Bill to Confiscate the Property of Rebels and Free Their Slaves* (Washington, DC: Congressional Globe, 1861), 6.

26. "The President's Appeal to the Border States," in McPherson, *Political History*, 217; William C. Harris, *Lincoln and the Border States: Preserving the Union* (Lawrence: University Press of Kansas, 2011), 161–162.

27. "Speech of John Quincy Adams," *Niles' Weekly Register*, June 18, 1836, 276–277; David Donald, *Charles Sumner and the Coming of the Civil War* (New York: Knopf, 1960), 388; "The Hon. C. Sumner on a War for Emancipation," *Anti-Slavery Reporter*, November 1, 1861, 246.

28. James Kent, *Commentaries on American Law*, ed. G. F. Comstock (Boston: Little, Brown, 1867), 1:67, 295–303; Louis Fisher, *Constitutional Conflicts between Congress and the President* (Lawrence: University Press of Kansas, 1991), 286; Alexander Hamilton, "No. 69," *The Federalist*, ed. G. W. Carey and James McClellan (Indianapolis: Liberty Fund, 2001), 357; Joseph Story, *Commentaries on the Constitution of the United States* (Boston: Hilliard, Gray, 1833), 1486.

29. Lincoln to Duff Green, Gustavus A. Myers, and Alexander Stephens, in Fehrenbacher and Fehrenbacher, *Recollected Words*, 182, 338, 421; Lincoln to William Otto, June 1, 1863, and Lincoln to Stephen A. Hurlbut, July 31, 1863, in *Collected Works*, 6:241, 358.

30. Jefferson Davis, "To the Senate and House of Representatives of the Confederate States," January 12, 1863, in *OR*, series 2, 5:807–808.

31. T. J. Barnett to Samuel Barlow, fall 1862, December 17, 1862, and December 30, 1862, in Samuel Barlow Papers, Huntington Library, San Marino, CA.

32. "Speech of T. Morris Chester, Esq., of Liberia, in the Cooper Institute," *Weekly Anglo-African*, February 7, 1863; Frederick Douglass, "January First 1863," *Douglass' Monthly*, October 1862.

33. Richard Hill, Edmund Parsons, and William Thornton quoted in *Report of the Joint Committee on Reconstruction at the First Session, Thirty-Ninth Congress* (Washington, DC: Government Printing Office, 1866), 55, 59, 53.

34. Joanne Pope Melish, *Disowning Slavery: Gradual Emancipation and Race in New England, 1780–1860* (Ithaca, NY: Cornell University Press, 1998), 88; Margot Minardi, *Making Slavery History: Abolitionism and the Politics of Memory in Massachusetts*

(New York: Oxford University Press, 2010), 8; James Kloppenberg, *The Virtues of Liberalism* (New York: Oxford University Press, 1998), 30.

35. *The Life and Times of Frederick Douglass: From 1817–1882*, ed. John Lobb (London: Christian Age Office, 1882), 297.

36. Lincoln to Stephen A. Hurlbut, July 31, 1863, in *Collected Works*, 6:358.

CHAPTER EIGHT

Abraham Lincoln's Kantian Republic

Steven B. Smith

Abraham Lincoln represents the high-water mark of the American Enlightenment.[1] He both completes and perfects many of the essential themes of early modernity. To say this, however, is already to stake a claim. Frequently, Lincoln is regarded as a shrewdly pragmatic politician, a pure Machiavellian cleverly tacking with the times to advance his ends.[2] Others see him as a disciple of the New England tradition of the American jeremiad, with its uniquely Calvinist blend of politics and conscience.[3] Neither of these views quite hits the mark. If, by a pragmatist, one means someone concerned more with results than with principles—a view brilliantly depicted in Steven Spielberg's *Lincoln*—then nothing could be further from the actual Lincoln. Lincoln was not a philosopher in any ordinary sense—he never wrote a book (but then again, neither did Socrates)—but he cared deeply for ideas and saw them as giving shape to public opinion, which is the only source of legitimate authority in a democracy. Nor was he simply a disciple of Jonathan Edwards and the Puritan tradition. While Lincoln could, on occasion, adopt the high pulpit style of the New England transcendentalists—consider the peroration to the Cooper Institute speech—he preferred to shape his arguments in terms of reason and certain shared moral sentiments rather than by appeals to the "inner light" and the private satisfactions of conscience politics.[4]

But if Lincoln was a man of the Enlightenment, the question is, which Enlightenment? On one account, Lincoln's Enlightenment belongs entirely to the natural law–based jurisprudence of the American founders. He was a faithful preserver and transmitter of the founders' principles of 1776. "I have never had a feeling," he said in Philadelphia's Independence Hall, "that did not spring from the sentiments embodied in the Declaration of

Independence" (324). Those sentiments embodied in the Declaration's appeal to "the laws of nature and nature's God" are said to derive, in turn, from Locke and the tradition of moral prudentialism going back to Aquinas and Aristotle. Lincoln's Enlightenment, on this account, is moderate if not conservative.[5]

Yet if Lincoln was the heir of the moderate Enlightenment associated with Aquinas and Locke, he was also a product of the radical Enlightenment associated with Spinoza and Paine. From an early period, Lincoln was an admirer of Paine's *Age of Reason*, and as a young man he had to defend himself from charges of religious infidelity (26–27). Although Lincoln has been described by the spirit of caution and prudence, there is also a powerful egalitarian, universalist, and progressive character to his statecraft. If Lincoln's Enlightenment contains elements of the empirical and experimental temper of Franklin, it also bears close affinity to the moral idealism and perfectionism of Kant. To be sure, in describing Lincoln's statesmanship as Kantian, I do not mean to say that he ever read or studied the works of Kant, nor do I ascribe to him anything as crude as a "system" of thought. Rather, I am suggesting that Lincoln's writings, speeches, and public actions evinced certain fixed principles that fall within a broadly Kantian frame of reference.[6]

To describe Lincoln as a Kantian has become something close to profanity in certain quarters. It is often taken as code for a kind of moral rigidity, even absolutism, that values the purity of intentions over the efficacy of results. Harry V. Jaffa deplores the fact that "German idealism in all its forms had come to possess a very great influence in the United States by 1857."[7] He singles out in particular the Kantian demand for moral consistency ("Act only on that maxim through which you can at the same time will that it should become a universal law") as the shared premise behind both Chief Justice Roger Taney's decision in the *Dred Scott* case (if slavery is right anywhere, it must be right everywhere) and the abolitionists' slogan of "No Union with Slaveholders" (if slavery is wrong anywhere, it must be wrong everywhere). The abstract formalism of the Kantian moral imperative, Jaffa suggests, allows it to be pressed with more or less equal plausibility in the service of both slavery and its opponents.[8]

Similarly, Allen Guelzo contrasts "the Enlightenment politics of prudence so dear to Lincoln's Lockean and rationalist sense of politics" to "a political ethic built on romantic Kantianism (and hallowed in our times by John Rawls)."[9] According to Guelzo, it is "precisely the intrusion of the Kantian ethic into American political thought" that has made it especially difficult to appreciate Lincoln's prudentialism. "Lincoln understood emancipation," Guelzo writes, "not as the satisfaction of 'spirit' over-riding the law, nor as the moment of fusion between the Constitution and absolute moral theory, but as a goal to be achieved through prudential means, so that worthwhile consequences might result."[10]

Both these arguments are caricatures of the Kantian position. Jaffa assumes that the only relevant aspect of Kantian ethics is the demand for a kind of moral resoluteness of will. On this account, any action, so long as it is willed with sufficient consistency, passes the test of morality. The result would be to empty Kant's categorical imperative of all moral content, since the morality of an action would be dependent on the firmness of the will that informs it. But this completely abstracts from Kant's view that no action can be deemed morally valuable unless it treats individuals as moral agents, that is, as "ends in themselves." At the core of Kantianism is a conception of dignity or moral respect for persons that is completely inconsistent with the institution of slavery and other forms of domination. Guelzo's references to "romantic Kantianism" seem to confuse Kant—a quintessential man of the Enlightenment!—with the Thoreauvian ethic of the "beautiful soul," which is more concerned with its own personal integrity than the moral consequences of actions. The mistake is understandable, but it rests on a deliberate conflation of Kant with his New England transcendentalist admirers. Kant never believed, as Guelzo implies, that the moral law can serve as an immediate standard for political action; rather, it is something like a North Star that sets the general direction for policy. Like Jaffa, Guelzo reduces Kantianism to a purely internal ethic of conviction.

At the core of this debate is not just an argument over influences and intellectual traditions. It is an argument over the nature—and future—of American democracy. Did Lincoln intend to return American politics to its founding principles in the Lockean-Jeffersonian conception of natural law, or did he envisage himself as a new founder undertaking a modification or even a transformation of these principles? Did Lincoln regard the American founding as a timeless model of political wisdom or as a noble but flawed beginning on which we must make progressive improvement? The answer is both. Lincoln often invokes the tradition of natural law when condemning the injustice of slavery and all forms of economic coercion, but his conception of emancipation as a moral struggle between right and wrong, his hope for a union purified from the stain of slavery, and his desire for a nation "dedicated to the proposition" of equality all bespeak a moral perfectionism—even a utopianism—that goes well beyond the Whiggish and contractualist language of natural law prudentialism.

Lincoln's republicanism was concerned with more than the protection of the rights to person and property. His idea of politics was not only protectionist but also progressive. Lincoln brings to a high level of theoretical self-consciousness a tension, even a bipolarity, within Enlightenment liberalism between the Lockean language of securing individual rights and the Kantian language of achieving moral perfectibility. This latter represented a reformist and pedagogical dimension of Lincoln's politics that was concerned with the cultivation of individual physical, intellectual, and moral capacities. The union was, for him, not just a legal or constitutional term of art but a site of moral self-development. "For Lincoln," J. David Greenstone has written, "there was a symbiotic relationship between individual self-development and the institutional life of a community. Lincoln thought that only a regime devoted to improving the capacities of its members for self-development could rightfully be called a Union."[11]

Lincoln's Kantianism is, above all, an expression of his confidence in the power of reason as a moral force in human nature. Throughout his writings, he repeatedly appealed to "ideas," "maxims," "the logic of principle," and "propositions"—all terms that express the rational foundation of political conduct. Furthermore, Lincoln believed that reason could serve as an independent cause of action rather than as a vehicle or smoke screen for certain ulterior motives or interests. Although he frequently traced these foundations back to the Declaration of Independence and its reference to the laws of nature, his appeal did not rest on veneration for authority—not even the authority of the framers. In his first major speech to the Young Men's Lyceum in Springfield in 1838, he defends the thesis that the preservation of our institutions cannot depend on sentiment and feeling but must be grounded in "the solid quarry of sober reason." "Reason, cold, calculating, unimpassioned reason," he told his audience, "must furnish all the materials for our future support and defense" (14).

To emphasize Lincoln as a man of principle, even Kantian principle, is not to deny that he was also a man of prudence or to suggest that he was some kind of moral absolutist. To invoke principle is always to court the possibility of violence, to draw a line in the sand beyond which compromise is impossible. As much as anyone, Lincoln understood the importance of addressing the "public mind" and adapting himself to what circumstances would permit. In fact, those closest to him, friend and enemy alike, were often baffled by Lincoln's apparent inconsistencies and his willingness to compromise even on such controversial issues as the fugitive slave law. But Lincoln saw no contradiction in this. Principle and prudence are not opposed but complementary moral dispositions. To adapt a Kantian turn of phrase: principle without prudence is empty; prudence without principle is blind. Despite the claim that he was vacillating and weak when it came to pressing for immediate emancipation or repeal of the fugitive slave law, with regard to the moral foundations of republican government, Lincoln was absolutely clear. Although particular policies must remain flexible and be adapted to circumstance, Lincoln reminded his audience in his last public speech that matters of principle "may and must be inflexible" (434).

"FOREVER WORTHY OF THE SAVING"

The first and most fundamental aspect of Lincoln's Kantian statecraft is his commitment to moral egalitarianism. By this, I mean Lincoln's belief that all human beings are rational—or potentially rational—moral agents and are therefore entitled to at least a minimum of moral respect. By moral respect, I mean, positively, an acknowledgment of human beings as rights-bearing agents, and negatively, an avoidance of policies that set out to systematically demean, humiliate, or deprive people of their dignity. In other words: no slavery. Equality had been enshrined in the Declaration of Independence, but Lincoln sought to give it independent philosophical worth. Equality was the principle—or "proposition," as he called it in the Gettysburg Address—on which free government rested. Lincoln realized that the abolition of slavery could not be accomplished by an appeal to morality alone ("the better angels of our nature"). To be effective—to give it teeth—morality required a certain kind of government. This is why Lincoln's defense of moral egalitarianism always went hand in hand with his efforts to preserve the union as embodied in the Constitution.

Lincoln's defense of the union has often been troubling to his readers. Why did it remain of such singular significance? Was there a tension between the equality principle enshrined in the Declaration and the Constitution's emphasis on federalism and the separation of powers? It has been argued—principally by his detractors—that the idea of union had a "mystical" significance for Lincoln, thus joining him with the nineteenth-century tradition of romantic nationalism. But in fact, there is little that is mystical or inexplicable in Lincoln's commitment to the union. Union represented for him the precondition for equality, for self-government. No doubt, Lincoln saw the original Constitution as a deeply flawed document, but he believed its preservation was necessary to make emancipation possible in the future. His opposition to secession followed from this premise. Secession made self-government impossible. "Plainly," he said in the First Inaugural, "the central idea of secession is the essence of anarchy" (329).

"My paramount object in this struggle *is* to save the Union and *not* either to save or to destroy slavery" (362). This statement, contained in a public letter to Horace Greeley written at the height of the war, has been gleefully cited by generations of Lincoln interpreters as evidence that political, not moral, considerations were paramount in his policy. There is no doubt that Lincoln attached primacy to preserving the union, but not in the sense this is usually understood. Lincoln inherited from the Whig tradition of Henry Clay and Daniel Webster a strong belief in the inviolability and sanctity of the union. But unlike the great Whig lawyers of the previous generation, the union that Lincoln sought to save was the one that had put slavery firmly "on the path of ultimate extinction." Preserving the union and abolishing slavery were not aspects of a zero-sum game for Lincoln but mutually constitutive parts of a single whole. The union that Lincoln set out to save was not simply a legal or constitutional framework but an object of moral aspiration. It was not the empirical fact of union but the moral idea of union to which Lincoln appealed in the letter to Greeley.

Lincoln's letter to Greeley has been widely (and sometimes maliciously) misunderstood because Lincoln's unionism has been misunderstood.[12] The union that Lincoln elevated to his supreme moral value was a union that put the principles of liberty *and* equality at its core. The conjunction of liberty and union, a standard trope of Whig rhetoric throughout the 1840s and 1850s, was given new meaning by Lincoln. The occasion for this conceptual innovation in the meaning of union was the Kansas-Nebraska Act of 1854, which threatened to introduce slavery into the territories where it had been expressly forbidden by the Missouri Compromise of 1820. Prior to 1854, Lincoln's most extensive public utterance had been devoted to opposition to the Mexican War during his one term in the House of Representatives. Prior to that, he had taken up such conventional themes as temperance and moral reform and the dangers to the rule of law posed by lynch mobs. Kansas-Nebraska was to Lincoln what reading Hume had been to Kant—a wake-up call from his "dogmatic slumber." Beginning in the mid-1850s, Lincoln turned the perpetuation of the union, not as something half free and half slave but as something devoted to the ideas of liberty and self-government, into something like a moral truth of reason.

Lincoln first publicly reflected on the moral idea of union in his famous Peoria speech on the Kansas-Nebraska Act. Here, he rebuked Stephen A. Douglas for his professed "indifference" to the fact of slavery, which, he accused, concealed a covert but real "zeal" for the spread of the institution (66). Douglas's solution to the problem of slavery in the territories was his doctrine of popular sovereignty. By allowing each territory to vote on whether to permit slavery, he hoped to defuse conflict. By removing slavery from federal jurisdiction and handing it over to the states or territories, Douglas hoped to deal with slavery in the same way one might address any local matter. But a mechanism for resolving conflict is not a principle, and Lincoln saw popular sovereignty as a substitute for the principle of self-government.

Lincoln regarded the union as resting not on the direct expression of the popular will—a kind of American version of Rousseau's "general will"—but on his "ancient faith" in the principle that all men are created equal. The difference between Douglas's doctrine of popular sovereignty and Lincoln's idea of self-government could not be stated more strongly than in the Peoria speech. One professes not to care whether slavery is voted up or down, and the other maintains that "there can be no moral right in connection with one man's making a slave of another." The idea that no one is good enough to govern another without that other's consent is, according to Lincoln, "the sheet anchor of American republicanism" (76).

Lincoln and Douglas did not just debate over slavery in the territories; they contested the very idea of union. At issue was nothing less than a struggle for the future and direction of the public mind. Slavery, Lincoln avers, is founded in the selfishness of human nature, which stands in "eternal antagonism" to our sense of right or justice. Attempt to deny that slavery is wrong, and you attempt to alter the very foundations of the moral sense. "You cannot repeal human nature," Lincoln warns. It is from "the abundance of man's heart" that our sense of slavery is wrong, "and out of the abundance of his heart, his mouth will continue to speak" (81). In contrast to Douglas's view that the slave is not a human being and that the doctrine of self-government is intended for the benefit of whites alone, Lincoln retorts that "the great mass of mankind take a totally different view." The feeling, the sense, that slavery is "a great moral wrong" is not evanescent but eternal and "lies at the very foundation of the sense of justice" (91).

Lincoln couches the debate over the future of the union in unmistakably moral, not merely legal or constitutional, terms. What Lincoln appears to object to is not so much the fact of slavery in the territories but the new principle by which slavery has been justified ("I particularly object to the NEW position which the avowed principle of this Nebraska law gives to slavery in the body politic" [83]). Whereas the framers of the Constitution had permitted slavery to persist out of arguments from "necessity"—that is, because slavery was an already established institution in colonial America—the new defenders have taken a fact and turned it into a "sacred right" (85). They are guilty of committing a version of the naturalistic fallacy, of confusing facts with rights. What is particularly loathsome from Lincoln's perspective is that a temporary concession to necessity has been turned into a sacred moral right. It is not, then, simply the empirical union that needs to be saved but the moral idea of union that must be made worthy of saving from the Douglas Democrats. "Our republican robe is soiled and trailed in the dust," Lincoln declares at the denouement of the speech. Let it be purified "in the spirit, if not the blood, of the Revolution" (85).

The source of Lincoln's political morality derives, above all, from his adherence to the principles of the Declaration of Independence. "I have never had a feeling politically," he declared in a speech at Independence Hall, "that did not spring from the sentiments embodied in the Declaration of Independence" (324). Despite what he says about his "ancient faith" in the principle of equality or his love of "the sentiments of those old-time men" like Washington and Jefferson, Lincoln's belief in the importance of self-government was not based on ancestral piety or love of tradition. Lincoln was not a Burkean Whig.[13] The principle of self-government is true not because it is ours but because it is right—"absolutely and eternally right," Lincoln adds (76). Earlier he had praised Henry Clay, who loved his country "partly because it was his own country, but mostly because it was a free country" (48).

The "sentiments" expressed in the Declaration are not simply "glittering generalities" or "self-evident lies," as the defenders of slavery had argued. Rather than viewing it as a period piece or as merely a legal document devised to secure independence from Britain, Lincoln regards the Declaration as enumerating nothing less than "the definitions and axioms of a free society." As he wrote to Henry L. Pierce of Boston on the occasion of the centenary of Jefferson's birth:

> All honor to Jefferson—to the man who, in the concrete pressure of a struggle for national independence by a single people, had the coolness, forecast, and capacity to introduce into a merely revolutionary document, an abstract truth, applicable to all men and all times, and so to embalm it there, that today, and in all coming days, it shall be a rebuke and a stumbling-block to the very harbingers of a reappearing tyranny and oppression. (244)

Lincoln's reverence for the Declaration was stated as early as his Lyceum address in Springfield, where he actually called for a "political religion" based on the principles that might serve as an oath to liberty (11). However, it was not until his speech on the *Dred Scott* decision in 1857 that he explicitly stated his understanding of the full meaning of the principle of equality and asserted his differences with the Douglas Democrats. "I think the authors of that notable instrument intended to include *all* men, but they did not intend to declare all men equal *in all respects*," he averred. "They did not mean to say all were equal in color, size, intellect, moral developments, or social capacity" (115). However, when it came to the capacity to have and enjoy the basic rights of life, liberty, and happiness, when it came to the right of each man to eat the bread acquired through the sweat of his own brow, each person was the full equal of all others. Lincoln adds to this understanding of the union an awareness of its incomplete nature; it is not a finished product but an object of moral aspiration that may be achieved only in the fullness of time: "They meant to set it up as a standard maxim for free society, which should be familiar to all, and revered by all; constantly looked to, constantly labored for, and even though never perfectly attained, constantly approximated, and thereby constantly spreading and deepening its influence, and augmenting the happiness and value of life to all people of all colors everywhere" (115). Lincoln's reference to "people of all colors" may be the first specific attempt to include blacks within the American family. It is this sense of moral universalism that makes the Declaration worth preserving and adopting. He disavows Douglas's historicist view that the document served merely to restore to the American colonists the rights of British subjects. Rather, the Declaration "contemplated the progressive improvement in the condition of all men everywhere" (116). If one were to believe Douglas, one would conclude that the Declaration is "of no practical use now . . . old wadding left to rot on the battle-field after the victory is won." The object of independence having been acquired, the Declaration would be left "shorn of its vitality, and practical value and left without the *germ* or even the *suggestion* of the individual rights of man in it" (117). It is, above all, dedication to the individual rights of man that will secure the moral foundation of the union.

There is more going on in Lincoln's invocation of the Declaration than the proper method of interpreting a historical document. The central issue, he declared in the "House Divided" speech, is "*where* we are and *whither* we are tending" (126). Lincoln does not invoke the Declaration and its principle of equality to argue for immediate emancipation. "For the extinction of slavery he could wait," Lord Charnwood writes; "for a decision on the principle of slavery he would not."[14] In fact, he declared a willingness to wait for up to a century for emancipation to run its course. It was not so much immediate results that interested Lincoln but the larger direction of national policy. His initial goal was no more than to return the slavery issue to where it had been established by the Missouri Compromise. His larger aim, however, was to stigmatize slavery as "a moral, social, and political wrong" (219). Only by readopting the principles of the Declaration could slavery be put where it belonged—on the course to ultimate extinction. Adherence to the principle that slavery is an unconditional moral evil affirms the priority of justice over self-interest. To Lincoln, the idea that "there is no right principle of action but self-interest" is a hateful and detestable maxim (66). Contrary, then, to the view that he was out to save the union at whatever cost, Lincoln's paramount objective was not merely to save the union but to make the union "forever worthy of the saving" (86).

"SUBLIME CHRISTIAN HEROISM"

The second element of Lincoln's Kantianism is a powerful streak of moral perfectionism and an emphasis on individual self-development. Running throughout his writings is a demand that human beings cultivate their individual moral, social, and intellectual faculties. Indeed, the system of slavery was especially vile because it barred an entire race of people from the opportunity for self-improvement. Lincoln's emphasis on improvement and development was more than the crude worship of economic success or a desire to be first in "the race of life," as he sometimes put it.[15] There was an important moral component in his perfectionism. Only with the full development and exercise of our distinctively human faculties can citizens become capable of self-government. "As I would not be *slave*, so I would not be a *master*" (150): this is Lincoln's pithy way of showing that neither servitude nor domination provides the grounds for self-development. The capacity for self-government requires careful cultivation and development, something "constantly looked to, constantly labored for, and even though never perfectly attained, constantly approximated," even if never fully realized (115). Lincoln's repetition of the word "constantly" brings out the progressive and probably unachievable nature of the commitment to equality.

Lincoln coupled his ethical perfectionism with a concern for the importance of labor, struggle, and, above all, history. "*We* cannot escape history," he told Congress in 1862 (392). But Lincoln deepened the standard Whig sense of history as the story of social and material progress with an almost Augustinian belief in the inscrutability of God's will and the mystery of his Providence. Lincoln came to see the war as much more than a sectional conflict, as much less a struggle between two competing sets of social and economic interests than a form of atonement for the national sin of slavery, which could be redeemed only through shared sacrifice. The war, "the fiery trial through which we pass," was bound up with the prophetic values of sin, guilt, atonement, and redemption. "The will of God prevails," Lincoln wrote in a private meditation from 1862. "He could have either *saved* or *destroyed* the Union without a human contest. Yet the contest began. And having begun He could give the final victory to either side any day. Yet the contest proceeds" (362–363). The ethical improvement of humanity is, in the final analysis, not up to human effort alone, but it can be achieved almost instrumentally through the hand of Providence.

Some of Lincoln's earliest and most pointed reflections on the possibility of moral reform occur in his 1842 address to the Washington Temperance Society. The speech is a testament to Lincoln's gradualism and moderation in reform. Though ostensibly directed toward temperance advocates—a cause in which Lincoln had little interest—it is in fact a lecture on the pace and tempo of moral reform. The greatest dangers come from neither drunkards nor saloon keepers ("denunciations against dram-sellers and dram-drinkers, are *unjust* as well as impolitic" [17]) but from those who would use the cause of moral reform to impose a new order of saintliness on the citizen body. Curbing the zealotry and intolerance of moral reformers and preachers is the real object of Lincoln's speech.[16]

Lincoln's address contains a speech about speech. He begins by telling his listeners that in attempting any reform, you must first convince your audience that you are their "sincere friend." "When the conduct of men is designed to be influenced, *persuasion*, kind, unassuming persuasion, should ever be adopted" (16). The old methods of reform that attempt to dictate judgment, command action, or even ostracize will inevitably fail. Such is the power of the passions that they resist all efforts at coercion, even if the cause is the truth itself. Lincoln's fundamental moderation is revealed later in the speech when he remarks that would-be reformers are characterized more by an "absence of appetite" than any mental or moral superiority (20). Lincoln flatters the Washingtonians for resisting the harsh and denunciatory moralism of earlier reform movements. But in praising his audience, he also warns against the danger of excessive moral zeal. He puts a certain distance between himself and the reform society. He is willing to use their cause, even though it is not exactly his cause.

The Temperance speech concludes with Lincoln's view on the relation between the political revolution of 1776 and the moral reform movements of the mid-nineteenth century. The one is presented as the complement and completion of the other. While the political revolution established "a degree of political freedom, far exceeding that of other of the nations of the earth," its work was left essentially incomplete. Political independence is but a first step toward the achievement of the moral independence of humanity. The moral improvement of mankind must attempt to overcome an even "viler slavery" and a "greater tyrant," that is, mankind's enslavement to the passions. Lincoln gives extravagant expression to the aims and goals of the moral revolution now under way. "Happy day," he says, "when, all appetites controlled, all passions subdued, all matters subjected, *mind*, all conquering *mind*, shall live and move the monarch of the world" (21–22). It is only at the end of his speech that Lincoln connects the temperance movement with the goals of abolitionism. The victory will be complete only "when there shall be neither a slave nor a drunkard on the earth" (22). Political freedom and moral autonomy are, then, the twin goals of Lincoln's perfectionism.

Lincoln's perfectionist temperament colored his views on labor and slavery throughout the second half of the 1850s. Just as he refuses to chastise drunkards in the Temperance address, he refrains from stigmatizing slave owners as a class ("They are just what we would be in their situation" [66]), but he criticizes the system of slavery and what it does to those living under it. He asks his audience to universalize the arguments now being used in defense of slavery. Lincoln makes none of the standard sentimental or emotional appeals to the cruelty of slavery; he is interested only in the logic of the arguments and what those arguments commit their holders to believing. "They are," he invites his listeners to consider, "the arguments that kings have made for enslaving the people in all ages of the world. You will find that all the arguments in favor of kingcraft were of this class; they always bestrode the necks of the people, not that they wanted to do it, but because the people were better off for being ridden" (149).[17]

Lincoln's most sustained argument regarding the prospects for moral self-improvement occur in the context of a speech given to the Wisconsin State Agricultural Society in Milwaukee in 1859. This speech has generally been treated by half-Marxists as the urtext of Lincoln's republican "free labor ideology," but such a view is overly reductionist.[18] In Milwaukee, Lincoln regrets the doctrine that he dubs "the mud-sill theory," which posits capital's tendency to maintain labor in a fixed condition of near servitude (274). This idea had gained particular traction in the South, where it was used to show that the northern system of free labor was no different from the southern slave system, but with the additional insult of hypocrisy. Such theories, Lincoln reminds his audience, are false to the experience of life, where there is generally considerable fluidity of movement between capital and labor.

On Lincoln's account, the mud-sill thesis is closer to the traditions of European feudalism, with its fixed ranks and estates, than to the fluid and mobile condition of the American workforce. In America, Lincoln argues, most people belong to neither capital nor labor but occupy a kind of middle state. Free labor is the precondition for moral self-development:

> The prudent, penniless beginner in the world, labors for wages awhile, saves a surplus with which to buy tools or land, for himself; then labors on his own account another while, and at length hires another new beginner to help him. This, say its advocates, is *free* labor—the just and generous, and prosperous system, which opens the way for all—gives hope to all, and energy, and progress, and improvement of conditions to all. (275)

The fundamental question posed by Lincoln in this speech, however, is the relation between labor and education. "How can *labor* and *education* be the most satisfactorily combined?" he asks (275). He rejects the view that labor and education are incompatible. "A blind horse on a treadmill" is the view of labor advanced by the defenders of slavery and the detractors of free labor. Labor is, for Lincoln, a form of cultivation in both senses of the word, a cultivation of both the land and the human personality. More than any other kind of work, agriculture combines labor with the possibility of education. "Every blade of grass," he observes, "is a study and to produce two, where there was but one, is both a pleasure and a profit" (276). Through the systematic application of science to agriculture, one can expect to develop a taste for reading, a facility for pursuing unsolved problems, and the arts and sciences. Furthermore, developing the agricultural arts is the best guarantee of political independence. "No community," he avers, "whose every member possesses this art can ever be the victim of oppression in any of its forms" (277).

Lincoln sums up his exhortation on a slightly chastened note. He recalls the story of an Eastern potentate who commissioned his wise men to come up with a sentence that would prove true for all times and all places. They came up with these words: "And this, too, shall pass away." Yet, Lincoln opines, let us hope that this statement is "not quite true": "Let us hope, rather, that by the best cultivation of the physical world, beneath and around us; and the intellectual and moral world within us, we shall secure an individual, social, and political prosperity and happiness, whose course shall be onward and upward, and which, while the earth endures, shall not pass away" (278).

The image of cultivating the self was familiar to Lincoln and his audience not only through literary works such as *Pilgrim's Progress* and *Robinson Crusoe* but also through the larger theological and ethical culture of American Protestantism. What makes the "free labor ideology" thesis so misleading when applied to Lincoln is that it is abstracted entirely from the larger ethical outlook of which it is a part. In an earlier speech given at Kalamazoo, Lincoln asks what explains the greatness of the American "empire" and discovers his answer in the cause that "every man can make himself" (103). It is this ethical, not economic, principle that is the root of American prosperity as well as free government.

Lincoln made the defense of this ethical ideal a central part of his war aims. The goal of government is to eliminate obstacles and artificial barriers not only to trade and commerce but also to human autonomy and self-direction. "This is essentially a People's contest," he told Congress in a special message delivered in 1861: "On the side of the Union, it is a struggle for maintaining in the world, that form, and substance of government, whose leading object is, to elevate the condition of men—to lift artificial weights from all shoulders—to clear the paths of laudable pursuit for all—to afford all, an unfettered start, and a fair chance, in the race of life" (345). Lincoln reiterated this theme near the end of the war when he reminded members of the Ohio Regiment that the war has been fought so that "you may all have equal privileges in the race of life, with all its desirable human aspirations," adding that "the nation is worth fighting for, to secure such an inestimable jewel" (424).

The economic interpretation of Lincoln's thought—that he was concerned only with securing free soil for free white men—fails to take into account Lincoln's repeated appeals to moral duty as a principal reason for action. We have already seen Lincoln reject the view that self-interest is the only motive for action. In his Temperance address he made the point that posterity is a distant goal, and few can be induced to work on its behalf (18), but throughout his life, Lincoln himself felt a powerful sense of duty and an obligation to future generations. He frequently reminds his listeners that the signers of the Declaration of Independence pledged not only their lives and liberties but their "sacred honor" for the cause of freedom. At the Cooper Institute he exhorts his audience to have the courage to do their duty "fearlessly and effectively," whatever the consequences (298). And in his annual message to Congress in 1862, he appeals to the sense of honor that alone will determine whether "we shall nobly save or meanly lose the last best hope of earth" (392).

Lincoln's writings express a desire to spread not only a doctrine of economic success but also a powerful moral principle that freedom requires acts of moral heroism that are often at odds with our interests. In a stirring letter he expresses his gratitude to the Workingmen of Manchester England for their support of the northern cause, even at the cost of great hardship to themselves. "It has been often and studiously represented," he writes, "that the attempt to overthrow this government, which was built upon the foundation of human rights, and to substitute for it one which should rest exclusively on slavery, was likely to obtain favor in Europe" (397). By resisting the pull of self-interest that would have favored the support of southern cotton, Lincoln adds, "I cannot but regard your decisive utterance upon the question as an instance of sublime Christian heroism which has not been surpassed in any age or in any country" (397).

"TO LIBERATE THE WORLD"

The final aspect of Lincoln's Kantianism focuses on the cosmopolitanism and progressivism of his republican ideal. His writings continually emphasize the open and inclusive character of the American republic, in contrast to the narrow and exclusive particularisms of his leading contemporaries. The American republic is defined not by religion, race, or ethnic identity but exclusively by adherence to the principle of rights embodied in the Declaration of Independence. He offers an enlarged reading of the Declaration's language as applying to a broader segment of mankind than those British descendants of North Americans who were already present in 1776. The American republic is the first nation built on a universal idea of awakening people everywhere to their right to free government. In an extraordinary statement of moral universalism in his speech on the Mexican War, Lincoln claims that "any people, anywhere, being inclined to rise up, and shake off the existing government, and form a new one that suits them better" have the right to do so. "This is a most valuable—a most sacred right," Lincoln concludes, "a right, which we hope and believe, is to liberate the world" (36).

Lincoln's enlarged republicanism took the immediate form of opposition to the nativist and anti-immigrant policies of the American Party, or the Know-Nothings. Regarding the wave of anti-immigrant fervor that swept over America at midcentury, Lincoln had nothing but contempt. "Our progress in degeneracy," he wrote to Joshua Speed, "appears to me to be pretty rapid" (96). Rather than acquiesce to the exclusion of not only blacks but also foreigners and Catholics from the principles of the Declaration, Lincoln claimed he would prefer to immigrate to some other country, perhaps Russia, "where they make no pretense of loving liberty" and "where despotism can be taken pure, without the base alloy of hypocrisy" (96).

Lincoln's cosmopolitanism revealed itself in his liberal treatment of recent immigrant groups, many of which had come to America to escape the wave of political repression in Europe after 1848. In Chicago he noted that the group who could trace their bloodline directly to the founding generation was growing smaller with the passage of time. But rather than deplore this fact, Lincoln used the occasion to welcome those of recent ancestry to the table. What makes a citizen is not direct genealogical descent from that race of "iron men" but adherence to the principles for which they fought. The principle of equality, "the father of all moral principle," is "the electric cord" that unites all "liberty-loving men" (148).

The same language pervades Lincoln's later utterances to a group of German immigrants in Cincinnati. Regarding the Germans and other foreigners, Lincoln says, he esteems them no better or worse than any other people. Yet he adds to this judgment a belief that it is important to remove obstacles or "weights" to their enjoyment of the rights of citizenship. "It is not my nature," he continues, "when I see a people borne down by the weight of their shackles—the oppression of tyranny—to make their life more bitter by heaping upon them greater burdens; but rather would I do all in my power to raise the yoke, than to add anything that would tend to crush them" (323). The language of lifting weights and burdens from the shoulders of men clearly connects Lincoln's language to the Puritan notion of a "calling" and a quest for salvation from original sin. However, for Lincoln, the original political sin was inequality, and the mission of the American republic is release from that fallen state. He reiterates this theme in his speech at Independence Hall on his way to the White House:

> It was not the mere matter of the separation of the colonies from the mother land; but something in that Declaration giving liberty, not alone to the people of this country, but hope to the world for all future time. It was that which gave promise that in due time the weights should be lifted from the shoulders of all men, and that *all* should have an equal chance. (324)

It is one thing to consider the inclusion of free white immigrants, even Catholics, from northern Europe. It is another matter to raise the issue of freed black slaves and their future place in the republic. The society that Lincoln inhabited was a deeply racist one, and such prejudice, "whether well or ill-founded," could not be "safely disregarded." Lincoln admits that such racial prejudices are unjust, but he goes on to say that justice is not "the sole question" (66–67). The question was what kind of society would whites and freed blacks inhabit after emancipation. Like his contemporaries, Lincoln had no clear idea of what such a society would look like. He knew that slavery was an evil and that blacks were entitled as human beings to the same rights as whites, but whether blacks and whites would live together, apart, or in some other way remained a vast conundrum.

Time and again, Lincoln stated his preferred outcome as the repatriation of freed blacks to a home in Liberia. The colonization of freed slaves had been the design of Lincoln's early political hero, Henry Clay, the man he called his "beau ideal" of a statesman (178). In his "Eulogy on Henry Clay" Lincoln quoted at length from Clay's "Address to the American Colonization Society" of 1827. In the creation of a colony of freed slaves in Liberia, Lincoln, like Clay, saw the possible redemption of the African American people, who, like the Jews in Egypt, could be free only in a land of their own. Long before he wrote the Second Inaugural, Lincoln had begun to see the resolution of the slavery problem in explicitly theological terms. He noted that despite the fact that Jefferson had been a slave owner, he could admit that "he trembled for his country when he remembered that God was just," and he chided Douglas for refusing to offer a similar sentiment (254). Colonization would help whites atone for slavery, the continuation of which threatened, in Clay's words, to "blow out the moral lights around us" (53).

Although Lincoln's "first impulse" was to free all the slaves and manumit them to Liberia, "a moment's reflection" was all he needed to realize the impossibility of such a plan (66). Nevertheless, he continued to consider the possibility of colonization even during his presidency.[19] In his annual address to Congress in 1861 he raised the issue of appropriating funds to purchase territory for newly emancipated slaves, using Jefferson's purchase of the Louisiana Territory as his model. And later when he met with a group of free blacks at the White House, he urged that, "for the sake of your race you should sacrifice something of your present comfort for the purpose of being as grand in that respect as the white people" (359). In expressing these views, Lincoln was not being callous. Rather, his continued belief in the prospects for colonization expressed his faith that blacks, as well as whites, were capable of self-government.

Still, colonization was not Lincoln's last thought—or his best thought—on the solution of the slavery problem. One way or another, he realized, blacks and whites would have to inhabit the same space. The only question that remained was what kind of relationship would develop between the races. Throughout his writings, he took pains to deny that emancipation entailed the "amalgamation" of the races. In a line he repeated several times for the effect it had, Lincoln protested the "counterfeit logic" that "because I do not want a negro woman for a slave, I do necessarily want her for a wife." The two races could simply leave each other alone and, as a consequence, "do one another much good thereby" (147). Even though Lincoln defensively denied that he favored full social and political equality ("my own feelings will not admit of this" [67]), he insisted that emancipation guaranteed blacks all the liberties granted to every other American. He worked assiduously for passage of the Thirteenth Amendment, but could he have imagined the election of an African American to the White House?

Lincoln never fully worked out the disparity between his insistence that blacks and whites were bound together under the same moral law of equality and his disclaimers that emancipation required full social and political equality. Lincoln could not say with any certainty what form race relations would take after emancipation had been achieved. Most likely, he crafted his words carefully to exert the maximum antislavery influence that he believed public opinion would allow. "Our government rests in public opinion," he wrote in 1856. "Public opinion, on any subject, always has a '*central idea*,' from which all its minor thoughts radiate" (107). Lincoln's great fear was that the combined forces of the Douglas Democrats, the Taney Court, and what he mockingly referred to as southern "pro-slavery theology" had entered into an unholy alliance to desensitize public opinion to the moral wrongness of slavery. "Whenever this question shall be settled," he told his audience in New Haven, "it must be settled on some *philosophical basis*. No policy that does not rest upon some philosophical public opinion can be permanently maintained" (302; emphasis added). Would public opinion be permanently in favor of slavery or against it? That was Lincoln's only question.

Lincoln's carefully shaded ambiguities over the future of race relations were dictated, I suggest, by a prudential, statesman-like regard for his goal of guiding public opinion back to the "central idea" of equality, which represented the moral core of American republicanism. "He who molds public sentiment," he stated in his first debate with Douglas, "goes deeper than he who enacts statutes or pronounces decisions" (176). Lincoln could have added that even war is a struggle to control the "public sentiment," but instead, he chose to tell a story about the American past. The framers of the republic, he liked to remind his listeners, had intentionally omitted the word "slavery" from the Constitution, not out of hypocrisy or squeamishness but to deny it even the patina of moral legitimacy. The only argument in favor of slavery that the framers were prepared to admit was the argument drawn from necessity alone—that slavery was an established fact and could be neither ignored nor argued away (84–85). Necessity was the only argument Lincoln was prepared to consider. But eventually, even necessity would have to bend to the moral law, the "is" would have to give way to the "ought." Lincoln's cosmopolitanism consisted in large part of preparing the public to accept a far more inclusive view of republican government than anyone had previously imagined or even he was willing to admit publicly.

Lincoln's contribution to American politics was not merely that of an architect of the Republican Party or a supreme wartime commander but that of a moral and political philosopher. By emphasizing the Kantian character of Lincoln's statecraft, I mean three things: a belief in the moral truth of human equality, a commitment to the rational self-development of every individual, and an adherence to the universal or cosmopolitan nature of republican government. To be sure, he often proclaimed that, in asserting the primacy of principle, he was doing no more than returning the American self-understanding to where it had been at the time of the founding. But Lincoln did more than this—much more. He added a dimension of political idealism and moral perfectionism that helped reshape and in part redirect the meaning and scope of American liberalism.

There is a deep resistance to thinking of Lincoln as a Kantian statesman. This, we have seen, derives in part from the enormous influence of the pragmatic tradition on our views about politics. There have been two versions of pragmatism. In one version, the peculiar "genius" of American politics is its aversion to matters of principle and abstract theory. As every schoolchild knows, the Constitution was the product of a series of compromises culminating in the "Great Compromise." In contrast to the ideological style of European political parties, American politics, it is claimed, is rooted in a Whiggish and ultimately Burkean devotion to prudence, compromise, and the avoidance of extremes. Flexibility and accommodation—what Arthur Schlesinger Jr. once called "the vital center"—are the watchwords of this older pragmatism.[20]

This older version of pragmatism has been superseded by a newer, postmodern variant of the creed. Similarly, it has an aversion to introducing moral principles into political argument, but in the name of the ostensibly democratic values of deliberation and dialogue. This newer pragmatism has its roots in the philosophy of William James and John Dewey and has been given powerful expression in the work of Richard Rorty.[21] For Rorty and the new pragmatists, there are no longer truths of reason but only interpretations or the stories we tell about ourselves. Principles cannot be justified by reference to nature or the logic of history (for there is no logic there); they are always bound up in what Wittgenstein called "forms of life," that is, part of an ongoing tradition or conversation. By viewing politics as the art of storytelling, the new pragmatists believe they have found a way to reinvigorate democracy. Democracy is a matter of talk, of conversation with fellow citizens over things they care about. The opinion of today's "deliberative democrats" is that laws and policies should be openly debated and discussed, so long as citizens refrain from introducing controversial moral and religious opinions into the dialogue.

The irony of our situation is that both these pragmatisms have more in common with the views of John C. Calhoun and Stephen A. Douglas than those of Lincoln. Calhoun and Douglas were, in contemporary parlance, "multiculturalists" who believed that the unique and indigenous character of peoples and cultures was more authentic than common and universal moral principles. Calhoun defended the view of slavery as a "positive good" rooted in a uniquely southern way of life and threatened by northern imperialism. Douglas's version of this position was that the federal government had no business legislating on controversial moral issues; it must maintain an attitude of studious neutrality toward whatever the citizens of a given state or territory chose for themselves. Whether a people voted slavery up or down might be a question of intense private concern, but it should be one of official indifference. All politics was local, and there was no sense destroying the union over what were essentially private and thus inherently contestable moral beliefs.

For the reasons examined earlier, Lincoln could not possibly accept either of these views. He could not abide Calhoun's idea that each state or section could claim its own morality tailored to the special requirements of its history, geography, climate, and institutions. This kind of ethical relativism was tantamount to admitting the falsehood of the Declaration's moral truth that all men are created equal. Lincoln read the Declaration and its principle of equality not just as a historical document but as a comprehensive system of justice against which particular practices and policies were to be judged. Similarly, Douglas's idea of bracketing questions of ultimate moral concern for the sake of preserving the union struck Lincoln as a violation of all that republican government stood for. A republic that was neutral to the difference between freedom and slavery was an oxymoron. Self-government, for Lincoln, was ultimately a matter of principle and conviction rather than pragmatism and the mutual accommodation of interests. The statements that "no one has a right to do wrong" and "if slavery is not wrong, nothing is wrong" are not the sentiments of a pragmatist out to save the union at whatever cost; they are the statements of a moral universalist with a Kantian conscience.

NOTES

1. Steven B. Smith, ed., *The Writings of Abraham Lincoln* (New Haven, CT: Yale University Press, 2012), 126. All subsequent references to this work appear parenthetically in the body of the text.

2. David Herbert Donald, "Abraham Lincoln and the American Pragmatic Tradition," in *Lincoln Reconsidered* (New York: Random House, 1984), 128–143.

3. John Patrick Diggins, *The Lost Soul of American Politics* (Chicago: University of Chicago Press, 1984), 296–333. See also Sacvan Bercovitch, *The Puritan Origins of the American Self* (New Haven, CT: Yale University Press, 1975), 150–151, 168.

4. For the danger of appeals to conscience in politics, see John Burt, *Lincoln's Tragic Pragmatism: Lincoln, Douglas, and Moral Conflict* (Cambridge, MA: Harvard University Press, 2013).

5. Allen C. Guelzo, *Abraham Lincoln as a Man of Ideas* (Carbondale: Southern Illinois University Press, 2009), 73–86.

6. For the influence of Kant on Lincoln, if not directly then at least on his larger public culture, see Daniel Walker Howe, *Making the American Self: Jonathan Edwards to Abraham Lincoln* (Cambridge, MA: Harvard University Press, 1997), 202–203, 209–210.

7. Harry V. Jaffa, *A New Birth of Freedom* (Lanham, MD: Rowman & Littlefield, 2000), 297.

8. Ibid., 292–295, 432–433.

9. Guelzo, *Lincoln as a Man of Ideas*, 99.

10. Ibid., 191.

11. J. David Greenstone, *The Lincoln Persuasion: Remaking American Liberalism* (Princeton, NJ: Princeton University Press, 1993), 278.

12. For a recent attempt to grasp the distinctiveness of Lincoln's unionism, see Rogan Kersh, *Dreams of a More Perfect Union* (Ithaca, NY: Cornell University Press, 2001), 153–197; see also Greenstone, *Lincoln Persuasion*, 230–240.

13. For a contrasting view, see Daniel Walker Howe, *The Political Culture of the American Whigs* (Chicago: University of Chicago Press, 1979), 290, 296, which defends the Burkean character of Lincoln's thought.

14. Lord Charnwood, *Abraham Lincoln* (1916; reprint, New York: Madison Books, 1997), 97.

15. James McPherson, "How Lincoln Won the War with Metaphors," in *Abraham Lincoln and the Second American Revolution* (New York: Oxford University Press, 1990), 96.

16. Harry V. Jaffa, *Crisis of the House Divided: An Interpretation of the Lincoln-Douglas Debates* (Seattle: University of Washington Press, 1959), 271–272.

17. Lincoln shows his ability to parse the logic of an argument in his "Fragment on Slavery" (58–59).

18. Eric Foner, *Free Soil, Free Labor, Free Men* (New York: Oxford University Press, 1970), 29–30, 38. For Lincoln's economic views, see also Gabor S. Borritt, *Lincoln and the Economics of the American Dream* (Memphis, TN: Memphis State University Press, 1978).

19. Eric Foner, *The Fiery Trial* (New York: W. W. Norton, 2011).

20. See Daniel J. Boorstin, *The Genius of American Politics* (Chicago: University of Chicago Press, 1953); Arthur M. Schlesinger Jr., *The Vital Center: The Politics of Freedom* (Boston: Houghton Mifflin, 1949).

21. See Richard Rorty, "The Priority of Democracy to Philosophy," in *The Virginia Statute of Religious Freedom*, ed. Merrill Peterson and Robert Vaughn (Cambridge: Cambridge University Press, 1988), 257–282; Richard Rorty, *Achieving Our Country* (Cambridge, MA: Harvard University Press, 1998).

Contributors

NICHOLAS BUCCOLA is chair and associate professor of political science at Linfield College, where he also directs the Frederick Douglass Forum on Law, Rights, and Justice. He is the author of *The Political Thought of Frederick Douglass*; his essays have been published in scholarly journals such as the *Review of Politics* and *American Political Thought*, as well as popular journals such as the *Claremont Review of Books, Dissent,* and *salon.com.*

JOHN BURT is the Prosswimmer Professor of American Literature at Brandeis University and the author of *Robert Penn Warren and American Idealism* and *Lincoln's Tragic Pragmatism: Lincoln, Douglas, and Moral Conflict.*

ALLEN GUELZO is the Henry R. Luce Professor of the Civil War Era and Director of Civil War Era Studies at Gettysburg College. He is the author of *Abraham Lincoln: Redeemer President*, which won the Lincoln Prize for 2000; *Lincoln's Emancipation Proclamation: The End of Slavery in America,* which won the Lincoln Prize for 2005; and *Lincoln and Douglas: The Debates that Defined America*, which won the Abraham Lincoln Institute Prize for 2008.

BRUCE LEVINE is the J. G. Randall Distinguished Professor of History at the University of Illinois at Urbana-Champaign. He is the author of several books, including *The Fall of the House of Dixie: The Civil War & the Social Revolution That Transformed the South, Confederate Emancipation: Southern Plans to Free and Arm Slaves during the Civil War, Half Slave & Half Free: The Roots of Civil War,* and *The Spirit of 1848: German Immigrants, Labor Conflict, and the Coming of the Civil War.*

DOROTHY ROSS is the Arthur O. Lovejoy Professor Emerita of History at Johns Hopkins University. Ross is the author of many scholarly essays and books, including *The Origins of American Social Science*.

MANISHA SINHA is professor of Afro-American studies and history at the University of Massachusetts–Amherst. She is the author of *The Counterrevolution of Slavery: Politics and Ideology in Antebellum South Carolina* and *The Slave's Cause: A History of Abolition*.

STEVEN B. SMITH is the Alfred Cowles Professor of Government and Philosophy at Yale University. He is the author of several books, including *Hegel's Critique of Liberalism*; *Spinoza, Liberalism, and Jewish Identity*; *Spinoza's Book of Life*, and *Reading Leo Strauss*. He is also the editor of *The Cambridge Companion to Leo Strauss* and *The Writings of Abraham Lincoln*.

MICHAEL ZUCKERT is the Nancy Reeves Dreaux Professor of Political Science at the University of Notre Dame. He is the author of *Natural Rights Republic* and is currently working on *Completing the Constitution: The Post–Civil War Amendments*.

Index

abolitionism, 22–23, 73, 111, 115, 122–123, 127, 132n4, 164–191
  and constitutional interpretation, 174–191
Ackerman, Bruce, 41n25
Adams, John, 87, 104n42
Adams, John Quincy, 184, 205–207, 214n27
Ahlstrom, Sydney E., 102n14
Alton, Illinois, 14, 22, 42, 117, 139, 156n1, 166
American Anti-Slavery Society, 176
American Colonization Society, 168–169
American Party (also known as the Know-Nothings), 139–163, 229, 230
American Revolution, 16, 19, 74, 77, 79, 223
Anbinder, Tyler, 141, 157n18, 158n26, 159n32
Anderson, Dwight G., 16–17, 40n9
Andreas, A. T., 160–161n55
Andrew, John A., 185
Aptheker, Herbert, 204, 213n20
Arendt, Hannah, 16, 39n5, 41n26
Arkansas, 47
Ashmun, George, 162n69
Ashworth, John, 157n14
Avineri, Sholomo, 102n9
Ayers, Edward L., 73, 100n1
Azbug, Robert, 189n19

Babcock, James F., 162n74
Bacon, Leonard, 169

Baker, George E., 103nn18–19, 157n16
Baker, Jean H., 102n13, 106n54
Bancroft, George, 195, 211n1
Barlow, Samuel, 214n31
Barnes, Gilbert H., 189n19
Barnett, T. J., 214n31
Basler, Roy P., 132n6, 156n1, 187n1, 211n2
Basson, Ralph, 161n63
Bates, Edward, 146, 151, 162n64
Beale, Howard K., 162n64
Beecher, Edward, 41n27
Bell, Daniel A., 102n11
Belz, Herman, 40n9, 107n57
Bender, Thomas, 102n12, 103n15, 107n64
Bennett, Lerone, 8n1, 133n26, 188n11
Bercovich, Sacvan, 236n3
Berdan, James, 160n54
Bergquist, James M., 158n30, 161n58
Berlin, Ira, 97, 106n50, 108n70, 108n72, 213n19, 213n22
Bible, 52, 65, 174
Birney, James G., 154
Blake, Ruel, 30
Blassingame, John W., 103n17, 107n65
Blight, David, 94, 106n50, 107n62
Blue, Frederick J., 189n21, 190n26, 190n28
Bodnar, John, 102n13
Bonaparte, Napoleon, 14, 16, 37
Boorstin, Daniel J., 237n20

241

Boritt, Gabor, 40n9, 157n13, 212n13
Brancaforte, Charlotte L., 158n30
Briggs, John Channing, 14, 28, 39n1, 39n6, 41n27, 57, 69n30
Brock, William R., 104n27
Bromell, Nick, 190–191n29
Brookhiser, Richard, 188n5
Brown, J. N., 125
Brown, John, 172
Brown, Joseph, 163n84
Browning, Orville, 151, 162n65, 196, 211n2
Brownlee, W. Elliot, 104n32
Bryant, William Cullen, 195
Buccola, Nicholas, 190–191n29
Burlingame, Michael, 14, 39n3, 108n67, 191n33, 212–213n13
Burns, Anthony, 181
Burt, John, 2, 61, 69n12, 70n39, 95, 108n69, 132n7, 134n42, 187n1, 188n14, 236n4
Bush, George W., 43n42
Bushnell, Horace, 29
Butler, Benjamin, 184, 202–203

Calhoun, John C., 173–174, 179, 235
Callicles, 15, 26
Calvin, John, 54
Calvinism, 216
Campbell, A. C., 212n7
Canisius, Theodore, 148, 150, 159n38
Cantrell, Gregg, 157n21
Carey, G. W., 214n28
Carlander, Jay R., 104n32
Carleton, Guy, 198
Cartwright, Peter, 54
Carwadine, Richard J., 101n7, 187n1
Catholicism, 7, 42n29, 140–143, 147, 160n55, 161–162n63, 230–231
Charlestown, Massachusetts, 14
Charnwood, Lord, 224, 236n14
Chase, Salmon P., 114, 124, 179, 180, 190n26, 214n24
Chester, Thomas Morris, 209, 214n32
Chicago, Illinois, 12
Child, Lydia Maria, 114

Christ, Jesus, 60
Christianity, 51, 54, 74, 75, 78, 92, 100n2
civic (or classical) republicanism, 17, 81
civil rights (for freedmen), 46, 76, 169, 172, 180, 186
Civil Rights Act (1866), 174, 211
Civil War, 6, 7, 38, 44–70, 164, 165, 169, 171, 174–175, 179–185, 196, 198, 204
Clark, Elizabeth B., 100n1
Clay, Henry, 29, 56–57, 84, 105n33, 146–147, 167–169, 199, 212n10, 221, 223, 232
  the "American System" of, 168
  Lincoln's eulogy of, 56, 199, 232
Clink, Patricia C., 213n19
Cobb, Howell, 156n7
Cole, Arthur Charles, 160–161n55
Colfax, Schuyler, 160n44
colonization (of African Americans), 76, 98–99, 168–169, 172–174, 182, 186, 199–201, 232
Compromise of 1850, 42–43n35, 147, 167, 173, 180
Confederacy, 46, 48, 89, 182, 185, 196, 201, 204, 205, 207, 209
Confiscation Acts, 89, 202
Constitution (US), 33, 43, 45, 46, 78–82, 85–88, 93, 95, 120–130, 164–191, 195–215, 218, 220, 233
  Bill of Rights of, 175
  interpreted as antislavery, 79–80
Continental Congress, 197
Corwine, Richard M., 162n75
Cotton, Joshua, 31
Cover, Robert M., 189n20
Cox, LaWanda, 101n7, 191n37
Crittenden, John J., 155
Current, Richard, 40n9
Curti, Merle, 102n13
Cushing, Caleb, 214n23

Dain, Bruce, 100n4
Davis, David, 213n15
Davis, David Brion, 74, 100nn2–3, 108n73
Davis, Garrett, 205, 214n24

Davis, Henry Winter, 47
Davis, Jefferson, 202, 209, 214n30
Declaration of Independence, 7, 15, 33, 34, 36, 51, 59, 79, 80, 84, 86, 88, 98, 110, 113–114, 118, 122, 126, 130, 147, 167, 171, 175, 216–217, 219, 220, 222–224, 229–231, 235
Delahay, Mark W., 159n39
Delaware, 196, 201, 206
Delbanco, Andrew, 187n2
Democratic Party, 92–93, 114, 142, 170
de-Shalit, Avner, 102n9
Deutsch, Kenneth, 8nn3–4
Dew, Charles B., 156n6
Dewey, John, 234
Diamond, Martin, 19, 40n16
Diggins, John Patrick, 2, 8n1, 236n3
DiLorenzo, Thomas, 8n1
Dirck, Brian, 188n8, 188n11, 191n33
District of Columbia, 206
Donald, David, 48, 63, 69n9, 69n16, 70n40, 101–102n8, 141, 156n12, 157n18, 159–160n43, 190n28, 214n27, 236n2
Douglas, H. Ford, 171, 186
Douglas, Stephen A., 13, 15, 24, 57, 85, 88, 110, 116, 123, 127, 139, 140, 156n1, 167, 221–223, 232, 235
Douglass, Frederick, 80, 95, 114–115, 125, 134n56, 140, 163n79, 170, 176, 181, 210, 214n32, 215n35
  on the Constitution, 181–183
draft riots (1863), 29
Dred Scott v. Sandford (1857), 86, 113, 116, 127, 129–130, 168, 171, 176, 211, 217, 223
Duberman, Martin, 190n23
DuBois, W. E. B., 119, 134n37
Dumond, Dwight L., 156n5, 189n19
Durley, Williamson, 104n27
Dworkin, Ronald, 25, 41n25

Edge, Frederick, 213n14
Edwards, Jonathan, 216
Egerton, Douglas R., 189n17
Egypt, 232

Eisenhower, Dwight, 37
Emancipation Proclamation, 8, 45, 62, 75–76, 90, 91, 94, 95, 99, 182–184, 195–215
Emerson, Ralph Waldo, 18, 19, 26
Endy, Melvin B., 106–107nn54–55
England, 198
Enlightenment, 55, 74–75, 92, 216–237
equality, 1, 2, 51, 53, 58, 86, 200, 210, 218, 220, 222–224, 231, 233–235
Ericson, David F., 189n18

Fahs, Alice, 106n48
Faulkner, William, 30
Faust, Drew, 100–101n4
Federalist Papers, 207
Federalist Party, 142
Fehrenbacher, Don E., 39n7, 69nn3–4, 84, 103n16, 104n32, 188n9, 190n23, 190n27, 213n15
Fehrenbacher, Virginia, 188n12, 213n15
Fillmore, Millard, 141, 152
Finkelman, Paul, 103n16, 189n20
First Inaugural Address (of Abraham Lincoln), 59, 91, 220
Fisher, Louis, 214n28
Fisher, Sidney George, 142, 153, 157n15
Flesch, William, 40n11
Fletcher, George P., 102n9, 134n51
Foner, Eric, 18, 40n12, 98, 103n15, 104n27, 109n76, 109n78, 141, 157n17, 158n30, 162n64, 187n3, 188n11, 190n26, 190n28, 237nn18–19
Foner, Philip S., 156n2, 190n29
Foote, Henry, 30, 42n35
Forgie, George, 40n9, 104n24
Fornieri, Joseph, 8nn3–4
Fortress Monroe, 202
Fort Sumter, 207
Fox, Richard W., 102n14
Fox-Genovese, Elizabeth, 104n27
Franklin, Benjamin, 217
Fraysee, Olivier, 157n13
Frederickson, George, 76, 85, 100–101nn4–7, 104n25, 104n32, 104n35, 133–134n35, 188n11

freedom. *See* liberty
Freehling, William, 30, 42n35, 163n84
free labor ideology, 18, 83, 89, 93,
    170–173, 182, 227–229
free soil doctrine, 82–88, 180
Fremont, John C., 47, 154, 184, 202, 205,
    213n18
Freud, Sigmund, 37
Fugitive Slave Act, 123–124, 143, 166, 180
Furstenberg, Francois, 100n4, 102n13

Gallagher, Gary W., 191n34
Garrison, William Lloyd, 79, 114,
    169–170, 172, 180–182, 189n22
Gates, Henry Louis, 188n11
Genin, Thomas, 173, 188n16
Genovese, Eugene D., 104n27
Gerteis, Louis, 42n29
Gettysburg Address, 14, 51–60, 90, 99,
    208, 220
Giddings, Joshua, 114, 143
Gienapp, William E., 101–102n8, 141,
    145, 156nn9–12, 157n23, 158n29,
    160–161n55
Gilbert, Alan, 212n6
God, 1, 6, 8, 20, 26–28, 38, 48, 50, 78, 87,
    91, 111, 183, 209, 217, 225, 232
Goodell, William, 176–178, 190n24
Goodwin, Doris Kearns, 187n1
Gorham, George Congdon, 213n19
Gospel of Matthew, 50
Grant, Susan-Mary, 104n27
Grant, Ulysses S., 45
Great Society, 195
Greeley, Horace, 90, 144, 152, 183, 199,
    212n9, 221
Green, Duff, 214n29
Greene, Gilbert, 213n15
Greenstone, J. David, 2, 15, 25, 39n4, 219,
    236n11
Grimsted, David, 30, 42n34, 43n36
Grotius, Hugo, 197, 212n7
Guelzo, Allen C., 39n2, 101n7, 106n52,
    106–107n54, 187nn1–2, 190n33,
    217–218, 236n5, 236nn9–10
Guyatt, Nicholas, 108n68

Haakonssen, Knud, 100n1
Haiti, 200
Halleck, Henry Wager, 197, 212n4
Halstead, Murat, 159n33
Halttunen, Karen, 100n1
Hamilton, Alexander, 184, 214n28
Hamilton, Charles Granville, 145, 158n28,
    160n46
Hamilton, Daniel, 212n5
Hanley, Mark Y., 102n14
Harding, Aaron, 196, 212n3
Harding, Vincent, 213n20
Harper, Frances Ellen Watkins, 186
Harris, William C., 214n26
Harrison, William Henry, 37
Hart, Albert Bushnell, 190n26
Hart, H. L. A., 41
Harvey, James E., 162n68
Hay, John, 201, 212n13
Hayek, Friedrich A., 133n22
Helvetius, Claude, 55
Herndon, William, 159n43
Herriot, F. I., 158n30
Hietla, Thomas R., 103n18
Hill, Richard, 214n33
Hobbes, Thomas, 55
Hodges, Albert, 212n4, 212n7
Holt, Michael F., 162n76
Holzer, Harold, 132n1, 191n33
Howard, Mark, 162n74
Howe, Daniel Walker, 236n6
Howe, Julia Ward, 60, 66–67
human nature, 56, 74, 113, 219, 222
human rights, 73–108, 110–135
Hume, David, 221
Hunt, Lynn, 100n1, 104n36
Hunter, David, 203
Hurlbut, Stephen A., 214n29, 215n36

immigration, 139–163

Jackson, Andrew, 14, 39n1
Jaffa, Harry, 2, 8n1, 14, 40n24, 70n35, 90,
    105n40, 106n53, 217, 236n7,
    236n16
James, Henry, 234

Jay, William, 212n7
Jefferson, Thomas, 34, 87, 90, 168, 169, 199, 212n9, 218, 223, 232
Jenkins, Brian, 213–214n22
Jim Crow, 211
Johnson, Bruce, 158n30
Johnson, Michael, 100n1
Johnson, Reverdy, 92
Julian, George, 143, 157n18, 163n78

Kahn, Paul W., 104n24
Kansas, 24
Kansas-Nebraska Act, 15, 127–129, 147, 167, 173, 221
Kant, Immanuel, 216–237
Kauffman, Eric, 103n18
Kellogg, William, 163n85
Kendrick, Paul, 187n3
Kendrick, Stephen, 187n3
Kent, James, 207, 214n28
Kentucky, 92, 196, 201, 205
Kersh, Rogan, 102n12, 103n18, 103n20, 107n57, 236n12
Kloppenberg, James T., 102n14, 106n54, 214–215n34
Know-Nothing Party. *See* American Party
Koch, Cynthia M., 102n13
Koerner, Gustave, 150, 159n40

Lacey, Michael J., 100n1
La Mettrie, Julien, 55
Latrobe, J. H. B., 200
Lawson, Melinda, 106n48
Lecompton Constitution, 40
Lee, Robert E., 45
legalism (in Lincoln's thought), 5, 110–134
Lehrman, Lewis E., 188n9
Lenin, Vladimir, 17, 32
Lenner, Andrew C., 103n20
Levering, Noah, 160n53
Levine, Bruce, 158n25
liberalism, 2, 6, 15–16, 24, 25, 76–77, 95, 110–134, 216–237
Liberia, 199, 232
liberty, 1–8, 24, 73–108, 114, 118, 120, 122, 123, 130–131, 143, 165, 171, 176–178, 186, 207, 210, 221, 223, 224, 230–231
  abuse of, 29
  civil, 19
  as non-interference, 170
  religious, 19, 121
Liberty Party, 176, 179
Lieber, Francis, 185
Lincoln, Abraham
  and the American founding, 17, 52, 121, 165, 173
  and the American Revolution, 19
  assassination of, 48
  and Christianity, 42–70
  on civil rights (of freedmen), 46
  on colonization (of African Americans), 168, 199–201
  Cooper Union Address of, 86, 172, 173, 216, 229
  on democracy, 14–37
  on *Dred Scott v. Sandford* (1857), 86, 113, 116, 127, 129–130, 171
  First Inaugural Address of, 59, 91, 220
  on Fugitive Slave Act, 123
  Gettysburg Address of, 50–60, 90, 99
  House Divided speech of, 21
  on labor, 226–230
  on law, 14–37
  Lyceum Address of, 14–37, 51, 95
  and natural law, 216–217
  Peoria Speech of, 75, 101n6, 113, 170–171, 222
  on political religion, 13, 33, 35, 81–82, 121
  pragmatism of, 216
  on property rights, 85
  providenitalism of, 225–226
  on the "public mind," 24, 36, 87
  and race, 75, 170
  Second Inaugural Address of, 42–70, 91, 183
  on slavery, 163–191, 198
  Temperance Address of, 226–227
Lind, Michael, 187n4, 188n114
Livingston, Mississippi, 30
Locke, John, 217–218

Louisiana, 47, 186
Louisiana Purchase, 232
Lovejoy, Elijah, 21, 22–23, 25, 28, 41n27
Lovejoy, Owen, 22, 147, 159n42
Lowenthal, David, 55–56, 69n20
Lubet, Steven, 189n20
Lucas, Josiah M., 159n31
Lukes, Steven, 104n30
Lusk, Edward, 161n57
Luther, Martin, 54
Luthin, Reinhard, 158n27
Lyceum Address (1838), 5, 13–43, 58, 81, 95, 121
lynching, 21–23
Lynd, Staughton, 190n23
Lyons, Richard, 205

Machiavelli, Niccolo, 17, 67, 216
Madison, James, 177
Magness, Philip W., 191n37
Maier, Pauline, 106n53
Mallard, R. Q., 213n19
Margalit, Avishai, 102n10
Marshall, John, 197
Marx, Karl, 204
Maryland, 201
Massachusetts, 144
Masur, Louis, 213n16
Mayer, Henry, 189n22
McClay, Wilfred, 187n2
McClellan, George B., 204
McCormack, Thomas J., 159n40
McDaniel, Caleb, 103n17, 189n22, 213n21
McFee, Ward M., 190n25
McIntosh, Francis, 14, 21
McPherson, Edward, 213n17
McPherson, James, 100n1, 106n45, 106n52, 109n78, 191n33, 236n15
Melish, Joanne Pope, 100n4, 214n34
Mellen, G. F. W., 176, 189n21
Melville, Herman, 17
Mercer, Hugh, 213n19
Mexico, 89, 147, 166
Miller, David, 102n9
Miller, Edward A., 213n18
Miller, William Lee, 101n7, 187n1
Mills, Charles, 115–116, 133n24

Milton, John, 16, 17, 27, 39n6
Minardi, Margot, 214n34
Missouri, 126, 127, 202
Missouri Compromise, 128, 155, 167, 221, 224
mob violence, 14, 21–28, 59
Moorhead, James H., 106n48
Morel, Lucas, 8n4, 44, 68n2
Morris, Christopher, 31
Morris, Thomas D., 189n20
Mosby, John Singleton, 212n3
Murrell, John, 31
Mussolini, Benito, 29
Myers, Gustavus A., 214n29

nationalism, 73–108, 220
nativism, 2, 139–164
natural rights, 2, 6, 7, 74, 80, 85, 97, 110–134, 171–172, 175, 178
Neely, Mark E., 101n8, 106n50, 165, 188n7, 191n33
Nevins, Allan, 162n70, 162n77
New Deal, 195
New Jersey, 199
New Mexico, 147
New York, 28, 199
Niebuhr, Reinhold, 53
Nietzsche, Friedrich, 34
Niven, John, 190n26
Noll, Mark, 53–54, 60, 69n14, 70n38, 100–101n4, 106n54
Northwest Ordinance, 175
Nozick, Robert, 133n22

Oakes, James, 96–97, 101n7, 106n52, 108nn70–71, 108n74, 132n10, 187n3, 188n11, 188n15, 190n27, 212n11
"On the Perpetuation of Our Political Institutions." *See* Lyceum Address (1838)
Orwell, George, 34, 43n39
O'Sullivan, John L., 83
Ottawa, Illinois, 110, 113, 124

Page, Sebastian N., 191n37
Paine, Eleazar A., 163n83

Paine, Thomas, 53, 217
Paludan, Philip S., 212n13
Panama Canal, 195
Pangborn, L. K., 159n31, 162n67
Parsons, George M., 157n13, 214n33
patriotism, 8
Pease, Theodore Calvin, 162n65
Pennsylvania, 146, 199
Peoria, Illinois, 15, 34, 113
Perkins, Howard Cecil, 156n3
Perry, Lewis, 100n1
Petacci, Clara, 29
Peterson, Merrill D., 101n5, 101n7, 212n9, 237n21
Phan, Hoang Gia, 190n29
Phelps, Alonzo, 31
Phillips, Wendell, 177, 190n23
Pierce, Edward L., 190n28, 202, 213n16
Pierce, Henry L., 213n15
Pinckney, Darryl, 187n2
Pinsker, Matthew, 160n53
political (or civil) religion, 13, 33, 35, 81–82
popular sovereignty, 1, 58, 221
Porter, Kirk H., 158n30
Posner, Eric A., 132n9
Potter, David, 101n8, 160n46, 163n81, 165, 188n6
presidential election of 1860, 46
Price, George R., 103n17
Prigg v. Pennsylvania (1842), 176

Quarstein, John V., 213n16
Quincy, Illinois, 114

Rael, Patrick, 103n17
Randall, James G., 162n65
Rawls, John, 217
reason, 27, 37, 219
Reconstruction (US), 45–47, 186–187, 210
Reed, H. Clay, 213n15
Reformation (Christian), 54
Republican Party, 61, 88, 124, 139–164, 170, 172, 184
    early platforms of, 145, 158n30, 167
Riker, William H., 157n15

Robespierre, Maximilien, 17
Rodgers, Daniel T., 103n16
Rodriguez, Junius P., 134n49
romanticism, 17
Rorty, Richard, 234, 237n21
Rosenblum, Nancy L., 102n9
Ross, Dorothy, 102n14, 106n48, 165, 188n6
Rousseau, Jean Jacques, 222
rule of law, 1, 5, 7, 8, 24, 42, 81, 125, 131, 166, 180, 221
Russia, 230

Satan, 17
Saunders, William, 31
Schlesinger, Arthur, Jr., 234, 237n20
Schneider, George, 149, 160–161n55
Schuckers, J. W., 190n26
secession, 51, 59, 75, 88–92, 97, 140, 167, 180, 182, 185, 204, 220
Second Inaugural Address (of Abraham Lincoln), 5, 42–70, 91, 183, 232
Selznick, Philip, 102n9
Seward, Frederick W., 157n19
Seward, William H., 80, 142, 143, 146, 157n19, 159n40, 173, 180, 188n16
Sewell, Richard H., 158n30
Sharkey, Patrick, 31
Shestack, Jerome J., 100n3
Shklar, Judith, 112, 121–122, 129, 132n5, 132nn8–9, 134n36, 134n45
Shore, Laurence, 31
Sierra Leone, 199
Silbey, Joel, 141, 156n7
Simon, Paul, 42n29
Simpson, Brooks D., 106n50, 213–214n22
Simpson, Craig M., 163n84
Sinha, Manisha, 95, 104n27, 108n70, 187n3, 189n18, 189n20, 191n30, 191nn36–37
Smith, Adam I. P., 89, 91, 106n48, 107n57
Smith, Anthony D., 102n11
Smith, Gerrit, 176
Smith, Rogers, 77, 97, 103n15, 103n18, 103n20, 108n75, 118, 133n34
Smith, Steven B., 236n1
Socrates, 26, 216

Speed, Joshua F., 101n5, 127, 147, 196, 212n3, 230
Sperry, Nehemiah, 159n32
Spielberg, Steven, 216
Spinoza, Baruch, 55, 217
Spooner, Lysander, 177–178, 190n25
Springfield, Illinois, 13
Stampp, Kenneth M., 158n24, 163n86
Stanton, Edwin, 203
Stephens, Alexander, 208, 214n29
Stewart, Alvan, 175, 189n21
Stewart, James B., 100n4, 103n17, 190n23
St. Louis, Missouri, 14, 28
Story, Joseph, 214n28
Strauss, Leo, 70n36
Striner, Richard, 101n7, 115, 133nn20–21, 187n1
Strong, George Templeton, 152, 154
Strozier, Charles B., 40n9
Sumner, Charles, 143, 179, 180, 190n28, 207, 214n27

Taney, Roger B., 179, 205, 207, 233
Tappan, Lewis, 43n37
Tarbell, Ida M., 160
Taylor, Zachary, 37, 143
Texas, 89
Thelwell, Mike, 188n10
Thirteenth Amendment (to the US Constitution), 16, 92, 93, 94, 183, 195, 233
Thomas, Milton Halsey, 162n72, 162n77
Thoreau, Henry David, 17, 19, 20, 40n20, 218
Thornton, William, 214n33
Thrasymachus, 15
Thurow, Glen, 44, 68n1
Tocqueville, Alexis Charles Henri Clerel de, 19–21, 40nn17–19
Treaty of Ghent, 198
Treaty of Paris, 198
Trumbell, Lyman, 92, 171, 205, 214n25

tyranny, 13–43, 78, 140, 172, 177, 197, 199, 223, 231

Ullmann, Daniel, 157n22, 161n63

Van Buren, Martin, 39n1, 154
Varon, Elizabeth, 189n22
Vaughn, Robert, 237n21
Vicksburg, Mississippi, 30
Volney, Constantin, 53
Vorenberg, Michael, 107n57, 107n61

Wade, Benjamin, 47
Wade-Davis Bill (1864), 45, 46, 47
Wainwright, Nicholas B., 157n15, 162n73, 163n80
Waldstreicher, David, 102n13
War of 1812, 198
Washburne, Elihu, 162n68
Washington, George, 17, 37, 223
Washington, John M., 213n19
Webster, Daniel, 57, 221
Weld, Theodore Dwight, 174–176, 189n19
Welter, Ruth, 102n13
Welty, Eudora, 31
Wheaton, Henry, 212n5
Whig Party, 14, 26, 82, 139–164, 180
White, Ronald C., 49, 69n11
Whiting, William, 185
Whitney, Thomas R., 157n20
Wiecek, William M., 189n20
Wilentz, Sean, 187n1
Wills, Garry, 106n53
Wilmot Proviso, 143
Wilson, Edmund, 16, 40n8
Wilson, Henry, 158n29
Wilson, Major L., 104n24
Witt, John Fabian, 191n35, 212n7
Wittgenstein, Ludwig, 235
Wolin, Sheldon, 3, 8n2

Yack, Bernard, 103n15

Zuckert, Michael, 134n38